D0907170

Planning document access: options and opportunities

Neil Jacobs
Anne Morris
Julie Woodfield
Eric Davies

Based on the work of the eLib project FIDDO

BOWKER
SAUR

London • Melbourne • Munich • New Providence, N.J.

© Reed Business Information Limited, 2000

Library of Congress Cataloging-in-Publication Data
A catalog record for this book is available from the Library of Congress

British Library Cataloguing in Publication Data
A catalogue record for this title is available from the British Library

Published by Bowker-Saur
East Grinstead House, Windsor Court
East Grinstead, West Sussex RH19 IXA, UK
Tel: +44(0)1342 326972 Fax: +44(0)1342 336198/190
Email: lis@bowker-saur.co.uk
Website: www.bowker-saur.co.uk

Bowker-Saur is part of REED BUSINESS INFORMATION LIMITED.

ISBN 1-85739-2698

Cover design by Amanda Barragry
Typeset by Florence Production Ltd, Stoodleigh, Devon
Printed on acid-free paper
Printed and bound in Great Britain by Antony Rowe Ltd, Chippenham

Contents

Preface

As this book is written, the whole structure of scholarly communication is in a state of flux. In particular, the world of document access is the site of considerable technological, legal and social changes. Existing players, such as libraries and publishers, are attempting to carve out new roles for themselves or to extend existing ones, and new players, such as web-based aggregator services, are entering the field. It could easily be argued that the quantitative changes of the past, such as increases in the size of the higher education sector or in the price of scholarly journals, are giving way to qualitative shifts in the structure of scholarly communication. In this context, it is a bold person who makes predictions of any kind about this structure.

In this book, which emerged from the work of the British eLib project FIDDO, we have tried to find ways of discussing some of the persisting issues in this dynamic world, while at the same time relating these issues to current developments. Indeed, even as this book was being prepared for publication (itself a changing process), initiatives were being announced by publishers' organizations and other bodies that could pave the way for the development of new ways for researchers to publish and to acquire academic papers. Furthermore, it is inevitable that more initiatives of this type will have been announced between the time that this is written and the time that it is read. It is vital, in such a dynamic environment, that those involved have some common understanding of the issues they are trying to address and, in a small way, this book is an attempt to lay out some of those issues.

There are many people who have helped in different ways to produce this book, although it is, obviously, the authors who accept responsibility for any mistakes or omissions in it. Firstly, we would like to thank all those who have been involved in FIDDO over the past four years, including (in no particular order) Steven Hirst, Mandy Webster, Sheila Price, Cliff McKnight, Emma Blagg and Steve Guest. We would also like to thank members of the FIDDO Project Advisory Group, especially John Blagden and Gordon Brewer, who kept us focused on issues relevant to library managers. In addition, we would like to thank the team in the Electronic Libraries Programme office, especially Chris Rusbridge, Kelly Russell and Elizabeth Graham, for their support throughout FIDDO. As a general rule, support staff do not get the credit they deserve for their contributions to research and development work, so we would also like to mention Shirley Horner, whose computing expertise and helpful, friendly attitude were much appreciated. Finally, and perhaps most importantly, we would like to thank all those people (who know who they are) who participated in FIDDO's field work, in a liaison role, as interviewees, completing questionnaires and so on. Without them there would have been no book.

Neil Jacobs
Anne Morris
Julie Woodfield
Eric Davies
Loughborough, February 2000

PART ONE: THE BOOK'S CONTEXTS

CHAPTER ONE

Document delivery, academic library management and the FIDDO Project

Introduction

Document delivery is not new; libraries have offered this type of service from the very beginning. However, the scope and demand for document delivery has increased dramatically in recent years. Document delivery was once seen as an admission of failure on the part of the local collection to support the needs of users, but not anymore. Every library now accepts that it cannot be self-sufficient and 'biggest is best' is no longer regarded as a true reflection of good library performance. Indeed, there is some evidence that larger libraries generate even more traffic in externally acquired material than smaller ones, thus reinforcing the notion that self-sufficiency is a fallacy (Exon and Punch, 1997). The purpose of libraries is shifting from one of acquisition to one of access. Libraries are becoming gateways to resources as much as they are custodians of those resources (Deegan, 1998).

What is document delivery?

Initially, books, conference proceedings, reports, articles and other bibliographic items were borrowed mostly from other local libraries, hence the use of the term inter-library loan (ILL). However, this term became a misnomer with the introduction of the photocopier. Photocopiers enabled copies of journal articles to be sent to requesters, which could then be retained, rather than borrowed, by library users. The term 'document delivery' was coined to overcome this problem. Document delivery, in its broadest sense, therefore means the provision to a library user of any type of document that may be borrowed from another library, or purchased from a document supplier for retention by the requesting library or individual. However, definitions do vary. Some librarians prefer to use the term 'document delivery' for documents that are retained by the requesting library or library user and the term 'ILL' for items that are borrowed and have to be returned to other libraries. Many academic libraries also retain the name 'ILL Department' for the section dealing with document delivery. The term 'document access' is also gaining in popularity as a substitute for 'document delivery'. The preference for 'document access' stems from the reasoning that documents obtained from the web are not delivered in the same sense as a photocopy of an article is from a commercial document supplier; they are accessed.

'Full-text access' and 'electronic document delivery' (EDD) are also terms widely found in the literature. Systems offering full-text access provide users with access to full-text documents online while EDD is when a document is supplied to the requester, either library or library user (often referred to as an end-user), electronically in the form of a PDF file, Email attachment or fax. Again definitions vary and, in the past, EDD has been used when any part of the document request and delivery process has been via electronic means. Systems offering full text or EDD are, in reality, specific types of document access or document delivery systems.

The growth in document delivery

The increasing inability of libraries to fulfil the needs of their users from library stock has given rise to an exponential rise in the demand for document delivery. The British Library Document Supply Centre (BLDSC), for example, which is the largest document supplier in the world, has reported a 132 per cent increase in the number of requests from 1973/4 (1 832 000) to 1997/98 (4 257 670) (British Library Bibliographic Services and Document Supply, 1999). Statistics collected by the Association of Research Libraries (ARL, 1998) also show increases of 69 per cent and 151 per cent over the past 12 years (1986 to 1998), for inter-library lending and inter-library borrowing, respectively, between the major research libraries in Canada and the USA. 'ILLs received' statistics from the Circle of Officers of National and Regional Library Systems (CONARLS) in the UK, which excludes traffic through the BLDSC, confirms this trend. The number of requests reported in 1993–94, for example, was 1 307 507, whereas this had risen to 1 543 302 in 1997–98, a rise of 18 per cent in just four years (Prowse, 1998). So why this increase and why is document delivery emerging from being a Cinderella-type facility to being recognized as an important mainstream library service? There are several reasons for this and they are outlined below.

Spiralling serial and book prices

The average prices of both serials and books have spiralled in the last decade forcing cash-stricken libraries to cancel subscriptions and cut down on the number of monographs purchased. The cancellations have led to increased document delivery requests as libraries struggle to fill the gap between what can be provided from local stock and user demand. Mean serial prices in the UK have more than trebled since 1988 when the mean serial price was £127.42. Today it is £392.01, whereas monographs have increased from a mean of £25.44 in 1988 to a mean of £41.96 in 1998, representing an increase of 65 per cent (Creaser and Murphy, 1999). Similar increases in the USA have also been noted. Brook and Powell (1994), for example, found that academic libraries had experienced a 52 per cent increase in serial prices in just four years from 1990 to 1994. The price of monographs has also increased in the USA by 50 per cent in the ten years, from 1988 to 1998 (Creaser and Murphy, 1999).

Budget constraints

In addition to the rise in serial and book prices, many libraries have had to contend with falling library budgets. Libraries have seen their purchasing power diminish considerably over the last decades as the economic climate has deteriorated. Barker, writing in 1996, for example, describes how university librarians in the UK had seen their purchasing power dwindle in the previous 20 years, instancing his own institution where the 1996 budget was 40 per cent of its 1976 value (Barker, 1996). Many library budgets have been cut or frozen when inflation and currency fluctuations have been taken into account. Although the proportions of library expenditure for periodicals and books have increased over the last 10 years, for example, the real periodical and book spend per person has decreased 62 per cent and 32 per cent, respectively, in the new British universities (Creaser and Murphy, 1999). Document delivery, therefore, has become a necessity in this climate, being viewed as a money saver, particularly when used in conjunction with imposed restrictions on the number of requests that users are allowed to make.

Increase in publications

Even if serial and book price rises had remained modest and library budgets had kept pace with inflation, libraries would still have found difficulty meeting the needs of their users from local collections. No library could possibly keep pace with the soaring rate of published information. The number of serial titles, for example, increased from 108 590 in 1988 to 157 173 in 1998 and the number of new book titles per year in the UK almost doubled from 56 514 in 1988 to 104 634 in 1998 (Creaser and Murphy, 1999). The increases are due in part to the 'publish or perish' syndrome where research output and tenure are linked, and to the increasing reliance on measures that relate research output to funding; one such example of this is the Research Assessment Exercise in the UK. Advances in technology, leading to more cost-effective and quicker publishing, the development of new research areas and the increase in cross-disciplinary research have also had a very big impact.

Advances in technology

Advances in computer technology, networking architecture and data compression techniques, coupled with the development of the Internet, have revolutionized the way information can be made available and transmitted from one library to another. This has provided huge opportunities for new, faster, more versatile methods of document delivery which have led to increased demand. Documents can now be ordered online and received in digitized form in a matter of seconds. Technological advances, therefore, have provided the opportunity to move to 'just-in-time' access rather than the 'just-in-case' local holdings scenario.

Increase in user expectations

The last two decades have seen the pervasive use of computers and networks both at work and at home. Library users have, therefore, become increasingly sophisticated in their computer use. This has led to greater awareness and stimulated demand for information. Users expect not only to be able to search databases and online catalogues world-wide but also to obtain any document they require instantaneously. They are familiar with being able to order pizzas and other consumer goods on the Internet at a touch of a button, so why not documents too?

Increase in student numbers

The number of students entering higher education has increased dramatically in the last decade. The number of full-time students in the UK increased by almost 70 per cent between 1989 and 1995, increasing the ratio of young people entering higher education to one in three, compared with one in six in 1989 (Department for Education and Employment, 2000a). This increase coincided with Government initiatives to promote life-long learning (Department for Education and Employment, 1988) and the change from a binary higher education system, of universities and polytechnics, to a unitary system (Department for Education and Employment, 2000b). This increase in student numbers and an ever more diverse student population (more mature students, more part-time students and more students from other countries and cultures) has led to a shift in teaching styles (Davies, 1998). Much greater reliance is now placed on student-centred and project work that puts even greater strains on local collections and document delivery services.

Increase in distance-learning students

Not only have student numbers been increasing but the modes of study have been changing too. Distance learning is becoming much more popular, made easier by advances in technology and boosted by the relatively low tuition costs when compared with residential, full-time, equivalent study (Unwin, Stephens and Bolton, 1998; Snyder and Fox, 1997). However, supporting distance learning students is staff-intensive and places huge demands on the library, particularly with respect to document delivery.

Other major influences

Various reviews and research programmes have also helped to raise the importance and awareness of document delivery. Some of these are discussed below.

Follett Report

The Follett Review of libraries in British higher education, which began in 1992 and reported its findings in December 1993, was commissioned by the UK Higher Education Funding Councils and was chaired by Professor Sir Brian Follett (Joint Funding Councils' Libraries Review Group, 1993). The driving force behind the Review was the need to address the concern, felt across the newly unified higher education sector, that university libraries were not coping with the pressures that had been caused by the massive increase in student numbers, given shortfalls in space, materials and funding. There was also concern that libraries were not making the most effective use of information technology (IT). The report sought to review the situation and provide recommendations. It stressed the need for:

- the development of institutional information strategies that encompassed library and related services;
- an integrated review of information resources;
- the consideration of organizational convergence.

The importance of effective information and communication strategies and infrastructures in universities was emphasized further in 1997 by the UK Dearing Committee Report (National Committee of Inquiry into Higher Education, 1997), which predicted that by 2005 most students will or should possess laptop computers.

The Follett Report also recommended that the Funding Councils provide the sum of £20 million to support a series of development projects designed to further the use of IT in selected areas. One of the areas highlighted by the Report was electronic document and article delivery. It pointed out that '[it] is neither feasible nor even desirable to expect each institution itself to provide for all the research needs of its users' – a view endorsed by The Joint Funding Councils' Library Review (1995), which is also known as the Anderson Report.

JISC and the Electronic Libraries (eLib) Programme

The UK Joint Information Systems Committee (JISC, 2000) was formed in April 1993 after the unification of the higher education sector, and succeeded the Information Systems Committee (ISC) that had, in turn, succeeded the earlier Computer Board. The JISC is funded by the Higher Education Funding Councils and its mission is 'to stimulate and enable the cost-effective exploitation of information systems and to provide a high-quality national network infrastructure for the UK higher education and research councils communities' (Rusbridge, 1998).

As part of this remit, and as a direct response to the Follett Report, the JISC established the Electronic Library (eLib) Programme (eLib, 2000). Initially, the Programme received funding of £15 million over a period of three years to support a variety of projects. The main aim of the eLib Programme was to engage the higher education community into developing and shaping the implementation of the electronic library (Deegan, 1998).

There were two phases to the early part of eLib. In response to calls for proposals in 1994 and 1995, almost 60 projects were supported in the following programme areas:

- electronic publishing;
- learning and teaching;
- resource access;
- supporting studies;
- training and awareness.

Document delivery formed one strand of the programme area 'Resource access', the other being 'Access to network resources'. The document delivery projects funded in phases one and two were:

- *EDDIS (Electronic Document Delivery the Integrated Solution).* The aim of this project was to produce an end-user service that integrated, through a web interface, the discovery of non-returnable items (such as journal articles), their location, request and receipt (Larby, 1999). t was an attempt to integrate the process of information access from discovery to delivery. Although funding for EDDIS has now finished, the product is being developed further by Fretwell–

Downing Informatics Ltd., who was part of the original project consortium.

- *Infobike.* The original aim of Infobike was to provide a service that would enable users to search journal databases, and then order and retrieve articles electronically. However, this mutated into the JournalsOnline Project (see Electronic Journals section below).
- *LAMDA.* Originally known as London and Manchester Document Access, LAMDA was a project designed to set up a document delivery service based on the journal holdings of libraries based in London and Manchester, and later Leeds (making 10 in total). In response to requests from customer libraries, dedicated staff provided by LAMDA scanned articles and then transmitted them using Ariel software developed by the Research Libraries Group (RLG, 2000) in the USA. At the end of funding in July 1998, LAMDA moved to a non-profit, full-cost recovery service with 50 member libraries at 67 sites. A charge, £4.20 at the time of writing, is made for each request (Taylor, 1999).
- *SEREN (Sharing of Educational Resources in an Electronic Network in Wales).* The main aim of SEREN was to produce a document delivery system for the Welsh higher education community based on MIME-compliant Email. A pilot operation was established in May 1998 that enabled requests to be sent via Email and articles to be supplied to the requesting library or directly to the user either as Email attachments, or by post in the case of returnable items (Prowse, 1999a). At the time of writing, the SEREN service was being developed further and merged with the regional library system for Wales to offer services to all eligible libraries.

The FIDDO (Focused Investigation of Document Delivery Options) project, introduced in more detail later in this Chapter, was funded under the Supporting Studies banner. Its findings are the main focus of this book.

The third phase of eLib was designed to have four components:

- hybrid libraries;
- large-scale resource discovery, or clumps;
- preservation;
- turning early projects into services.

The hybrid library component, according to Rusbridge (1998), was 'designed to bring a range of technologies from different sources together in the context of a working library, and also to begin to explore integrated systems and services in both the electronic and print environments'. Projects sponsored under this component included AGORA (2000), BUILDER (2000), HEADLINE (2000), HYLIFE (2000) and MALIBU (2000); they are discussed further in Chapter 11. The clumps component was an attempt to enhance co-operation between libraries, as recommended by the Anderson Report and the realization from the document delivery projects that there was a need for virtual union catalogues to identify the location of documents. Three of the clumps projects, CAIRNS, M25Link and RIDING, have now developed prototype gateways that allow users to conduct searches across one or more libraries (see CAIRNS, 2000; M25Link, 2000; RIDING, 2000). In the case of the RIDING Project, the concept of a broker is used, offering the ability to carry out parallel simultaneous searching from a single query (effectively large-scale resource discovery) with the scope for adding other user-oriented services. A document ordering and delivery facility is included in the system. The fourth component of eLib Phase Three saw funding being given to enable EDDIS and LAMDA to become commercial services.

Needless to say, the eLib Programme has had a significant effect on the way document provision has been perceived and managed in universities.

Electronic journals

Electronic journals have the potential to make a considerable impact on document delivery. In 1995 the Pilot Site Licence Initiative (PSLI) was launched to provide higher education institutions with electronic access to journals published by four publishers (Academic Press, Blackwell's, Blackwell Scientific and the Institute of Physics) for a lump-sum payment. Following the success of this project, which resulted in the JournalsOnline service giving access to over 425 leading academic journals, the National Electronic Site Licence Initiative (NESLI) was set up on January 1 1999. NESLI, a three-year programme funded by the JISC, was given the remit to deliver a national electronic journal service to the higher education and research communities.

Another interesting development is JSTOR, which has the aim of making available to the higher education sector electronic versions of journal backruns, rather than current journals for at least 100 titles in 10–15 subject fields, mostly in the humanities and social science area.

It will be interesting to see whether these initiatives and others elsewhere in the world will have an effect on traditional document delivery statistics.

Other research influencing document delivery

Considerable research has also been undertaken outside the UK higher education sector. The Telematics for Libraries Programme of the European Union DG XIII, for example, has funded a number of projects with a direct or an indirect emphasis on document delivery (EU Telematics for Libraries Programme, 2000):

- *DALI*. The main aim of the *Document and Library Integration* project was to develop and evaluate a prototype multimedia document delivery system based upon open system standards. The project focused on all delivery methods, including print and electronic delivery, in the domain of oceanography. The project ended in December 1996 and, according to the Echo web site, it 'promoted the positive positioning of libraries and librarians in the context of distributed delivery services and the exploitation of information highways as gateways to networked catalogues' (Echo, 2000a).
- *FASTDOC*. Funded initially for two years ending in March 1996, this project involved the development and testing of a prototype high-speed electronic document delivery service based upon an existing chemical journal image collection. Additional studies covered user requirements, copyright and administrative components. This project proved that chemical information could be scanned to high standards and potentially be distributed on demand over different channels, to anywhere in Europe (Echo, 2000b).
- *UNIverse*. This project began in October 1996 and ended in June 1999. The aim was to create a pan-European large-scale network of Z39.50-compliant connected catalogues to facilitate the provision of advanced library services, including electronic document delivery, to end-users and libraries (UNIverse, 2000). The final phase of the

project saw the software being demonstrated and evaluated by approximately 45 libraries across Europe (Murray, 1999).

In the USA, the American Research Libraries' (ARL) 'Interlibrary loan and document delivery (ILL/DD) performance measures study' has received much publicity (Jackson, 1998). This study provided 1996 base-line data to enable librarians to identify and understand local performance of ILL/DD operations and compare them with those of other institutions. Economic and non-economic indicators of ILL and DD services in 119 North American research and college libraries were studied using four performance measures:

- direct costs: costs that a library incurs to fill a borrowing or lending request;
- fill rate: percentage of borrowing or lending requests successfully filled;
- turnaround time: number of calendar days to complete a borrowing request;
- user satisfaction: level of user satisfaction with timeliness of the borrowing service, quality and completeness of material, and inter-action with ILL staff (Jackson, 1998).

The study identified the characteristics of low-cost, high-performing ILL/DD operations and provided libraries with the opportunity to maxi-mize access to remote resources while at the same time minimizing costs.

Several developments have also taken place in Australia. Document delivery here, as in the USA, is characterized by a high degree of co-operation between libraries. The most recent development has been the Local Interlending and Document Delivery Administration (LIDDA) Project and the development of a centralized physical union catalogue marketed by Kinetica (Wells and Amos, 1999). The catalogue, together with a web interface, (commercially known as Libri/Vision) will provide holdings maintenance, copy cataloguing and ordering of bibliographic prod-ucts. Kinetica are also developing the Kinetica Document Delivery Service (KDDS) using OLIB VDX client software, which will enable participating libraries to send and monitor requests and exchange messages with each other through the lifecycle of a request. Enhancements taking place include incorporating directory services, the Z39.50 standardized Item Order

Extended Service, links between citation and bibliographic databases and the development of a national ILL Profile. Further details of the LIDDA Project and Kinetica can be found in Wells and Amos (1999). Also included in this paper are details about the forerunners to the LIDDA Project: the Joint Electronic Document Delivery Software Project (JEDDS), the Regional Electronic Document Delivery (REDD) Project and the Co-ordinated Inter-Library Loan Administration (CILLA) Project.

Discussion of other research and project web sites can be found in Jacobs, Chambers and Morris (1999). An overview of earlier research prior to 1996 in the document delivery field can be found in Price, Morris and Davies (1996).

Range of systems available

The increased demand for document delivery and the flurry of research in this area have led to a number of different providers each vying for a share of the market. Traditionally, the higher education sector in the UK has relied heavily on the BLDSC to meet its document delivery needs. This was still the case in 1997 when FIDDO carried out a survey to deter-mine document delivery practices in UK university libraries (Morris and Blagg, 1998). However, many libraries were seriously looking at alterna-tives, especially electronic document delivery.

An alphabetical listing of document suppliers is given in Appendix A. One could argue that two main types of document access systems are emerging; mediated, where libraries act as mediators at some stage of the process, and unmediated, where end-users order, pay and receive documents at their desk-top. However, since most current systems have some form of mediation, if only to set budget limits, it is perhaps easier to think of the different type of products and services as described below.

General collection-based suppliers

Suppliers in this category generally have a large in-house collection of material to enable them to satisfy the majority of requests. The BLDSC is the obvious example, where 89 per cent of the requests are satisfied from its own stock (Vickers, 1994).

Specialized collection-based suppliers

These suppliers have specialized collections or access to specialized material that supports a limited, but necessary, document delivery service for researchers or professionals in specific subject disciplines. Examples include Engineering Information Inc., which provides services for engineering professionals (Ei, 2000), and the Institute of Electrical and Electronic Engineers (IEEE, 2000), which gives access to major collections in electrical engineering, computing and physical sciences.

Non-collection-based suppliers

These suppliers do not hold a collection of documents, but merely act as a brokerage between the requester and document supplier. They take the request and find the most appropriate supplier. Instant Library Limited (2000), for example, offers this type of service.

CAS–IAS suppliers

Current awareness service/individual article supply (CAS–IAS) suppliers offer both a citation-level awareness service and a document delivery service. Often unmediated, these types of suppliers provide tables of contents of journals and the facility to order required documents at the point of discovery. Infotrieve (Infotrieve, 2000) and Carl's Uncover (Uncover, 2000) offer this type of service.

Publishers

Several publishers are making their journals available electronically either for access through an intermediary, typically serial subscription agents, or directly themselves. Often they also provide a facility for some form of user profiling. Examples of publishers offering almost exclusive, direct networked access to some or all of their journal titles include Aslib Electronic Journals (Aslib Electronic Journals, 2000), Elsevier's Science-Direct (ScienceDirect, 2000), MCB (MCB, 2000) and Cambridge Journals Online (Cambridge University Press, 2000). Examples of systems offering networked access to full-text journals across a range of publishers include Blackwell's Electronic Journal Navigator service (Blackwell's, 2000),

IngentaJournals (Ingenta, 2000) and Faxon e-journal services (Faxon, 2000). However, to obtain online access, subscriptions to the printed journals are generally required. Some services, such as SilverLinker (SilverPlatter, 2000), provide a common interface for searching across several of these types of systems and offer options for linking with a range of document suppliers.

Full-text subscription-based products

There are two types of full-text subscription-based products: CD-ROM products and web-based products. The former have been available for a long time; they are well established, generally easy to use and provide exact images of the hard copy. Adonis and Business Periodical Ondisc are typical examples of CD-ROMs in use. However, the full-text web-based products that enable access to journal articles across a range of publishers, irrespective of whether the printed journals are subscribed to or not, are rising in popularity and are probably superseding the CD-ROM products in the West. Infotrac (Infotrac, 2000), ProQuest (ProQuest, 2000) and EBSCOhost (EBSCO, 2000) offer this type of access. Infotrac, formally known as SearchBank, and ProQuest, formally known as ProQuest Direct, are both discussed in detail later in this book.

Library-to-library

Obtaining or borrowing documents from other libraries is also popular, especially in the USA, but increasingly so in the UK too, encouraged by eLib projects and advances in technology that make transmission of documents easier. There are fee-based services, like LAMDA (LAMDA, 2000), where each transaction costs a fixed amount (see discussion above) and non fee-based services, where libraries may have consortium-type arrangements offering reciprocal services for free. The eLib 'clumps' projects mentioned earlier are investigating and promoting this type of service. However, it is worth noting that previous research, investigating a consortium arrangement between East Midlands Universities, found that, when staff time was taken into account, it was cheaper to pay for and obtain documents from the BLDSC than to obtain them from the libraries in the consortium (McDougall, 1989). Whether this is still the case, given advances in technology, remains to be seen.

Management criteria for selecting systems

The range of document delivery services can be overwhelming for library managers. Which service or services should they choose and what criteria should they use in the selection process? Obviously, the needs of library users are paramount. For example, it is no good selecting a service because it is cheap if documents arrive past their 'use by' date. However, do we know enough about the needs of users to make informed decisions? Little research has been done in this area, which is one of the reasons why the FIDDO Project was undertaken. Traditionally, the criteria used by managers have been:

- *total cost.* Factors include basic document costs, copyright fees, page costs, delivery charges, extra costs for urgent delivery, indirect administrative and telecommunication costs and/or subscriptions;
- *copyright.* An important consideration here is whether documents are 'copyright fee paid' or supplied under the 'fair dealing' option (see Chapter 8 on Copyright);
- *costing mechanisms.* The options are subscription-based systems, 'pay-as-you-go' or, as in the case of consortia, possibly 'free'. Factors of interest here include the potential usage of the system (will a subscription-based system be used sufficiently to warrant a large outlay?), the local library collection (if the collection is extensive then 'pay-as-you-go' may be better), whether the institution operates a central or a devolved budgeting system and whether the service includes budgeting or limiting facilities;
- *mediated vs. unmediated access.* Library managers must consider whether potential services are mediated by the library or 'bypassed' and operated solely by end-users. The implications of using either mode should be examined;
- *coverage/fill rate.* Factors concerned with coverage include types of material, (journal articles only or conference papers and monographs too?), the subject matter (a general or a specialized supplier?), period of coverage (does the supplier have access to backruns?) and journal coverage (does the system cover the journals required by users?). Suppliers will differ in the number of document requests they can satisfy because of coverage. If the fill rate is low then library staff

and users are forced to use more than one supplier. There are implications for this in terms of staff and user time;

- *response time*. This is concerned with how quickly a service provides
  the document requested. It is also known as turnaround time;
- *feedback*. Ideally, library staff and users should be kept informed of
  the progress of a request. Early notification when requests can not
  be satisfied is essential;
- *ordering options*. The range of options available includes the use of
  dedicated ordering services, such as ARTel as in the case of the
  BLDSC, telephone, fax, Email and the web. The last is most often
  used by end-users;
- *delivery options*. The options that may be available here include mail,
  courier, Group III fax, Group IV fax, Ariel, Email or full-text online;
- *document quality*. Documents need to be readable and complete.
  Time and money is wasted if documents have to be requested again;
- *service reliability*. Any document delivery supplier selected should
  provide a consistent and reliable service;
- *availability of service*. Some suppliers, particularly the full-text online
  services, provide 24-hour access, while others are more restrictive;
- *technology requirements*. Specific software and hardware may be
  needed to use some suppliers;
- *standards compliance*. Not all services adhere to the same standards.
  It is important, therefore, to ensure that the service selected will
  conform to those standards operating elsewhere;
- *ease-of-use*. Any system chosen needs to be easy to use and have
  good search facilities. The need for user training and support needs
  to be minimized and the degree of integration with other library
  modules must be considered. The provision of a good online help
  system and backup from a help desk are essential;
- *archive position*. Important to note here is that the subscription-
  based services may only provide access to their service while a
  subscription is active and that some services only provide access to
  relatively recent material;
- *provision of management statistics*. All managers need to have access
  to statistics to make informed decisions. These can be provided
  online or be paper-based but some suppliers are better than others
  in providing statistics that are both timely and in a useable format;

- *vendor stability*. Vendor credibility is important: how long have they been established and are they likely to continue trading in the future?

Just how these criteria relate to user requirements and how managers can be better informed about user needs formed part of the FIDDO research.

FIDDO research

The FIDDO research commenced in November 1995 and was completed in December 1999. The main aim of the FIDDO project was to disseminate reliable and objective data to enable library and information managers to make informed decisions about the feasibility, selection and implementation of document delivery services within their own institutions. The main objectives were:

- to provide managers with up-to-date information throughout the Project on the types of document delivery services available and their relative merits;
- to develop and apply criteria for measuring the performance of document delivery systems in real working environments;
- to examine the cost benefits of document delivery services in the working environment;
- to examine routines and methods for identification, ordering and receipt of documents;
- to assess various technical factors such as networking reliability;
- to measure end-user reactions, behaviour and attitudes;
- to ensure that the findings had portability across institutions.

One of the earliest tasks was to develop a FIDDO General Advice Point (FIDDO, 2000). This web site provided details about the options available and an extensive list of document delivery suppliers. It also contained a Frequently Asked Questions page, a contacts page listing people who would be willing to share experiences in using different services, news about current developments, the research outcomes of FIDDO, workshop details and much more. Although this web site is still available, the list of document delivery suppliers was transferred to the

Aslib web site at the end of the Project, to enable this section to be kept up-to-date (Aslib, 2000).

Early research also involved a review of research in the document delivery field and a survey to determine current practices, trends and experiences relating to document delivery within British academic libraries. The outcomes of this research are posted on the FIDDO web site (FIDDO, 2000).

The main bulk of the research has been involved with investigating user reaction to different document delivery services. t is the outcome of this research, together with an examination of the management perspective, that has been used as a basis for this book.

CHAPTER TWO

The FIDDO Project and its methods

At the core of this book are the results from a four-year research project called FIDDO (Focused Investigation of Document Delivery Options). Chapter 1 introduced the background to the FIDDO Project: UK higher education in the 1990s, the Follett Report, Electronic Libraries Programme (eLib) and, later, 'hybrid libraries'. In this chapter the methods used during the FIDDO Project to investigate document delivery to the user are examined. The first half of the chapter is important background to the rest of the book, and follows on from Chapter 1. The second half of the chapter is fairly specific to the FIDDO Project and, although those reading this book as a research report would find it essential, others may prefer to omit it.

Scope and definitions

In a world of fluid definitions, FIDDO (as a research project) had to set some ground-rules against which to work. Since this book follows those ground-rules, they should be understood at the outset. The scope of the Project can be summarized as those issues that relate to *full-text document access for academic researchers*. This scoping phrase probably needs some explanation.

- The research focus is on users as much as on document access. There are many initiatives focusing on the technology of hybrid libraries; FIDDO, as a supporting study, was allowed the freedom to put users in the picture. In addition to end-users, FIDDO included the views of library managers, to reflect its place as a part of the Electronic *Libraries* Programme.

- End-users, so far as FIDDO was concerned, were those undertaking academic research[1]. That is to say, within UK higher education we excluded explicit discussion of issues of teaching and learning support. However, the development of lifelong learning, distance education and resource-centred programmes means that 'research' is becoming an activity that is universal throughout higher education and beyond. Hence, FIDDO's findings are relevant beyond academic research.

- FIDDO's title specified 'document delivery' but, as noted in Chapter 1, we considered that 'delivery' was too narrow a term in a world where the web was becoming a ubiquitous phenomenon. It is, surely, stretching a point to say that a web page is delivered to a user in the same sense as a photocopied article from the BLDSC is delivered. However, what both of these have in common is that they are examples of document access for the user. The idea of 'document access' is taken further below.

- FIDDO's scope excluded resource discovery; we felt that this was necessary in order to prevent the Project becoming unmanageable. However, although FIDDO has concentrated on full-text access, the difficulty in focusing on that, rather than including issues of resource discovery, has revealed some of the significant links between them.

In discussing FIDDO's scope, the phrase 'document access' has been used frequently, hinting that it might have been central to our understanding of FIDDO's mission. In fact, it was. Because of the importance of this concept to FIDDO's work, it may be worth explaining how it emerged.

Much of the FIDDO research agenda was developed at the same time as a highly influential series of workshops (Tavistock Institute, 1998) run by the eLib project MODELS. The MODELS Information Architecture (MIA) (Russell and Dempsey, 1998), described during these workshops and shown in Fig. 2.1, specified a horizontally integrated system deployment

---

[1]   We have tended to favour the word 'researchers' rather than 'end-users' in this book, since FIDDO's user focus aimed to see these people as partners in our work, rather than as subjects of it (Zeitlyn, David and Bex, 1999).

or library broker, consisting of user access, an applications framework, service description and mapping and distributed service access.

This evolving architecture (Gardner, Miller and Russell, 1999) has been the basis for most of the eLib phase three hybrid library projects, and for many of our developing ideas of the technologies of the hybrid library (see Chapter 11). One aim of this architecture was to hide the 'vertical' options from the end-user. That is to say, end-users should not have to decide between obtaining documents from their local library, an electronic subscription or from a document supplier – such decisions would be made within the 'Hybrid Library Management System'. The first thing to note about this arrangement is that it introduced a certain tension into FIDDO's objectives: on the one hand FIDDO was committed to being user-centred, and on the other hand the options (the 'O' in FIDDO) were not being presented to the end-user. The second thing to notice about the MODELS architecture is that it aimed to integrate what the eLib AGORA project has termed the 'four basic user needs: discover, search, locate and deliver' (Newton-Ingham et al., 1999). That 'seamless access' is a good thing for end-users is, apart from anything else, a strong finding of the FIDDO research. However, because FIDDO is focused (the 'F' in

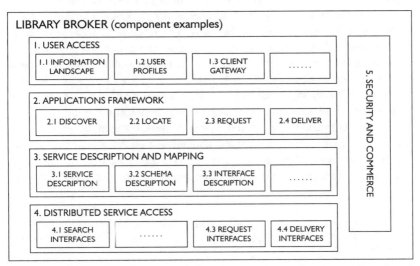

Figure 2.1. The MODELS Information Architecture (from Dempsey, Russell and Murray, 1999)

FIDDO) on just one aspect of seamless access – delivery (the second 'D' in FIDDO) – then developing a research agenda for FIDDO within the MODELS architecture was highly problematical. The FIDDO team considered that there were several questions relating to full-text access that were left unasked within the MIA framework. In particular, how would library managers (on behalf of end-users and universities) decide which options to include within their version of the applications framework? In order to make those decisions, library managers would need information about user requirements and the performance of systems. It was this information need that was the rationale for FIDDO, and it led to the development of the concept of a *document access system* and to the creation of a *methodology tool-kit* that investigated the requirements of both end-users (researchers) and library managers.

Document access systems: a definition

A document access system is any means by which the full text of documents is available to users in the appropriate format/medium. Although the future of information distribution is certainly electronic, at this point we assert that the appropriate final format for documents is paper; later in the book (Chapter 5) we explain why. The document access system is a user-centred concept, and includes everything necessary from the identification of an information need to the delivery of a paper document (Fig. 2.2). In this sense, it could be described as an example of 'joined-up' or holistic thinking about user needs, because it encompasses features that overlap conventional organizational and technical boundaries.

One example of a document access system might be journals on the shelf in a local university library, coupled with adequate photocopying facilities and researchers who are willing and able to put in the work to use these resources. Another example might be an online collection of

Figure 2.2. The document access system

full-text journals, available from the researcher's desktop, along with the appropriate technical and support infrastructure to make the system work (Fig. 2.3). Clearly, there are also options other than these two, and creating seamless access to them is the job of what has come to be called the 'hybrid library', based on the MIA framework.

However, taking the document access system as a unit of analysis meant that FIDDO could look at how each one performed in terms of its potential administrative burden for library managers and its value to researchers. Just as the MIA framework enables systems to be integrated without reference to their physical characteristics, so the concept of the document access system enabled us to compare approaches to full-text access that varied in their physical and organizational characteristics.

Methodology tool-kit

The detailed methodology tool-kit is described fully in Appendix B, and on the FIDDO web site (FIDDO 1999b). The principles of the methodology are described in the remainder of this chapter. The tool-kit was developed by the FIDDO team to reflect the relationships between the three primary

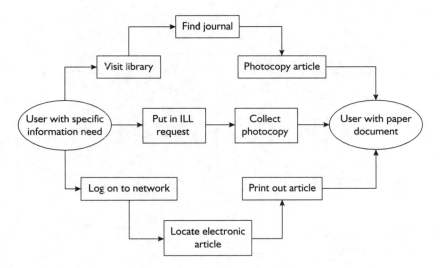

Figure 2.3. Examples of user tasks defining document access systems

relevant entities involved within the university: researchers, library managers and document access systems. Fig. 2.4 shows these relationships.

In a day-to-day working scenario (the plain lines), library managers administered document access systems and had a service relationship with library users. Library users – researchers – made use of document access systems in their work, a relationship described in the diagram as 'practice'. These three relationships (indicated by the plain arrows) represented the research field for the FIDDO Project (represented by the shaded area).

In the FIDDO scenario (the dashed lines), we were concerned with how each of these relationships may have been modified in the case of various systems. Hence, we needed information from or about the system, the end-users (researchers) and the library managers. These analytical relationships (indicated by the dashed arrows) are the ones described in the methodology tool-kit. Information from end-users related to their use of systems and to their service from the library, information from library managers related to the administration of systems and to the library's users, and information about systems related to how they were used and to how they were administered.

The methodology tool-kit includes specific approaches for all of these relationships. These are summarized below and there is a fuller

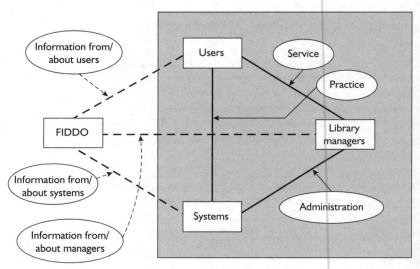

Figure 2.4. Overview of the context of the methodology tool-kit

description in Appendix B. The human actors in the above diagram – researchers and library managers – did not operate in isolation. That is to say, the working relationships shown in Fig. 2.4 were not the only ones in which these actors were involved. We took account of this by developing the idea of 'contexts of action'.

Contexts of action

Dempsey (1999) has noted that:

> 'The user is not only a visitor to the library; he or she is an inhabitant of a network space which is crowded with opportunity ... They [users] will expect resources to be available through digital libraries, learning environments, games, their customary work and workflow habitat.'

FIDDO's aim was to look at how various systems were (or could be) used and administered. We found it helpful to break down the 'network space' of users and library managers into a number of 'contexts of action'. We defined these as being the working practices and structures in which document access systems were used by researchers and supported by libraries. Academic researchers, as end-users, had contexts that were related to their work. This meant that the ways they needed to use systems, and were able to do so, depended on such things as the protocols of their subject area, the demands of the department in which they worked and the technical infrastructure available to them. Other end-users might have different contexts of action. For example, the manager of a private company might work in the contexts of expected profit figures and board and shareholder meetings, rather than in a subject area. However, even here there will be some similarities. Librarians, on the other hand, as local system administrators, had to make document access systems available to end-users effectively, legally, reliably and within a highly constrained budget; these were library managers' contexts of action. They are unlikely to be very different in principle wherever library managers work. The main body of this book is structured according to these various contexts of action. The rest of this chapter, after a description of the particular field-work sites and systems, is devoted to descriptions of how we approached each one.

The field-work sites

Conducting empirical research involves choosing field-work sites. Being based in the English Midlands, a region rich in both quantity and variety of universities, gave FIDDO an opportunity to include a diverse range of institutions within its remit. This we did, concentrating our work at five universities. Two of these became universities in the 1990s, and have a strong tradition in teaching and learning. The others were post-war universities, each with strong research and teaching traditions.

Clearly, we could not sample all the researchers from five entire universities! Therefore, we focused our attention on three subject areas. FIDDO's regional basis limited the choice to those subjects undertaken at most or all of the participating universities. A second criterion for the choice of subjects was that a substantial proportion of their formal scholarly communication should be in the form of journal articles, because that was the strength of the systems then available. A further, self-imposed restriction was that the subjects selected should have an element of interdisciplinarity. Chapter 1 noted that such subjects may be becoming more common, and they can be more difficult to support than traditionally discrete disciplines. The subjects that best fitted the criteria were business studies, geography and manufacturing engineering, although there was a geography department at only four of the five universities.

These, then, were the planned field-work sites: the departments of business, geography and manufacturing engineering at five (or, in the case of geography, four) Midlands universities, along with the relevant libraries at each institution. Since research in the real world is subject to such prosaic pressures as researcher time and the availability of participants, much of the field-work was limited to a subset of 11 of a potential 14 departments.

The products and systems used

Once we had decided on the field-work sites, FIDDO had to settle on a number of document access systems to evaluate. We had a number of criteria for this decision. Firstly, each component/product in the systems had to be available as a working example in 1998–9, rather than being just a plan or proposal. Secondly, the systems had to represent a variety of models of document access, so that FIDDO would be able to concentrate more on the issues with generic models, rather than with rapidly superseded individual products. Thirdly, they had to cover one or more of the subject areas chosen for the field work. On the basis of these criteria, we chose a number of document access systems. They are described below and references to them can be found in Appendix C. Firstly, two traditional systems were included, mainly as a baseline against which newer systems could be compared. These traditional systems were *local holdings* and *ILL–BLDSC*.

Local holdings

The journal holdings of a university library is a document access system familiar to all in higher education. Its essential features are well known. Librarians select journal titles, perhaps with some knowledge of local demand, and arrange subscriptions, usually via agents. Librarians then check in and catalogue journal issues as they are received, and perhaps arrange binding. They also arrange for the journal stacks to be maintained, used journals shelved, photocopiers maintained, and so on. Researchers access the journals at the shelves and generally need to photocopy articles in order to read them outside the library. Invoicing for journals is generally handled via serials agents. Photocopying costs are generally borne by researchers or their departments, although the library may have a role in maintaining a payment infrastructure.

ILL–BLDSC

ILL–BLDSC as a document access system is also familiar to most in British higher education. A major survey conducted by FIDDO in 1996 (Morris and Blagg, 1998) showed that *ILL–BLDSC* was then by far the most common document delivery mechanism in UK higher education. Typically, ILL request forms are received by a dedicated library unit. Each request has to be accompanied by a physical copyright declaration signature if the BLDSC 'library privilege' service (see Chapter 8) is being used. Librarians then check for availability via local holdings and, perhaps, via other priority systems such as LAMDA. They then rekey the requests and transmit them to the BLDSC using either Artel or ArtE-mail. The ILL unit receives documents from the BLDSC, checks them in and forwards them, or notifications of their arrival, to researchers. Invoices are sent from the

BLDSC to the ILL unit, which may pass on some costs to researchers or their departments (see Chapter 7).

The descriptions of these current UK access arrangements include both particular entities (such as journals and the BLDSC) and the infra-structure necessary for researchers to use them to obtain a paper copy of the article at their desktop. This reflects the inclusive definition of docu-ment access system (see above), and was a principle that carried over to our evaluation of newer systems. These newer systems were based on *BL inside* (British Library), *ProQuest Direct*, *SearchBank*, *EiText* and *SilverLinker*. The following descriptions of document access systems relate to these enti-ties, including their supporting infrastructure, as FIDDO used them in 1998.

BL inside

The British Library's *BL inside* service as used by FIDDO consisted of a web interface to the British Library's list of the 20 000 journal titles most frequently requested from the BLDSC. Copyright fee paid documents could be ordered online and were delivered by fax. A user of the system searched the *BL inside* database and ordered a document, giving a fax number. BL staff then retrieved the document and faxed it, and the user received the faxed document at a convenient machine. Invoices were sent in the post later.

ProQuest Direct

ProQuest Direct was marketed in 1998 by UMI, and subsequently as 'ProQuest' by Bell and Howell Learning Information. In 1998 it was a web-based database system offering access to many titles full text (text, text+ or PDF format) and many others as abstracts or citations. Its subject coverage was taken by FIDDO to be general. Clearly, researchers needed adequate computing and printing equipment to use it. *ProQuest Direct* was available on a subscription or a pay-as-you-go basis; we took the subscription option.

SearchBank

SearchBank, now InfotracWeb, worked very similarly to *ProQuest Direct*. It was marketed in 1998 by the Information Access Corporation, and subsequently by Gale Group. Like *ProQuest Direct*, it was a web-based database carrying a proportion of full-text material, along with abstracts and citations to other material. Users had to search the database and could then view and print documents, if available, in either text or PDF format. *SearchBank* was a subscription service, and its subject coverage was focused on business and marketing.

EiText

EiText, now Ei Electronic Text, was marketed by Engineering Information Inc., which merged in 1998 with Elsevier Science. The document delivery service at that time was often linked with Ei's Compendex database, but this was not possible for the UK-based FIDDO trials. Hence, we included *EiText* as a stand-alone service. Users Emailed document requests to Ei, whose staff then located the document in their stock or from satellite collections and scanned it into a TIFF/PDF ('internet fax') format. Users received their documents directly as Email attachments. Its subject coverage was, obviously, focused on engineering. Invoices were sent to the FIDDO office. As with *ProQuest Direct* and *SearchBank*, adequate computing and printing equipment were an essential part of this document access system.

Geo–SL–BL

In 1998 SilverPlatter Information marketed 'SilverLinker'. This was a linking technology, along the lines of the MODELS application framework. It supported seamless searching, location, requesting and delivery, so long as the appropriate resources were linked into the system. The options for the search function were limited to the databases hosted by SilverPlatter. In 1998 the options for request and delivery were being negotiated by SilverPlatter. For the purposes of FIDDO, the Elsevier database *Geobase* was linked via SilverLinker to the supplier BLDSC. This combination made up a composite document access system, called *Geo–SL–BL* in the remainder of this book. The subject coverage of this composite document access system was geography. Hence, during the FIDDO trials users searched Geobase, found documents that they required, ordered them from the BLDSC and received them directly as photocopies via the mail. As with the *ILL–BLDSC* system, BLDSC invoices were received later in the post. Sections of the SilverLinker system trialled were in fact software beta releases, and so the FIDDO trials must be seen, at least partially, as part of ongoing system development by SilverPlatter.

The document access systems included in FIDDO's work are summarized in Table 2.1. Where document access systems are described in this book, they are denoted in italics as above. In these cases, we are referring to the systems as defined here, as they existed in 1998. So much for the systems; what about the users?

The contexts of action of academic researchers

Researchers are not just end-users; they operate in a number of different contexts (see above), and we felt that we had to address this in our methodology. Our starting point for breaking down the working environment of academic researchers was a series of interviews that we undertook as a baselining exercise for field trials with a number of document access systems. The interview schedules are shown in Appendix B as a part of the FIDDO methodology tool-kit. In terms of

Table 2.1. The document access systems included in FIDDO's work

Label	Brief description
Local holdings	Local university library journal subscriptions + photocopying facilities
ILL–BLDSC	Inter-library loan via the local ILL department and BLDSC
BL inside	British Library BL inside + fax machine
ProQuest Direct	ProQuest Direct (now supplied by Bell and Howell Learning Information) + computing and printing equipment
SearchBank	SearchBank (now InfotracWeb supplied by Gale Group) + computing and printing equipment
EiText	Elsevier Information EiText + computing and printing equipment
Geo–SL–BL	SilverPlatter's SilverLinker system with Geobase as the front-end database and BLDSC as the supplier + computing equipment

their baselining function, the interviews are described in the section below devoted to the field trials themselves. In terms of identifying contexts of action, we wanted researchers to tell us about the way they worked, and about the things that enabled and constrained their work in terms of access to full text. From an early analysis of these interviews it became clear that these things could be grouped into three contexts of action: their subject area or discipline, the local department and their physical environment. The last of these could be subdivided further into the technological infrastructure and the document itself. At this point we should point out that, however useful for the analysis, splitting researchers' work into these three contexts of action was rather artificial. There were several issues that overlapped two, or even all three, contexts. It might be helpful to think of researchers as working within an area defined by these three overlapping contexts, shown by the shaded area in Fig. 2.5.

Thinking in terms of the three contexts of action helped us to structure FIDDO's work with researchers. We used field trials with document access systems as the core of our investigations, and then added specific supplemental methods for each context of action. The structure of the approach is shown in Table 2.2.

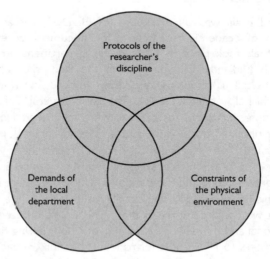

Figure 2.5. The researcher and her/his contexts of action

Table 2.2. The structure of FIDDO's approach

Context of action	Discipline	Local department	Physical environment
Attribute(s) of systems	Coverage of the system	Time necessary to use the system	Infrastructure and documents
Methodologies used	Field trials + citation analysis	Field trials + time trials	Field trials + survey
Relevant chapter in this book	3	4	5

The following section details the methods used to assess document access systems with respect to each of the researchers' contexts of action. The results of these investigations are presented in Part Two of this book (Chapters 3–5).

Methods appropriate to the contexts of action of researchers

General: the field trials

A set of field trials was the backbone of FIDDO's research into the requirements of academic researchers for document access systems. These field trials took place in 11 academic departments in universities in the English Midlands. The purpose of the field trials was to allow researchers to tell us about the way they worked and how particular systems would help or hinder them. The basic structure of all the field trials was simple. First, the researchers were interviewed on the ways they typically obtained documents, and on the advantages and problems of these methods (see Appendix B). Second, researchers were briefly introduced to one of the newer systems described above, and were left to use it for between one and three months. Third, they were interviewed again, with this interview following closely the pattern of the initial interview, so that we could compare as directly as possible between the use of the traditional and the newer systems. In addition, during the trials, we asked researchers to fill in short forms (see Appendix B) each time they used a system. These forms not only gave us some relatively hard data about system performance during the trial, but also reminded researchers in the second interview about their experiences. The interviews were transcribed verbatim and these transcripts were entered into the NUDIST v.4.0 software package. NUDIST is a fairly sophisticated package supporting qualitative data analysis which we used to manage the data and to select particular coded sections from the interviews.

Contexts of action 1: the discipline/coverage

Researchers discussed their disciplines in terms of scholarly communication, both formal and informal. That is to say, they discussed their disciplines in terms of relationships with other researchers working in similar areas, with funding bodies and with 'the literature'. In terms of access to full text, this translated into the key concern with system **coverage**. Researchers often talked about contributing publicly to their subject area, by submitting funding proposals or speaking at conferences, and on these occasions the key concern was not to have missed important documents. From this perspective it was clear that FIDDO would have to assess the coverage of document access systems.

Measuring coverage is not necessarily straightforward. At its most basic, the coverage of a system is simply a list of the full text available from it; but how much of that coverage is relevant? And how much that is relevant is not on the list? These questions can only be answered by reference to user requirements. Of course, measuring user requirements is itself anything but straightforward. As long as 25 years ago, Maurice Line (Line, 1974) felt it was necessary to try to clear up confusions between want, need, demand, use and requirement. Line suggested that these terms referred, respectively, to what users want, what they should have, what they say they want and what they use. He suggested 'requirement' as a terminological compromise – one that FIDDO has been happy to adopt in this context. In thinking how to measure user requirements in terms of coverage, we started by considering 'use' because it has a definite, if undefined, relationship with requirements, and because it is often easy to measure. The two principal problems with 'use' measures were that they were retrospective, and that they were limited to what was available to users at the time. One approach to solving the latter problem was by using citations as a measure of use, since researchers were not then bound by a particular collection. This is not the place to enter deeply into the thorny debate over the value of citations and their relationship with 'use' and 'requirements'; we have done that elsewhere (Jacobs, Woodfield and Morris, in press). Suffice to say that we considered that local citation figures would be a reasonable indicator of local use, and would be relatively easy to collect. However, the former problem, that 'use' is a retrospective measure, remained (Line, 1985). We were left to rely on the oft-quoted maxim that the best predictor of the future use of library materials is past use. Unfortunately, no measure of user requirements is perfect, and it must remain for others to suggest how better figures might be obtained practically.

User requirements were, therefore, indicated by counts of the citations to journal titles made over the previous five years by researchers in the departments included in the FIDDO field-work[2]. Librarians often want to divide journal titles into high and low use categories, or 'core' and 'peripheral' titles, to match the dividing line between subscription access (traditionally to printed journal titles) and pay-as-you-go access (usually via document suppliers such as the BLDSC). Consequently, as well as being used complete, the citation counts were also divided according to a number of definitions of 'core', there being little consensus in the literature on such definitions.

System coverage was indicated by the current full-text journal subscriptions of each system – again an imperfect but practical measure. User requirements, as citation counts, were then matched against coverage, and some assessment made of the adequacy of coverage of the various document access systems. We compared this assessment with that of the researchers using each system in the field trials. The results of this work are presented in Chapter 3, along with a discussion of their significance in terms of user requirements.

Contexts of action 2: the local department/time

Researchers are short of time; it is certain that this comes as no surprise to anyone – except, perhaps, to undergraduates. Our initial interviews

---

[2]   FIDDO would like to acknowledge the help of the Institute for Scientific Information in the generation of the citation figures used in this part of our work.

confirmed that, when discussing the practicalities of their work, time was of the essence in a number of ways. Furthermore, it was local pressures, of teaching and administration, that were cited as imposing most on research time. Hence, we characterized **time** as being a parameter related closely to the local department, and we developed an approach for evaluating document access systems in these terms. However, as noted above, there are issues that overlap contexts of action and of these time was, perhaps, the most obvious. Aspects of researchers' disciplinary context (for example, research proposal deadlines) impinged on their schedules, but in a different way from local pressures.

The approach we used for assessing the time aspects of document access systems was based around time trials, and took advantage of the slightly reflexive status of ourselves, as academic researchers, investigating the requirements of academic researchers. We put ourselves in the place of researchers (which we were) and ordered documents from various systems to see how much time they took to order, how long they took to arrive and, if necessary, how long they took to print out.

Before describing the method in detail, we need to note an over-whelming view from the field-work interviews that informed this part of our work: researchers read from paper. Short texts, abstracts, Email messages and the like were acceptable on the screen, but anything longer, certainly anything of a scholarly nature, needed to be on paper for a whole variety of reasons. These reasons will, we are sure, be clear to anyone who has done research, but in any case it is not necessary to go into them here; the issues are discussed in Chapter 5. Suffice to say that, when assessing the time needed to access documents, the end result we were waiting for was a paper rather than an electronic version of the document. Perhaps it is necessary to make clear that reading, although the focus of this part of FIDDO's work, was not the only thing researchers did with documents. They also stored and indexed them, searched them, informed colleagues about them and so on. Electronic texts were often much more acceptable for these other functions than they were for reading.

In the time trials themselves, we identified two samples of 20 documents each, one of business documents and one of engineering documents. Unfortunately, the timing of the field-work meant that we were unable to do time trials using geography documents, although the field-work itself did reveal some interesting figures (discussed, along with the rest of the findings from this part of FIDDO, in Chapter 4). The 20 documents in each set were obtained from the appropriate subject-specific document access system, and from the general systems, and the times were recorded at various points in the process, including final delivery of a paper copy. Admittedly, trials of 20 documents are small-scale, but we were able to generate statistically significant findings from them.

We were able to combine the figures available from these experiments with the perhaps more impressionistic data from the interviews that were a part of the field trials, to give a rounded picture of the consequences in terms of time of choosing one system over another. The results of this work are presented in Chapter 4, along with a discussion of their significance in terms of user requirements.

Contexts of action 3: the technical infrastructure and document qualities

During the initial round of field-trial interviews, researchers talked about obtaining documents by using a number of tools or infrastructures, whether these were computers, printers and networks or photocopiers and mail services. Whatever the material basis of the infrastructure, it affected how researchers saw the reliability of document access systems and the quality of the physical document at the end of the process. Obviously, apart from the field-trial interviews, we could also derive some indication of the reliability of the general infrastructures upon which particular systems relied from the time trials described above. However in terms of the quality of the physical documents we needed a specific approach.

As with the features of coverage and time, we took an approach to assessing document quality that was highly focused on the requirements of researchers. We asked them what they wanted, giving them alternatives to choose from, and asked for their reasons. As with our assessments of time, our approach to 'document quality' was based on the overwhelming view, expressed during the field-work interviews, that paper copies were preferred to electronic for reading purposes. So we compared paper copies (photocopies or printouts).

The physical quality of any copies of documents can be assessed in two ways: firstly, by how well it reproduces the original and the quality of the print; and secondly, by assessing the copy as a document in its own right, by qualities that may differ from the original, such as its format and layout. Document quality, therefore, extends beyond legibility to other criteria that together measure the 'readability' of any document. We developed these from Dillon's three levels of human stimulation involved in the reading process (Dillon, 1994), and these are embodied in the characteristics listed in Table 2.3.

We undertook a 'balanced paired comparison' experiment (David, 1988) in order to assess user preferences, using these criteria, for documents from different document access systems. In this approach, judges are presented with every possible combination of pairs in a sample of objects, and they are asked to express a preference in each case. From this data, cumulative choice scores for each document and probability scores are calculated to denote the number of cases in which one object is preferred over another.

For our purposes the 'objects' were paper documents and the 'judges' were researchers – a small sample taken from those who had trialled various systems. One example of a business document and one of an engineering document were chosen, both of which had a range of text and graphics. Copies of the business document were compared from *ProQuest Direct* (printed on laser and inkjet printers), *SearchBank* (on both printers) and *ILL–BLDSC*. Copies of the engineering document were compared from *ProQuest Direct* (laser and inkjet printers), *EiText* (both printers), *BL inside* and *ILL–BLDSC*. The results of this work, along with relevant findings from the interviews and other aspects of the field-trials, are presented in Chapter 5.

Table 2.3. Readability variables, derived from (Dillon, 1994)

	Characteristics	Readability variable
Physical characteristics	Size	1. Ease of handling
Perceptual characteristics	Headings, spacing, colours	2. Effective layout
	Legibility	3. Text print quality
	Clarity of graphics	4. Graphic print quality
Cognitive characteristics	Superstructure, contents list	5. Navigation aids

Investigating the 'contexts of action' of library managers

Although highly focused on the requirements of end-users (researchers) in the hybrid library, FIDDO's mission was always to support library managers in their decisions relating to document access systems. Our end-user studies should be seen in that light. We needed to know how academic researchers and document access systems fitted into the work of library managers, which we divided into administrative, budgetary and legal contexts of action. In contrast to the end-user studies detailed above, we did not have specific approaches for each of these contexts. Instead, we relied on three sources of information for all of them: the end-user studies, our experience of administering the various systems during the studies, and a series of structured interviews with senior library staff. The end-user studies have been described above. This section describes the interviews with library managers.

The aim for the interviews was for us to understand the way library managers viewed the present and the future of document access, what were the major issues for them and how they saw themselves dealing with those issues. It is sometimes difficult to talk about what are often very practical issues in these abstract ways, and so we developed a set of four hypothetical scenarios on which to base the interviews. These described different ways in which end-users could obtain documents, with different potential roles for the library and others in the information chain. The descriptions of the scenarios were left fairly vague, so that library managers would be able to focus on the significant unresolved issues in them. The four scenarios are described below.

- Scenario 1: users search a new subject-based full-text database on the web, viewing those documents in which they are interested, with an option to print them out. There are options to view and print documents in text-only or in PDF format. All full text is copyright fee paid, and the database provider charges a flat-rate access fee, depending on how many simultaneous accesses are allowed. The average delay between a user's decision to have a (printed) document and actually having it is generally around 10 minutes.

- Scenario 2: users search a known and familiar subject database on the web, ordering photocopies of those documents in which they are interested by clicking on the appropriate button. The documents are then sent by a supplier directly to the users via the postal service. The documents are available under the 'fair dealing' provisions of British copyright law. There is a subscription charge to the database, plus a charge for each document ordered, depending on the supplier. The library can set the system to try certain suppliers for particular journal titles or publishers. The average delay between a user's decision to have a (printed) document and actually having it is generally around three days.

- Scenario 3: users input their requests for documents to the university library via a web form, or via Email. The library decides on the best supplier for each article and makes the order. The document is delivered to the library, checked in and forwarded to the users via the internal mail. There is a charge for each document. The average delay between a user's decision to have a (printed) document and actually having it is generally around five days.

- Scenario 4: users send their requests for documents via Email to a document supplier. The documents are supplied in PDF format as Email attachments within a couple of days if the item is in the supplier's collection, or within one or two weeks if not. There is a charge for each document, consisting of a flat-rate delivery charge plus a variable copyright charge depending on the publisher of the document. The documents are therefore copyright fee paid. The average delay between a user's decision to have a (printed) document and actually having it is usually at least two days.

In order to prompt library managers to focus on all of the contexts that we had identified (administrative, budgetary and legal), we asked specific questions relating to each one, as well as a question asking for their overall reaction to each scenario. The questions are shown in Appendix B (methodology tool-kit). This approach had the advantage of structuring the interviews systematically, making their analysis somewhat easier than it might otherwise have been.

The interviews with library managers took place in the same universities as the end-user studies. There were 19 interviews, so that each university contributed around four interviewees. The interviews were tape-recorded and transcribed verbatim. As with the field-trials, we used the NUDIST v.4.0 qualitative data analysis package to help us manage and analyse the data. Again, although NUDIST is designed to support theory-building techniques, such as grounded theory (Glaser and Strauss, 1967), we used it mainly as a means of focusing our attention efficiently on relevant parts of the interview transcripts. Within these interview segments, we then used our judgement and NUDIST's Search-Text facility to draw together library managers' discussions of particular issues, such as authentication (see Chapter 6), quotas (see Chapter 7) and copyright (see Chapter 8).

The findings from the interviews, along with FIDDO's experiences in administering the end-user studies and relevant findings from those studies, make up the empirical background to Part Three of this book.

Summary

This chapter has introduced two key concepts in FIDDO's work. Not only are these concepts important in understanding the rest of this book, but we think that they have wider relevance, and could usefully be employed in a wide range of information research and development. The key concepts are:

1. **Document access system** – how end-users obtain the documents they require. A document access system is likely to include particular named products or services, along with appropriate technical, budgetary and support infrastructures. It is the corollary of 'seamless access' as described in discussions of the hybrid library.
2. **Context of action** – those aspects of users' worlds that are relevant to their interaction with a document access system. A context of action is an analytical category, and can relate to commonly accepted divisions of users' worlds, such as legal, technical and budgetary issues. However, it is important to look for emic (i.e. internal) categories as much as possible, rather than having the analyst impose categories.

The concepts are not original. For example, Davies (1997) uses the term 'electronic library system' in a way similar to 'document access system' and Kling (1991) looks at the contexts in which technological systems are used. Furthermore, the two concepts of document access system and context of action are very general and, it could be argued, amount merely to calling for investigators to take a broad view of systems and users. We do feel that much product and user research takes an approach that treats its subjects in isolation from their contexts. Product research often ignores the realities of the workplace in which the product is supposed to work and, even when it includes reference to users, often treats them as isolated individuals with stable preferences over, for example, interface design. We argue that products are only a part of the systems that people use, and that any one role (such as that of 'academic researcher') is only one hat that people wear. Using the concepts of document access system and context of action offers a way for analysts to broaden and deepen their understanding of what is going on when people use full-text information systems in their work. Furthermore, they are concepts that apply equally well to end-users and to others, such as library managers, who come into contact with full-text information systems. We consider, therefore, that FIDDO's methodological approach is robust and widely applicable.

PART TWO: RESEARCHERS' CONTEXTS

Introduction to Part Two

Researchers are not just researchers

We were interested in how document access systems support academic research, an activity that is not confined to one particular group of people. Within higher education, research is undertaken to some extent by both undergraduates and professors. There are also major research centres outside higher education. However, for the purposes of the FIDDO study, we defined 'researchers' as being PhD students, post-doctoral researchers, research assistants and academics working in universities. Of course, these people are not just researchers. For example, they are always researchers in particular subject areas or disciplines. It has been known for a long time that disciplines not only differ in their knowledge content, but also differ in terms of acceptable research practice. Researchers need to pay attention to the accepted protocols of their discipline, such as the ways in which articles and grant proposals should be written. This affects their requirements when it comes to literature sources. Chapter 3 explores these differences, and concentrates on **journal coverage** as a key indicator of document access.

As well as working within disciplines, researchers generally work in departments. Often, they are teachers and administrators as well as researchers. From this perspective, the key issue is **time**. Researchers often cannot dedicate as much time to research as they would like, and what time they have is fragmented by their other duties. Sometimes this means that they prefer to work at home. Chapter 4 explores the ways in which time is a factor in the use of document access systems, and how well these systems fit in with the busy schedules of researchers. Finally, researchers work in a physical environment of infrastructure and documents. They use networks, computers, mail systems and photocopiers in order to obtain and then use both paper and electronic documents. Chapter 5 reflects these two aspects of the physical environment of researchers, focusing firstly on the **infrastructure** and secondly on the **documents** themselves.

Contexts of action

Researchers are not just researchers; this is because they work within disciplines, departments and physical infrastructures. We have called these the contexts of action. As noted in Chapter 2, there were issues that over-lapped two or more contexts of action. An example of this is the issue of time, which forms the core of Chapter 4 on the departmental context of action. However, there are effects on the schedules of researchers from their disciplines, so that time also makes a secondary appearance in Chapter 3. One way in which we have tried to allow for these overlaps is to introduce distinctions between the actual and the effective coverage of a document access system, and between the actual and the effective time necessary to use it. In each case, 'effective' refers to the overlapping issues. There are more detailed explanations in Chapters 3 and 4.

Of course, if we were looking at other end-users besides academic researchers, then different contexts of action might be relevant. However, they might not be very different. Two examples might illustrate this. Firstly, others in higher education, such as distance learners and students being taught using student-centred learning techniques, have a lot in common with academic researchers. They too are working within a 'disci-pline', mediated by their course, and a technical infrastructure not too dissimilar to that of academic researchers. They may have constraints on their time other than teaching and administration duties, but they have constraints. Secondly, researchers in industrial settings can be understood as being similar to some academic researchers in important respects. Certainly, time is likely to play a similar role for them. Hence, although we have taken the three contexts of action from the world of academic researchers, they are likely to play a role in the work of people beyond the confines of the university. These issues are taken further in Part Four, especially in Chapter 10.

CHAPTER THREE

The contexts of action of academic researchers: the discipline

Introduction

Researchers are not just researchers; they are specialists within their chosen fields, each implementing the various stages of research in ways prescribed by their particular disciplines. This chapter is concerned with the need for literature that is central to several of these stages – that is to say, the need for researchers to receive ideas from and communicate their own ideas to the rest of the research community. The first part of the chapter takes a closer look at the different types of information need that correspond to the stages of the research cycle, concentrating particularly on dissemination. Related to this is a brief exploration of the inter-relationships between the three contexts of action already outlined. Derived from these discussions are the notions of 'actual' and 'effective' coverage of documents. These are the concepts around which the remaining sections of the chapter (the methodology, results and conclusions) are then structured.

The research cycle

In Chapter 2 we described how we chose three disciplines for inclusion in FIDDO's trials: business studies, geography and manufacturing engineering. These are distinct subject areas. That said, there are also inevitable areas of overlap and interdisciplinarity across certain research strands within them. At the broadest level, there are common features and incentives that are fundamental to the way research is undertaken in practice and that bridge departmental and institutional divides. Typically, our interviews with researchers showed that research was seen in terms of a cycle (Fig. 3.1) of between one and three years, wherein a project was planned, proposed, undertaken and written up. This model contains similar elements to the 'user scenario' constructed by the MALIBU Project (Wissenburg, 1999), although Fig. 3.1 also incorporates funding and assessment strands. Financial incentives for research work in the UK can be divided between those that are geared to publication, such as funds linked

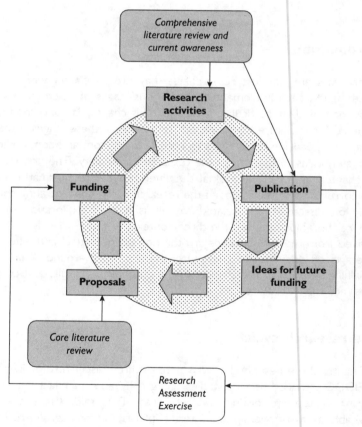

Figure 3.1. The research cycle schematic

to the Research Assessment Exercise (RAE) and those geared to more direct, project-based funds from bodies such as the Economic and Social Research Council.

The stages of the research cycle and the different funding regimes generate different types of information need. The information need corresponding to the initial stages of project design is to gain an up-to-date overview of research areas and to have enough information about these areas to filter out unpromising potential lines of research. This is currently supported by existing databases, core journals, the professional press and, increasingly, the web. As soon as the project is underway (the second stage of the research cycle), the information need is to ensure comprehensive access to the whole relevant scholarly literature. This is traditionally supported by academic libraries and their ILL departments.

Basically, the two types of information resource associated with these needs can be conceived as, firstly, the 'core' of information resources that provide a quick overview of any subject and, secondly, more 'peripheral' materials that provide relevant but less central information to the study of the subject area.

Communication and dissemination among researchers each function to maintain the momentum of the research cycle. Scholarly communication in all its aspects covers:

- proposing research and approaching funding bodies;
- identifying similar research interests among colleagues and researchers further afield, either for direct collaborative purposes or to establish wider interest links;
- disseminating research findings in the form of conference, seminar and journal papers and other publications.

Each of these relies on access to documents. Research proposals have to show an awareness of other related research interests and gaps in the literature that are worthy of study. The discovery of common interests relies on the ability to search for research published by others, especially of those not personally known to the researcher. By the same token, dissemination relies on others being able to access the publications of that same researcher. Clearly, document access systems play a central enabling role in scholarly communication practices.

Links with other contexts of action: actual and effective coverage

Successful document access is also affected by the departmental and technical contexts of action as described in Chapter 2 and the introduction to Part Two. Firstly, document access must fit in with other departmental work commitments, be they teaching, preparation of teaching materials or administrative duties, which are usually less movable than research-related tasks (see Chapter 4). Comprehensive full-text coverage can only be effective if it operates sufficiently well within the time constraints imposed by the combination of departmental schedules and personal circumstances. Of course, we recognize that, unlike lecturers, who are likely to be involved with both research and teaching, post-graduates and those engaged in contract research posts are not usually coping with the additional demands of a teaching timetable. Their favourable research position is slightly offset by the fact that full-time researchers are less likely than lecturers to have access to adequate computing and printing resources.

Secondly, and rather obviously, the use of systems that provide full-text document coverage involves accessing these systems; documents then need to be requested and materials of an acceptable quality need to be delivered. None of this is possible without the appropriate technical resources and infrastructure support (Chapter 5). These depend on the type of document access system in question. However wide a system's coverage may be, it has to be accessible in order to be of any use.

The impact of time and technical factors on the issue of coverage leads us to suggest that what we have termed the 'actual' coverage of a document access system may be different to its 'effective' coverage, as perceived by academic researchers. This actual coverage is the full list of journal titles that are theoretically available, assuming that requesting and delivery is straightforward. It does not take into account the possible negative impact of the three contexts of action on the individual's capacity to access the maximum coverage levels offered by any particular system. The qualities needed for a document access system to be effective, reflecting the three contexts of action, include an extensive and relevant coverage of full-text documents that can be accessed easily. This leads to the reliable and quick provision of good-quality printed documents. In reality, document access systems may not provide consistent satisfactory coverage of and access to full-text documents, perhaps offering, for example, access to citations or abstracts only or to standardized layouts. Ordering processes may be less flexible than is desirable, delivery may be slow and the printed quality of documents may be unsatisfactory. Seen in this way, all systems are partial as they cannot hope to satisfy the innumerable and diverse needs of their end-users. FIDDO has generalized from the different user requirements identified, to reveal patterns of common experience and need. This has allowed us to evaluate both the actual and the effective coverage of the different systems trialled, and to assess the important factors in such evaluations.

Any single library can only support a finite number of document access systems. Library management decisions about which to use require information about the actual coverage of systems and some impression of the requirements of users. The following section describes how FIDDO assessed various systems in terms of both their actual and their effective coverage.

Methodology: actual coverage

As described in Chapter 2, we used citation analysis to assess levels of actual coverage by selected document access systems. User requirements were represented by citation data, and these were divided into 'core' and 'peripheral' requirements. The coverage of actual systems was represented by their journal listings. The following sections describe this data in more detail.

The citation data

The citation data were generated using lists of the names of researchers currently engaged in research which were provided by each of the participating departments. The Institute for Scientific Information (Institute for Scientific Information, 2000) used these lists to identify the journals that were cited by the researchers during the period 1992 to 1997. Each citation generated a score of one for the journal in question. The citation scores from each researcher were added together to give a total citation score or frequency for each journal.

We matched the citation frequencies against net current coverage lists supplied by each document access system (see below), using Microsoft Access database software. As the objective of our analysis was to assess potential coverage, we decided not to consider the length of journal back-runs covered by systems. The ISSN field was the preferred point of comparison, but not all the systems' listings provided these. Instead, we compared lists by the journal title field. This was problematical because suppliers used different conventions (such as word order, abbreviations and punctuation) and we were only partially successful in our attempt to standardize them. We were able to estimate a random error factor for each system by comparing manually matched fields and equivalent auto-mated matches. Even when figures were adjusted for this random error, it did not eliminate completely a few apparently anomalous results. However, in general, our findings showed a degree of robustness; for example, they concurred for the most part with figures such as the BLDSC's request satisfaction rates (British Library Bibliographic Services and Document Supply, 1999).

Core Journals

The basic criterion for inclusion of a journal in the citation data was that it should have been cited at least once at a single institution during the six-year period between 1992 and 1997. This would be neither a realistic nor an economic basis on which to support selection and sourcing deci-sions by library managers. Up to now, the journals perceived to be the most useful have generally been held as printed copies in local journal collections, while other materials have been obtained as required from various remote sources, normally via ILL. Despite the evolution towards the hybrid library environment (Pinfield et al., 1998), a distinction between subscriptions and pay-per-document financial regimes persists, as does the requirement to identify and select material according to need. For this reason, our analysis needed to rank journal titles, reflecting the split in library provision of journals between important and less important jour-nals, in terms of user requirements.

The various attempts to define a core of journal titles in any disci-pline have been contested. Gaining widespread agreement about two sub-jectively-defined qualities (what are the central tenets of a subject area and which journal titles encapsulate those tenets most completely) appears to be problematical. The difficulty of agreeing on a single definition of core, regardless of what that definition is for, has been identified by White and McCain (1999), who note that '[i]n practical work, cores are identified by investigators' purposes and can be expanded or contracted at will, no matter what someone's algorithm says'. Our purposes, in comparing coverage by document access systems with the requirements of users, were exploratory, so that we settled on not one, but the following three definitions.

Core 1:   Bradford's 'nuclear zone' (Brookes, 1969) derives from Bradford's Law that states that most cited articles in a particular discipline relate to a small number of journals that are central to that discipline. The exact number is derived by graphical means from a plot of citations against the logarithm of journal rankings (Jacobs, Woodfield and Morris, in press).

Core 2:   The number of journals in Goffman and Warren's core (1969) is found by halving the number of journals cited only once, and adding one. If this number is N, and the journals are ranked according to citation frequency, then Core 2 consists of the top N journals.

Core 3:   This is the smallest number of journals that covers 80 per cent of citations, and is based on the Pareto 80/20 principle.

For each core there was a corresponding 'periphery' of journals that were cited, but not sufficiently to be included in the core. Each core plus its periphery accounted for all citations made.

In terms of notation in the rest of this chapter, core 1 is denoted by {1}, and the corresponding periphery by {1'}. Our citation analysis included the three cores and the three peripheries across the three subject areas, providing 18 categories of data for analysis. The subject areas are identified as business {B}, geography {G} and manufacturing engineering {M}. Therefore, as an example, {B1'} denotes those journals cited by business researchers between 1992 and 1997, but not cited sufficiently to be included in the Bradford 'nuclear zone'.

The document access systems data

The defining principles of a document access system were discussed in Chapter 2. Those systems included in FIDDO's work were summarized there in Table 2.1, and are denoted using italics. For the purposes of the citation analysis, the data used to represent the coverage of each document access system require further brief explanation.

Unfortunately, so far as *Local holdings* was concerned, only four of the five participating libraries were able to supply us with a list of the journals held. For the purposes of the citation analysis, these lists were combined into a list called *Combined holdings*. This consisted of 12 226 journal titles, covering a wide range of subject areas. While aware that not all researchers would visit other libraries and that, therefore, this consolidation was not ideal, we considered it to be reasonable to suppose that many would, given the close proximity in which the participating institutions were located. There was also evidence from FIDDO interviews and other studies (Crotteau, 1997) in support of this. For those curious, the journal collections of the four libraries who supplied us with a holdings list covered 20, 36, 67 and 82 per cent of the citations made by researchers at the relevant institutions.

ILL–BLDSC was based on the standard BLDSC service, offering coverage of 34 000 current journal titles in a range of subject areas.

BL inside was based on a product offered by the British Library, offering coverage of the 20 000 most requested current journal titles from the BLDSC.

ProQuest Direct was based on a desktop search and retrieval system, which claimed to offer general coverage and to be 'one of the world's largest collections of information, including summaries of articles from over 8000 publications, many in full-text, full-image format' (UMI, 1999). In fact, only 622 journals were available as full text at the time of the study.

SearchBank was another desktop search and retrieval option, although it was restricted to business and marketing sources. A total of 564 journal titles were offered in full-text and PDF formats at the time of the study.

So far as the *Geo–SL–BL* system was concerned, we decided to add *Georef*, a second geography-oriented database hosted by SilverPlatter, in conjunction with *Geobase*. This resulted in the document access system, *Geo–SL–BL + Georef*, shown in Fig. 3.2. We made this potential enhancement of *Geo–SL–BL* as we felt that it offered a more accurate reflection of the potential of the system. A user only received a document if it was covered by both the BLDSC and either Geobase or Georef, so that the

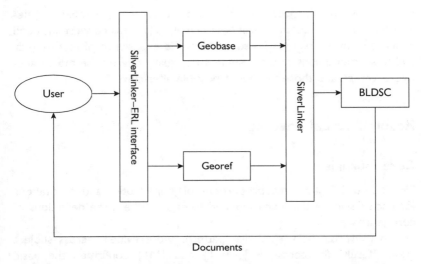

Figure 3.2. The *Geo–SL–BL* document access system with an additional database, Georef

relevant journal listing was a two-stage matching of Georef plus Geobase results with BLDSC holdings. The relevant coverage of the system as a whole was 2900 journal titles.

EiText supplied subject-specific (engineering) documents. It was selected as a standalone supplier although it was more usually linked with the Compendex database. Over 7000 titles were covered, although not all of these were journals.

Methodology: effective coverage

Effective coverage refers to the coverage of document access systems as they were used in the real world of research, and the perceptions of them by researchers. We took a more qualitative approach to assessing the effective coverage of document access systems. The general approach taken in the field trials is described in Chapter 2 and Appendix B. In the initial interviews, we asked researchers about their typical methods of obtaining documents. We urged them to complete diary-type forms each time they used a system, which asked them about the number of relevant hits found. Questions about subject coverage, number of relevant hits and the academic quality of the materials obtained were included in subsequent interviews. These revealed the experience of researchers, and their impressions of the systems that usually offered the most effective coverage and those that were possible alternatives.

Results: actual coverage

Core journals

Figs 3.3 to 3.5 show the proportions of journal titles and of citations for each discipline that corresponded to each of the three definitions of core journals.

Unsurprisingly, very similar patterns were evident across subject areas. Results for cores {B1}, {G1} and {M1} confirmed the basic premise of Bradford's law as small proportions (less than 10 per cent) of journal titles accounted for more than a third of all citations. In cores

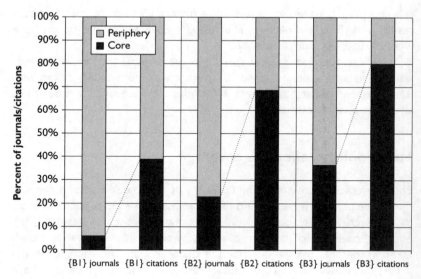

Figure 3.3. The proportions of citations accounted for by the three definitions of 'core' journals: BUSINESS STUDIES

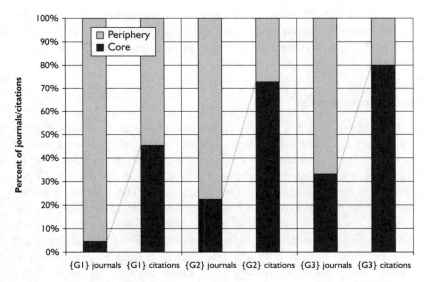

Figure 3.4. The proportions of citations accounted for by the three definitions of 'core' journals: GEOGRAPHY

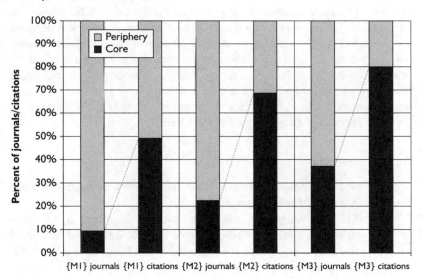

Figure 3.5. The proportions of citations accounted for by the three definitions of 'core' journals: MANUFACTURING ENGINEERING

{B2}, {G2} and {M2}, about 20 per cent of journal titles accounted for 70 per cent of citations, and in the third category of core, {B3}, {G3} and {M3}, approximately 40 per cent of titles covered 80 per cent of citations.

Interdisciplinarity

It should be noted that user requirements for literature coverage cross disciplinary boundaries. The mean overlap between departments was 18 per cent. That is, within each institution, of all the journal titles cited by researchers from the three (or, in one case, two) departments, 18 per cent were common to at least two departments. There were, however, wide variations between universities on this figure, from 6 to 26 per cent. Taking a disciplinary, rather than an institutional, view gave us a slightly different measurement. We calculated the proportion of journal titles cited by researchers in each discipline that were also cited by researchers in another discipline. This gave figures of 33 per cent for business, 77 per cent for geography and 19 per cent for manufacturing engineering. There was some evidence that those journals in core {1} were more likely to be used across disciplines in any institution than those that were in periphery {1'}. These results led us to believe that assessments of demand for journals that are based on institutional structures, such as departments, may not reflect demand accurately and may lead to inefficient use of library resources. Ideally, it is more appropriate to use either the individual researcher or the institution as a whole as the unit of analysis for document demand. Some budgetary implications of this are discussed in Chapter 7, and are taken further in Part Four.

Actual coverage

Tables 3.1 to 3.3 show that similar coverage patterns by suppliers were evident across the three subject areas.

ILL–BLDSC emerged as the most successful system as virtually all core and most peripheral citations were met. *BL inside* and *Combined holdings* had roughly equivalent coverage at around 80 per cent. With the exception of *BL inside*, coverage by the electronic systems was much lower, with *ProQuest Direct* covering between one and 10 per cent of all citations across subject areas. The subject-specific electronic systems were

Table 3.1. Percentage business coverage of the document access systems

System	All citations	BI	BI'	B2	B2'	B3	B3'
Combined holdings	78	88	71	83	66	82	60
ILL–BLDSC	98	100	97	99	96	100	93
BL inside	79	76	81	79	81	80	79
ProQuest Direct	7	10	6	9	3	9	3
Searchbank	11	16	7	14	4	12	3

Table 3.2. Percentage of geography coverage of the document access systems

System	All citations	GI	GI'	G2	G2'	G3	G3'
Combined holdings	77	82	72	84	59	82	56
ILL–BLDSC	90	85	85	91	89	91	88
BL inside	73	64	81	72	75	72	76
ProQuest Direct	1	1	1	1	1	1	2
Geo–SL–BL + Georef	39	43	55	43	26	43	23

Table 3.3. Percentage of manufacturing engineering coverage of the document access systems

System	All citations	MI	MI'	M2	M2'	M3	M3'
Combined holdings	85	99	71	93	68	91	62
ILL–BLDSC	97	98	97	97	98	98	96
BL inside	79	73	85	77	84	78	83
ProQuest Direct	3	3	3	2	4	3	3
EiText	37	48	26	42	26	40	26

more successful than this. For business, *SearchBank* covered 11 per cent of all citations. *Geo–SL–BL + Georef* and *EiText* each covered roughly 40 per cent of all citations. The limiting factor for *Geo–SL–BL + Georef* was certainly the databases rather than the BLDSC component.

There are, perhaps, two anomalous findings that are apparent in Tables 3.1 to 3.3. Firstly, the figures in Table 3.2 are generally lower than those in Tables 3.1 and 3.3. Secondly, some systems seemed to cover a higher proportion of wider core categories than of narrower ones (for example, *BL inside* M1:M3). Both of these apparent anomalies might be explained by the imperfect title matches as discussed in the methodology section.

Results: effective coverage

As background to the rest of this section, we start by outlining the various ways by which researchers obtain documents. These findings from the field-trial interviews should be seen as indicating users' impressions of the relative effective coverage of various document access systems available to them at the time. We then describe how users saw the effective coverage of the specific systems included in the FIDDO research. Finally, we look at the impact on this of time and infrastructure issues. It should be remembered that the experience of researchers was varied and that the notion of 'effective coverage' is based on both the actual and perceived performance of the systems trialled.

How do academic researchers obtain documents?

The usual routes that researchers used for obtaining full-text documents are shown in Table 3.4. Unsurprisingly, locally-based facilities (*local holdings* and ILLs) accounted for most of their document access. Of all the available options, these local facilities were seen to be sufficiently comprehensive and convenient to cover most document needs. However, researchers regularly supplemented their local collection coverage by visiting other library collections. The reported frequency of this behaviour offers an alternative perspective to that taken by library managers at the Anderson Report seminar (Pat Wressel and Associates, 1997), where researchers were described as reluctant to travel, preferring an appropriate collection to be held by their own institution. We found that researchers saw both other university libraries and the web as significant supplementary sources of documents. This pattern was fairly consistent across all three subject areas, except that engineers were more likely to use the web, and geographers were more likely to use other libraries. Not surprisingly, researchers predicted that the web would increasingly be used as a means of accessing directly full-text documents.

Table 3.4. Usual routes by which full-text documents are accessed by researchers

Route by which researchers get hold of documents	Percentage of interviews in which each route was cited
Using their local library holdings	86
Using ILLs	86
Web	24
Making a visit to another library	37
Asking a colleague at another university to visit that library	9
Other electronic sources (i.e. not the web)	9
Direct approach to the author	5
Ask a colleague in the department	7
Other	3

Effective coverage by suppliers[1]

Some of the qualities identified by researchers as contributing to the effective coverage of a system were that it should:

- include key journals in any chosen field;
- be comprehensive;
- include suitably academic content;
- provide full-text documents;
- provide document availability information.

The more that researchers felt in control of their document access, bearing in mind the above points, the more they felt that the systems had effective coverage. So, how did researchers discuss each of these points?

Effective coverage included the provision of key journal titles, necessary in the first stage of the research cycle as outlined earlier. Researchers had a greater sense of effective coverage from libraries that held predominantly research rather than teaching collections. They considered that *ILL–BLDSC* and *Combined holdings* succeeded in providing core subject area journals. The more electronic document access systems varied in

---

[1] *BL inside* was not part of the end-user trials and was not therefore included in the interviews.

their coverage but were generally seen to be much less likely to include key titles.

Effective coverage consisted of comprehensive listings that met the majority of user requirements. This relates to the second stage of the research cycle as outlined in the introduction. Researchers saw *Local holdings*, *Combined holdings* and *ILL–BLDSC* as offering such comprehensiveness. For the newer models of document access, perceptions of the above criteria for effective coverage varied. Generally, researchers said that considerable numbers of requested journal titles were not available through *SearchBank*, *ProQuest Direct*, *EiText* and *Geo – SL–BL*. However, researchers trialling the systems recorded fill rates of known-item searches of 45 per cent via *SearchBank* and 32 per cent via *ProQuest Direct*, which were much higher than the figures in Table 3.1. A possible reason for this was that researchers may have accessed abstracts only, which they then counted as successful finds, despite instructions to the contrary. Of course, an abstract alone might have satisfied a researcher's particular information need. Perceptions of coverage were also higher than in Table 3.1, possibly due to researchers' preference for the kind of efficient search engines operated by *SearchBank* and *ProQuest Direct*. Only 22 per cent of known item searches using *Geo–SL–BL* resulted in the delivery of a full-text document, which is only about half that of the coverage rates in Table 3.2. However, researchers reported that all requested documents were received. This confirmed that any limitations on coverage were due to the Geobase database, rather than to the BLDSC, and that these might be lessened by searching both Georef and Geobase using the SilverLinker technology.

Effective coverage in the higher education sector requires a high level of refereed material of a suitably academic nature. One of the main detractions from the effective coverage of *ProQuest Direct* and *SearchBank* was a relative absence of heavyweight academic journals and a bias toward trade and professional material. This resulted in too many inappropriate hits in open-ended searches, leading to problems in the selection of documents of sufficient academic quality. This was less of a issue for *EiText* and *Geo–SL–BL*, which appeared to be targeted more directly at the academic community.

Effective coverage required the provision of full-text documents. Some document access systems, such as *ProQuest Direct* and *SearchBank*, could not supply these consistently because many documents were available only as abstracts. The dual functions in these systems, of resource discovery (of all documents) and document delivery (as full-text documents only), confused the issue of effective coverage for researchers.

Effective coverage required the availability of full holdings information, prior to requesting. Its importance was demonstrated by the difference between the trial fill rate of *EiText* (35 per cent – approximately the same as the figures in Table 3.3) and the perceptions of researchers who thought it the worst of all the systems trialled. These negative perceptions were based partly on the fact that researchers had no way of checking the availability of documents prior to requesting. Although this also held for *ILL–BLDSC*, it seemed that its importance to researchers was minimized by the overall satisfaction rate of the ILL service.

Effective coverage and the impact of time

Issues of time (see Chapter 4) which were perceived by researchers as reducing the effective coverage of document access systems were:

- time spent locating and requesting documents;
- delays in document delivery;
- non-receipt of documents.

Researchers often found the use of traditional document access systems to be excessively time-consuming. Travelling to local and particularly to alternative libraries took time, as did locating the required documents once there. Using the ILL system also took time. Delays and non-delivery of documents applied to both traditional and electronic systems. For example, despite a reported *EiText* fill rate of 35 per cent, the majority of researchers who used it commented that requested documents did not arrive, arrived late or that there was no response to requests from *EiText*. User support is discussed further in Chapter 6.

Effective coverage and the impact of infrastructure

Infrastructure and technical issues (see Chapter 5) that impacted on the effective coverage of document access systems were the availability and reliability of:

- mail services;
- photocopying services;
- computers;
- printing resources;
- network services.

Failures in any of these areas could detract from users' perceptions of the effective coverage of systems. For instance, queues for photocopiers often dissuaded researchers from using the local collection as they might, thereby reducing its effective coverage. Conversely, the existence of network services, through which researchers had desktop access to systems such as *Geo–SL–BL*, led to high levels of perceived effective coverage.

Summary and conclusions

There are clear general patterns of 'actual' coverage by systems within the core/periphery categories that we have used. It is no surprise that *ILL–BLDSC* covered the most citations of any system and that its coverage rates were generally over 95 per cent. Coverage by the other general systems varied, with *BL inside* maintaining coverage of around 75 per cent of all citations. At the other extreme, coverage by *ProQuest Direct* was disappointing at less than 10 per cent for practically all categories of core and periphery. Admittedly, *ProQuest Direct* made no claims to be aimed exclusively at the academic world or to be a 'one-stop-shop'. Of the three new commercial, subject-specific document access systems tested, *SearchBank*, *EiText* and *Geo–SL–BL*, none really lived up to expectations although, like *ProQuest Direct*, *SearchBank* did not claim to be wholly focused on academic journals. Finally, the *Combined holdings* of the four universities provided high levels of coverage that were comparable with those of *BL inside* and, in several cases, even with those of *ILL–BLDSC*.

The notion of 'effective coverage' has added a further dimension to the overall success of these systems, which is related to:

- the amount, relevance and quality of information;
- the cost-benefit of use;
- preconditional technical and infrastructure support.

Whether a system provides coverage that fits with the changing needs and constraints of the research cycle, as experienced by individual researchers, depends on these factors. Applying these criteria, none of the systems trialled had adequate effective coverage, although they were each found lacking in different ways. *SearchBank* and *ProQuest Direct* would have benefited from improved ratios of academic to non-academic documents, or a means to filter out inappropriate material. Some indication of document availability was required of *EiText*. Unfortunately, the field trial with *Geo–SL–BL* was too small to be conclusive, although the linking principle employed is a potential way forward for document access in the developing hybrid library.

In this chapter we have drawn attention to some of the shortcomings of newer, electronic document access systems. However, their main advantage to users appears to be the potential to provide speedy and seamless document access. This potential would suggest that they will have an important role as partial but supplemental sources of document access. In this chapter we have shown that in order to realize this potential a better alignment of actual and effective coverage levels is needed.

CHAPTER FOUR

The contexts of action of academic researchers: the local organization

Introduction

Researchers are not just researchers. Lecturing staff, especially, are normally expected to pursue research in their area of expertise in addition to their main teaching-related and administrative tasks. Even full-time researchers, including post-graduates and post-doctoral researchers, have only a finite period in which to carry out their work as research contracts are often short and schedules ambitious. Furthermore, although we contend that research time is dictated mainly by such local organizational structures, we also recognize that the time that can be usefully dedicated to research may be further reduced by the effects of narrow coverage available from some document access systems (see Chapter 3) and by the impact of infrastructure and technical factors on both paper-based and electronic document delivery. Finally, aspects of non-working life pose additional limitations on the working day.

Clearly, in terms of document delivery, the issue of speed is important. Studies have found that, in general, end-users expect to have to pay more for a speedy service, although their willingness to do so depends on their ability to pay (Webster, 1997a). Express delivery services are perceived to be directly related to cost. This perception is confirmed by FIDDO trials reported elsewhere (Morris, Woodfield and Davies, 1999) and by other studies (Cornish, 1996; Dade, 1997; Evans, Bevan and Harrington, 1996; Williams, 1997). However, some studies have suggested that there is no direct correlation between user satisfaction and the actual delivery time of a document (Higginbotham and Bowdoin, 1994; Mann,

1998), although Weaver-Meyers and Stolt (1996) did find a correlation between user satisfaction and *perceptions* of timeliness (only 17 per cent of which were based on actual delivery times). FIDDO's interviews with researchers suggest that the speed at which documents are required reflects the different stages of the research cycle (see Chapter 3, and Jacobs and Morris, 1999b).

This chapter presents the results of our experimental testing of the various document access systems, together with researchers' experiences and perceptions of those systems. In this way, there is a dual analysis of both quantitative and qualitative measurements of time. Although we interviewed both lecturing staff and full-time researchers, the impact of some of the findings reported here is likely to be felt more by those who are carrying out simultaneously both teaching and research roles.

Aspects of time

As in Chapter 3, the terms 'actual' and 'effective' are used but, in this case, they are used in the context of time:

*   actual time is the time necessary to use a document access system, as measured experimentally;
*   effective time is the time necessary to use a document access system, as perceived and used by academic researchers.

There are two additional facets of time related to document delivery, which we have called 'dedicated' and 'delivery' time:

*   dedicated time is that which is necessary to dedicate exclusively to using a document access system – this time cannot be used for another purpose;
*   delivery time is the delay between requesting a document and receiving a paper copy – this time can be used for another purpose.

The rest of this chapter is organized around these four facets of time and their inter-relationships. The structure is summarized in Table 4.1, with each cell further explained below.

Table 4.1. Aspects of time used by FIDDO; numbers refer to sections in this chapter

	Actual time	Effective time
Dedicated time	1. Experimentally measured time necessary to dedicate to using a document access system	3. End-user perceptions of the time necessary to dedicate to using a document access system
Delivery time	2. Experimentally measured delay between requesting a document and receiving a paper copy	4. End-user perceptions of the delay between requesting a document and receiving a paper copy

1. Actual dedicated time

This represented the time taken by FIDDO staff and researchers to search for, find and request a required document in the appropriate format using a document access system. It was time during which a researcher was unlikely to be able to carry out other tasks, and time during which a computer, if a part of the document access system, was likely to be tied up with this exclusive task. It could also have been time spent filling in an ILL form, photocopying a journal article in the library or searching an online database. It was quite straightforward to measure this time from start to end by experimental testing. Recorded times by researchers were also taken from the completed trial forms; the more qualitative feedback from these was used to assess effective time (see below).

2. Actual delivery time

Actual delivery time represented the time from the point of requesting to the moment when the document arrived into the hands of the requester. This was time when researchers could do other things and when their computers, if a part of the document access system, were available to them. Actual delivery time was less accurately quantifiable than actual dedicated time because several components may have been involved in a single document access system. For example, the delivery time for ILLs via the BLDSC was made up of the time taken by ILL staff to process and send the request, the time for the BLDSC to satisfy the request, the time taken to deliver the document to the institution and, finally, the time for the document to reach the requester, perhaps via internal mail systems. Delays could be encountered at any of these stages and therefore may not have been a direct reflection of the BLDSC in isolation, but rather of the various elements and linkages that together make up a document access system.

3. Effective dedicated time

This represented several possible concepts, including the perceptions of researchers based on their experience of using of a system, and on the ways in which the necessary dedicated time fitted into the fragmented time available for research tasks. This is discussed further in the results section below. Our assessments of effective dedicated time were based on interview data with researchers and some sections of the completed trial forms, and were essentially subjective.

4. Effective delivery time

This represented the extent to which the time taken to deliver a document to a researcher fitted with the time available for a particular piece of research – was a document still useful when it arrived? Directly related to this is the issue of research momentum which again is discussed further in the results section below. Research momentum could be jeopardized by an excessive wait for a document. Again, effective delivery time was assessed through interview discussions and completed trial forms, and was subjective and impressionistic, based on individual ways of working and workloads.

Methodology

We used two sources of data to measure the actual time necessary to use document access systems. Firstly, we conducted some experiments and, secondly, we obtained some quantitative data from the field trials. The data on which we based our assessments of effective time were exclusively from the interviews that formed another part of the field trials.

Actual time: experimentation

We measured both actual dedicated and actual delivery times by experimentation using time-trials. The document access systems involved in these time trials were:

- *ILL–BLDSC*
- *BL inside*
- *ProQuest Direct*
- *SearchBank*
- *EiText*

In Chapter 2 document access systems were defined as including the infrastructure necessary for particular services or products to work, so that where necessary we have included photocopiers, printers, mail services and so on within the definition of a document access system. While this was only occasionally relevant in Chapter 3, it is absolutely central to this chapter.

The sample of documents used is described in Chapter 2. The times recorded depended on the system in question, but variously included the time to locate a document on the system, download and print it or wait for it to arrive. For *ILL–BLDSC*, we recorded the time between submitting the request to the ILL department and receiving it via the internal mail. For faxed *BL inside* documents, we recorded the search time, the time between requesting and receiving the document, the stated fax time, the actual fax time (in total and per page) and the total time. The data recorded for *ProQuest Direct* and *SearchBank* included the time taken to locate the document record entry within the database, the downloading time, the printing time and the total time. In the case of *EiText*, the data recorded were the time taken to Email the request, the time between requesting and receiving the Email attachment, the total printing time and the total time. Unfortunately, neither the actual time taken to photocopy locally-held journal articles, nor the actual time taken to complete an ILL form were measured, although most library managers will be able to supply their own estimates for such figures.

The time trials assumed that users required a hard copy of any document, since there was evidence from work discussed in Chapter 5 that users preferred to read from paper rather than from the screen.

Therefore, the end point of all the time trials was when a paper version of the document was finally received.

Actual time: quantitative data from the field trials

The researchers who took part in the FIDDO trials agreed to undertake some form of record-keeping of their use of the particular document access system and some evaluation of it. The aim was to reveal the issues and concerns of researchers with document access systems and the factors that were important in their assessments of them. The systems concerned were *ProQuest Direct, SearchBank , EiText* and *Geo–SL–BL*. Each researcher was asked to use the system to access documents over a period of one to three months and, when so doing, to complete 'diary-type' forms each time they used it (see Appendix B). Researchers were asked to record the time of day when they used the system, the number of documents obtained and the duration of their session.

Effective time: qualitative data from the field trials

Both effective dedicated and effective delivery times were assessed using interviews that formed a part of the field trials. In the initial inter-views (Appendix B), researchers were asked how much time they typically dedicated to obtaining documents by their usual routes, and how much delay there was. Overwhelmingly, these usual routes coin-cided with the document access systems *Local holdings* and *ILL–BLDSC*. This was followed up in the final interviews when researchers were asked to compare their usual routes with their experience of dedicated and delivery times using the newer systems (*ProQuest Direct, SearchBank, Geo–SL–BL* and *EiText*). These questions generated wide discussions of researchers' document needs and the constraints under which they worked.

Results and discussion

The structure of this section follows the four-part structure of Table 4.1; actual dedicated time, actual delivery time, effective dedicated time and effective delivery time.

Actual dedicated time

For all document access systems, actual dedicated time was that spent searching for, requesting and receiving a document. This applied perhaps more directly to *SearchBank* and *ProQuest Direct* than to the other systems trialled because these two required the end-user to be logged on to the system until the document was delivered (that is, printed out). Using *SearchBank* and *ProQuest Direct*, the whole document access procedure was online, so that the distinction between dedicated and delivery time was less than clear[1]. As a result, there is unavoidable overlap in the presentation of the dedicated and the delivery time results for *SearchBank* and *ProQuest Direct*. For example, is waiting for a printer to print a document downloaded from *ProQuest Direct* to be counted as dedicated time (the printer cannot be used for another purpose) or delivery time (the user can undertake other tasks)? We decided that the latter definition was more persuasive, although we understand that the point is arguable.

Table 4.2 shows a comparison for business documents between *SearchBank*, *ProQuest Direct* and *BL inside* in terms of dedicated time. T-tests revealed that there was no significant difference in these times for business-related documents requested from the first two systems. Search times for *BL inside* were much slower in comparison. In fairness, all three systems have installed improved interfaces since our trials took place, which may now result in faster search times.

Table 4.2. Mean dedicated times for business-related documents

System	Search/order time (hrs:mins:secs)
SearchBank	00:00:55
ProQuest Direct	00:00:37
BL inside	00:03:43

Table 4.3 shows that, for engineering articles, search and order times for *BL inside* were considerably slower than order times for *EiText*. This was partly because there was no search facility for *EiText*, so that we had only to key in an Email request. However, requesting documents

---

[1]   This was, in part, an example of the difficulty in distinguishing between 'resource discovery' and 'document access' in some systems, as noted at the start of Chapter 2.

Table 4.3. Mean dedicated times for engineering-related documents

System	Search / order time (hrs:mins:secs)
BL inside	00:04:38
EiText	00:00:28

from *EiText* was problematical. Orders had to be sent by separate Emails to generate a response; even so, repeated requests for documents not received frequently evoked no explanation or reaction. We also experienced initial problems with ordering from *BL inside*, but this appeared to be due to accidental processing delays associated with a new account. Results for *BL inside* do not, therefore, reflect these particular delays.

As noted in Chapter 2, we were unable to conduct experimental time trials with *Geo–SL–BL* owing to scheduling constraints within FIDDO.

In principle, each of the new systems (*SearchBank, ProQuest Direct, EiText* and *Geo–SL–BL*) could be accessed at any time and documents ordered, provided that researchers had access to a networked computer. During the field trials, researchers recorded the time of day at which they attempted to use the systems, as it was thought that this could have a possible impact on access. The results are shown in Figs 4.1 to 4.4. It is arguable that these periods include delivery times for *SearchBank* and *ProQuest Direct*. The results for *Geo–SL–BL* should be treated with some caution because the sample was so small.

The vast majority of use of the systems during the field trials was during office hours and this, surely, reflected the times at which researchers were most likely to be at their place of work. As described in Chapter 6, *ProQuest Direct* was available away from campus, whereas *SearchBank* was not, and the off-campus use of *ProQuest Direct* shows up clearly as 'After 6 pm' use. Both *SearchBank* and *ProQuest Direct*, which involved searching a database over the web, were used predominantly during the morning, perhaps in order to maximize internet use before the USA goes online at lunchtime British time. Interestingly, there was a smaller dip in lunchtime use of web-based systems than the ordering-based *EiText* system. This may have reflected a general identification of the use of the web as a leisure time activity that, in this case, extended to work-related document access.

In terms of the length of time researchers spent using the document access systems during the field trials, Figs 4.5 to 4.7 show that the

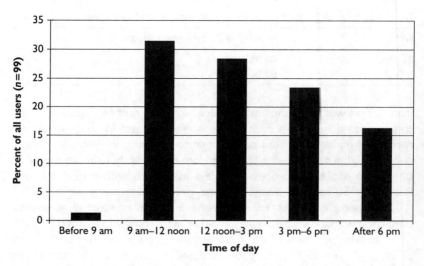

Figure 4.1. Time of day at which researchers used *ProQuest Direct* during the field trials

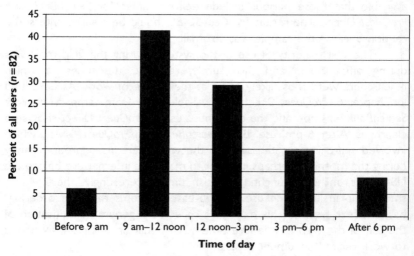

Figure 4.2. Time of day at which researchers used *SearchBank* during the field trials

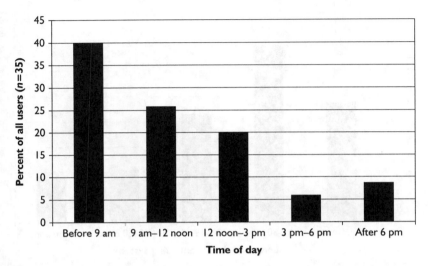

Figure 4.3. Time of day at which researchers used *Geo–SL–BL* during the field trials

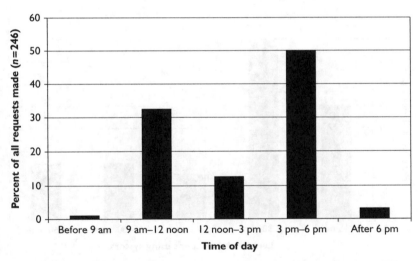

Figure 4.4. Time of day at which researchers requested documents from *EiText* during the field trials

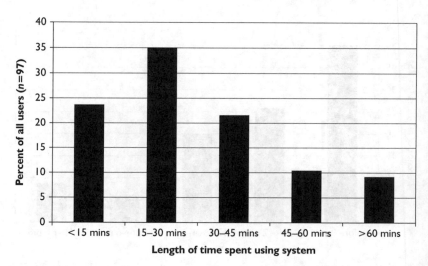

Figure 4.5. Length of time spent by researchers using *ProQuest Direct* during the field trials

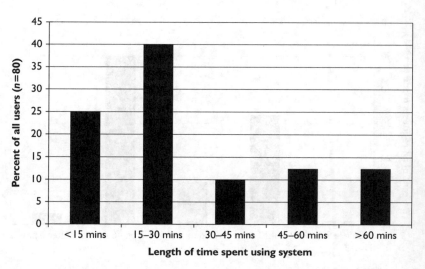

Figure 4.6. Length of time spent by researchers using *SearchBank* during the field trials

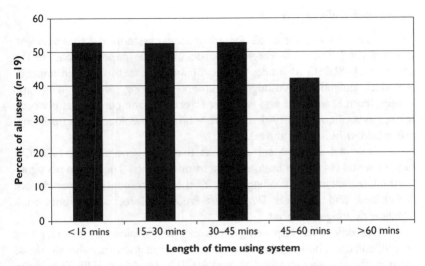

Figure 4.7. Length of time spent by researchers using *Geo–SL–BL* during the field trials

systems tended to be used in relatively short sessions. *EiText* is excluded because of its lack of a database component, and again the results for *Geo–SL–BL* should be treated with caution owing to the small sample size.

Assuming that the mean length of sessions over one hour long was 90 minutes, then the mean duration of sessions was remarkably consistent over the three systems (*SearchBank*: 32 mins; *ProQuest Direct*: 32 mins; *Geo–SL–BL*: 29 mins). These figures compare with at least a half-day for library visits, as reported in the field-trial interviews in many cases, especially where the library was geographically distant from the researcher's department, or where the researcher preferred to work at home. Of course, this is not comparing like with like, since in such cases many tasks were batched together and included in each library visit; the functional flexibility of the library is not comparable with the scheduling flexibility of the desktop electronic resources. However, the facility to search for, order and receive documents at the desktop meant that these functions were more likely to be carried out than if a library visit had been necessary.

2. Actual delivery time

The actual delivery time for all document access systems was that between the request for and the receipt of a document in paper format. In the cases of *ILL–BLDSC*, *BL inside*, *Geo–SL–BL* and *EiText*, this was an unproblematical definition. Although document ordering, downloading and receipt from *SearchBank* and *ProQuest Direct* was one continuous process, for reasons of consistency their delivery times (downloading and printing) are included here (see above).

Table 4.4 shows a set of results that was generated by FIDDO's experimental testing on business-related documents. There was no significant difference in downloading times for these documents requested from *SearchBank* and *ProQuest Direct*, but *ProQuest Direct* documents took significantly longer to print.

This difference in printing times can be explained by the fact that *SearchBank* documents included full text and some graphics, whereas those from *ProQuest Direct* included all graphics. It is, therefore, difficult to draw meaningful comparisons between them for printing times. The mean total time for *BL inside* was 2.5 hours, five times slower overall than *ProQuest Direct*. Because *ILL–BLDSC* is perhaps not set up as a desktop delivery service, its results are shown separately in Fig. 4.8. Using *ILL–BLDSC*, delivery times were generally from four to six days, although the BLDSC required further information three times between eight and 16 days after ordering. The presence of one significant outlier[2], delivered 251 days after requesting, suggested that the most meaningful statistic for *ILL–BLDSC* was the mode (rather than the mean or median), which was five days.

Fig. 4.8 indicates that the time taken to receive engineering-related documents using *ILL–BLDSC* was similar to that for business-related ones, with a mode of five days. The results for the two other systems from

Table 4.4. Mean delivery times for business-related documents

System	Download time (hrs:mins:secs)	Print/fax time (hrs:mins:secs)	Total delivery time (hrs:mins:secs)
SearchBank	00:00:48	00:06:35	00:07:23
ProQuest Direct	00:02:08	00:27:28	00:29:36
BL inside	N/A	02:27:04	02:27:04

[2]   This outlier is counted as 'not supplied' in Fig. 4.8.

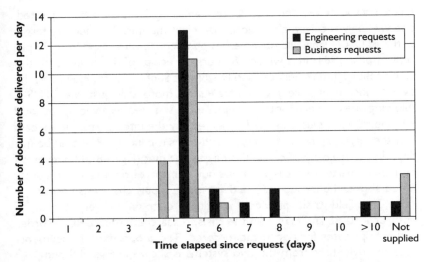

Figure 4.8. Delivery time for documents requested during the time trials from *ILL–BLDSC*

which engineering-related documents were requested are shown in Table 4.5. As noted above, we experienced some initial problems with *BL inside*. Table 4.5 therefore shows two results for this system, the second of which excludes the documents affected by these problems. There was no question that *BL inside* offered the faster total mean delivery time, which, even before this adjustment, was more than three times faster than *EiText*.

We encountered various problems during the experiments, even apart from the early problems with *BL inside* already noted. Of the 20 business-related documents, only 14 were received from *BL inside* because six were unavailable. One *SearchBank* document and five *ProQuest Direct* documents caused our computer to lose communication with the printer. Three of the 40 requests to *ILL–BLDSC* were abandoned because a

Table 4.5. Mean delivery times for engineering-related documents

System	Delivery time	(hrs:mins:secs)
BL inside	12:34:31	
BL inside (adjusted)	02:15:53	
EiText	40:35:03	

reference source was required. Of the remaining 37 documents requested, one was only received after more than eight months. The delivery target of the BLDSC's standard document supply service is to respond to 90 per cent of post-1984 titles within 48 hours of receipt of the request (British Library Bibliographic Services and Document Supply, 1999). However, the overall document access system relies on more than just the BLDSC. Allowing one day each for the requests to be sent and received by the local ILL department, plus one day for delivery by the internal mail, it appears that the target, so far as delivery to end-users is concerned, should be five days. In the majority of cases, this target was met (Fig. 4.8). However on perhaps a quarter of occasions it was not and, apart from the four requests noted above, the location of the delay in the supply chain was unclear.

The field trials provided additional data on delivery times for both *Geo–SL–BL* and *EiText*. In the trials, researchers recorded the order and receipt dates for documents ordered. The proportion of documents received over time from the two systems is shown in Figs. 4.9 and 4.10 and, for comparison, a similar chart (Fig. 4.11) has been generated from the experimental data discussed above relating to *ILL–BLDSC*. In each case, the proportions are of all documents successfully delivered.

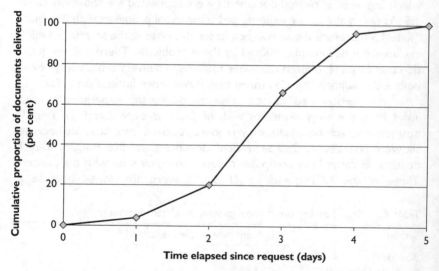

Figure 4.9. Proportion of documents delivered over time for documents requested by researchers during the field trials from *Geo–SL–BL*

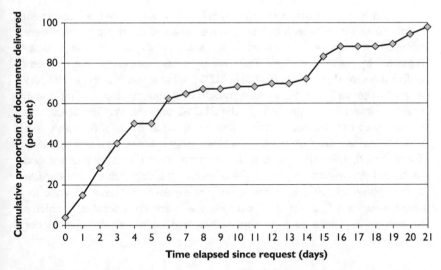

Figure 4.10. Proportion of documents delivered over time for documents requested by researchers during the field trials from *EiText*

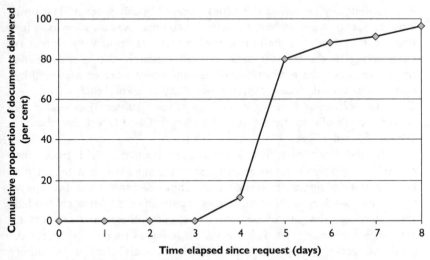

Figure 4.11. Proportion of documents delivered over time for business and engineering documents requested during the time trials from *ILL–BLDSC*

Delivery of documents from *EiText* showed a wide scatter of response times. A few documents were received on the day they were ordered; the longest recorded delay was 31 days. The mean delay reported by researchers for *EiText* was eight days, compared with a mode of five days for documents from *ILL–BLDSC*. Therefore, electronic delivery is not necessarily quicker than traditional paper systems. The mean delivery time of documents from the BLDSC ordered via *Geo–SL–BL* and delivered to the desktop was 3.1 days, with a maximum of five days. We should however emphasize again that this result is based on a small sample. If confirmed, this result would demonstrate that direct requesting and receipt of documents, bypassing the university ILL department, has considerable potential to reduce the time that researchers have to wait for documents (see Chapter 9). Obviously there are considerable problems to overcome before such an approach would be practical within higher education.

3. Effective dedicated time

For all document access systems, the effective dedicated time is that spent by real users locating and requesting a document (if applicable), taking into account any perceived difficulties involved in this process. The time input required of researchers to access documents was a major issue for them as they saw it as both disruptive to their 'day-to-day' work and as contributing to the fragmentation of their research. We examined the degree to which these difficulties were either reinforced or alleviated by current document access systems (*ILL–BLDSC*, *Local holdings* and the *Combined holdings* of libraries in the region, see Chapter 3) as well as by newer models of document access including *ProQuest Direct*, *SearchBank*, *Geo–SL–BL* and *EiText*.

In the interviews that formed a part of the field trials, the overwhelming impression given by most researchers was that they had a large number of demands on their time. These demands came principally from their teaching and administrative commitments. Research tended to occupy the margins of time for most researchers. In many cases, researchers affirmed that they worked at home as much as they could, partly to protect their research time from encroachment by other commitments. How did the various document access systems fare in this context?

At several of the universities in which FIDDO interviewed researchers, the academic department was some distance from the library. Although some viewed the opportunity to break up the working day in a positive light and others were ambivalent, most researchers interviewed perceived the trip to the library as cutting into their day-to-day schedule.

'Even having to actually go and visit our library here – just the fact of actually going down there and getting in and getting yourself settled – all takes time and the rest of it. You might not do it if you know you're going to be teaching a class in another forty five minutes.'

[Researcher, Business School]

Visits to the library were necessary to photocopy articles from journals (or to hand in forms to have the work done) and, possibly, to hand in ILL request forms. Each of these tasks had the potential for complications; journals can be missing from the shelves, and references for ILL forms can be incomplete. Not only did these tasks break up the workflow, but researchers saw them as trivial and clerical.

'Well I don't think there are any best aspects [to the current options]. The worst aspects are the time consuming and trivial nature of the activities. When I search round the library I think, 'God, this is a waste of time, why is this journal not here?' The vast amount of time you spend in non-value-added activities.'

[Researcher, Manufacturing Engineering]

Similarly other libraries, as a secondary source of documents for researchers (see Chapter 3), were seen to waste time on non-productive activities.

'. . . if time is a scarce resource anyway, then every three hours that you use searching for something or driving to [nearby university] or whatever, is time that you could have spent physically writing.'

[Researcher, Business School]

When they could, senior researchers delegated as much of this work as possible to research assistants and post-graduate researchers. However, some researchers did note that library searching, although slow, could be seen as a positive research experience; it was seen to be particularly valuable for browsing and for providing a broad-brushed literature search that included current research.

> 'So I have a habit of going to the library once a week and browsing through current issues, because once a week, more or less, new issues might arrive on the shelves.'
>
> [Researcher, Business School]

Clearly, this aspect of researchers' information work is more difficult to delegate.

To minimize the 'wasted time' in the library, some researchers talked of batching their document requirements, so that they would save up ILL requests and journal articles to be photocopied until they had enough to make a library visit worthwhile. Of course the corollary of this was that there could be a significant delay between identifying a document requirement and doing something about it.

One major advantage which researchers saw in newer models of document access was that documents could be requested as the need for them was identified.

> 'You can also do it when you want. You can have five minutes of doing it, whereas going to the library or whatever means time to actually physically cross campus.'
>
> [Researcher, Business School]

Due to their other commitments, researchers reported that they did not have major 'chunks' of time available to devote to literature-related tasks; they tended to have fragmented time at the margins of their days. For this reason, they noted that desktop access could improve both the quantity and the quality of their research. Desktop document discovery and access could utilize the small bits of otherwise 'dead' time in researchers' fragmented schedules, and so free up larger chunks of time for research work. However, some noted that administrative duties would be more likely to colonize this newly liberated time than genuine research. Researchers also claimed that they would probably be less worried about going down blind alleys in their literature review practices if they were using desktop systems. This, they noted, would improve their awareness of the literature and enable them to have a broader critical view of their work.

Some researchers even maintained that the greater convenience of desktop access had directly motivated them in their work.

'I think [*SearchBank*] has made me enthusiastic as well, in terms of wanting to do stuff as well. You know, you have better time; you think, 'I've got half an hour now, I'll just onto SearchBank for half an hour'; you may find something useful.'

[Researcher, Business School]

Attitudes varied concerning the downloading and printing of documents via *SearchBank* and *ProQuest Direct*, especially when this meant that the computer (as well as the printer) could not be used for other purposes until the document was printed out. Some researchers saw this as enabling them to go off to do other things; others were frustrated by the fact that they could not use their machines.

In summary, users viewed traditional methods of document access as inefficient uses of their time, which did not lend themselves to the real-life conditions imposed upon research activities. In comparison, newer systems offered fast requesting procedures that, most importantly, could be carried out from the desktop, making the most of the odd moments between other timetabled tasks, and maximizing the total time available to the researcher.

4. Effective delivery time

The effective delivery time relates to the delay between requesting and receiving a document as it is experienced by the end-user in their work context. This concept can be related to the other contexts of action of end-users. In FIDDO's case, these were issues of system coverage and of the technical infrastructure. Hence, the first part of this section examines researchers' experiences of the effective delivery times of document access systems. This is followed by a discussion of the impact on these experiences of coverage and infrastructure issues.

Document access systems: effective delivery time

Delivery time was important to researchers because the longer the delay, the less likely it was that the momentum of their research would be maintained. For some, an ideal world would be one in which the local library could subscribe to every required journal title, making delivery unnecessary.

> 'I'm happier if the library has the journal in question and I can therefore get the paper quickly.'
>
> [Researcher, Manufacturing Engineering]

However, electronic document access systems have presented an equivalent and, for many, better (that is, more convenient) means of document provision. This section presents the perceptions of users about the delivery times and performance of the various systems included in the field trials.

Delays impacted on the already fragmented time of researchers. While the dedicated time required to use systems impacted on the day-to-day schedules of researchers, the delivery time of documents impacted on the continuity of the research effort over a longer period. The ILL service was criticized because of the uncertainty over the document delivery date and the delay in receiving documents, both of which could impact on researchers' workflows and schedules, sometimes seriously.

> '[T]here will be times when I'll be frustrated because I want this now and ILL's going to take days, and so I'm not going to order it anyway because in two weeks' time I'm not going to need it.'
>
> [Researcher, Business School]

'Access delayed can be access denied' (Rutstein, DeMiller and Fuseler, 1993). The problem, as hinted above, was that an information (document) need was specific to a particular research context, and because research is dynamic (it is a process) this context could change, sometimes very quickly. As one researcher put it:

> 'At the moment that two week delay or whatever that we've talked about – that four week delay – that sometimes means you've got to go back in your memory and recreate that moment and it's not necessarily that easy.'
>
> [Researcher, Business School]

Furthermore, several researchers, especially – but not exclusively – in manufacturing engineering departments, noted that deadlines for research grant applications could be measured in days or weeks, not months. They commented that they were often less aware of the relevant literature than they would like to be when making decisions about their research paths. In general, most researchers interviewed confirmed that their research output was probably (or certainly) affected by the fact that documents were not available when they were needed.

A minority of researchers, perhaps more humanities-oriented, did note that they appreciated the way that ILLs gave them a steady trickle of papers to read.

> 'Let's face it, whether you use the canal or the motorway to distribute your goods, if it's a constant stream, as long as it's continually arriving it doesn't really matter how long it takes, does it?'
>
> [Researcher, Geography]

Others commented that the costs, in terms of time, of obtaining documents meant that they were not confronted with information overload; the delays were effectively acting as a filter.

Desktop delivery by *SearchBank* and *ProQuest Direct* was a very popular option with researchers because it was convenient and fast, with requesting and delivery merging into a single process. Both *EiText* and *Geo–SL–BL* could deliver documents within a few days and researchers were generally very satisfied in these cases. However, because so many requests to *EiText* were not satisfied promptly (if at all), then the majority of engineers' responses were critical of it.

To summarize, despite some variations in reported attitudes, researchers generally maintained that the fast delivery times offered by desktop systems were useful in progressing a research project, and in pursuing funding possibilities. They affirmed that slower systems further exacerbated the fragmentation of the research process already in place as a result of their other departmental commitments.

Effective delivery time and the impact of coverage

Issues relating to coverage (see Chapter 3) that impacted on the effective time of researchers using document access systems were:

- inadequate coverage by document access systems;
- loss or use of documents by others;
- lack of document availability details.

The ideal for most researchers would have been a local collection whose coverage could meet all their requirements. Locally held journals that were then unavailable, for whatever reason, forced researchers either to wait for them or to get them from other sources. The narrow coverage by some alternative systems meant that researchers could not take full advantage of potential speed benefits offered by these electronic systems. Added to this, researchers had no way of knowing whether a particular document could be provided by *EiText* prior to requesting, which could therefore be a complete waste of time.

Effective delivery time and the impact of infrastructure

Infrastructure and technical issues (see Chapter 5) that researchers noted as impacting on their effective time using document access systems were the availability and reliability of:

* mail services;
* photocopying services;
* computers;
* printing resources;
* network services.

Problems with any of these slowed down document access, whether it was due to inadequate internal mail distribution, broken or overcrowded photocopiers, inadequate printers or the need for resources such as the Adobe Acrobat reader. In the case of electronic document access systems, researchers had to be at a networked computer. This effectively tied many of them to their offices for the trial, although some were able to use *ProQuest Direct* from home. Such systems ultimately rely on a functioning network and adequate printing facilities, which were not consistently provided by all institutions during the field-trials.

Summary and conclusions

Speed is generally a desirable attribute for any document access system. A wide variation in document delivery times was apparent from our experimental testing and from the end-user field trials of the various systems.

The comparison is complicated by the different requesting procedures and the various methods of delivery employed. It is not always a straightforward case of comparing like with like. One useful way of approaching it is to look at total requesting and delivery times. In this case, the electronic online systems appear to offer huge advantages over more traditional methods as requesting and delivery are instantaneous within the constraints of the technological infrastructure. We also found that the delivery of paper documents requested from and delivered directly to the desktop might offer substantial time improvements over traditionally mediated methods.

Our research has also shown that the 'actual' speed of document access may be different from the 'effective' time taken by researchers to obtain documents. Desktop document access options appear to offer the best fit with their often fragmented research cycle. Researchers can make requests in the intervals that may sometimes be wasted between other tasks. Delivery might then be immediate, with electronic documents being printed out while the user is otherwise occupied, or it might be delayed if the documents are not electronic. Furthermore, both requesting and delivery require no relocation, electronic documents are never lost or in use and direct access is less likely to lead to the delays associated with a chain of providers. However, there are still important weaknesses inherent in the fastest systems that render them, as yet, unacceptable alternatives to more traditional methods. Without a wider coverage, as described in the previous chapter, the systems remain partial and supplemental. Communication and technical difficulties, relating both to products and local networks, can let researchers down and make desktop-based systems far less than instant (see Chapter 5). Copyright-fee paid electronic delivery also generally costs more than the BLDSC's 'fair-dealing' service (see Chapters 7 and 8). There is probably a future for both electronic and paper-based document delivery, as there are significant advantages to both. What is also clear is that as traditional information services move increasingly toward the hybrid library model, all forms of document access will need to tailor their services much more closely to the needs of their users.

CHAPTER FIVE

The contexts of action of academic researchers: infrastructure and documents

Introduction

Chapter 3 was concerned with the disciplinary context of academic researchers and the coverage of systems, and Chapter 4 was concerned with the local departmental context of researchers and the time factors involved in using systems. This chapter is not quite so easy to characterize. It is not quite a 'miscellaneous' chapter because there are meaningful links within the FIDDO work described below. As noted in the introduction to Part Two, researchers are not just researchers; they work in a context comprising a technical infrastructure and a set of work tasks which influence the kind of documents that are appropriate. This chapter discusses these issues, but we admit that its focus is a little more 'fuzzy' than that of Chapters 3 and 4.

The first topic of this chapter is the technical infrastructure available to researchers, and how it affected their use of document access systems during the field trials. When the word 'infrastructure' is used, people often think of cables and servers. However, we are using the term to include not only the network infrastructure but all the implied aspects of a document access system. For example, the document access system *Local holdings* includes access to photocopying equipment. It simply does not work properly without photocopiers. However, the operation and maintenance of adequate photocopying equipment is not usually included in our idea of a printed journal; rather it is implied. Such implied aspects of document access systems, such as photocopiers and printers, often affect the quality of the paper document as it reaches the end-user. This leads us on to the second topic of this chapter, which is the document itself. Although we have assumed in the definition of document access systems that paper is preferred to electronic for reading, we questioned this assumption in interviews with researchers. What are the features of print and electronic formats that are valuable to researchers? And what features of some paper documents make them better than others for researchers?

Infrastructure

Some of the infrastructures upon which document access systems rely have been mentioned in Chapter 4 because they affected the time that researchers needed to spend to obtain documents. Examples include the local area network and internal and external mail services. In this section we focus specifically on these infrastructures and on their effects on the work of researchers.

Photocopying

Although photocopying is not often seen as directly or organizationally relevant to document access, the researchers we interviewed made it fairly clear that they wanted portable paper copies of documents (see below). They did not see printed journals on shelves in a library as adequate in themselves. In Chapter 4 we saw how researchers viewed photocopying as being essential but a source of wasted time. Here we discuss how researchers' routines interacted with the photocopying arrangements common in higher education.

The photocopier was the means by which most researchers gained effective access to locally held journals. Researchers described the technology as reliable, but the arrangements for its use as problematical. Library photocopiers were public resources; departmental ones less so. Their public character meant that they were time-consuming to use – queues of undergraduates were frequently mentioned.

'[The system is] archaic in comparison. And the large student population doesn't help either. I mean, I would never chuck a student off the photocopier; they have every sympathy and every right to be there, but it's a

damn sight easier out of term time. There's a huge demand on the system
– a real, real pain.'

[Researcher, Manufacturing Engineering]

For researchers to have effective access to photocopying facilities, at some point undergraduates had to be excluded. Researchers also voiced another complaint familiar to library managers – that photocopying in the library was expensive. Since library photocopiers were viewed as time-consuming and expensive, researchers took every opportunity to do as much photocopying as possible on departmental machines that were, in general, inaccessible to undergraduates. This meant that researchers relied on libraries to lend journal issues (even very briefly), and needed the departments to make machines available. Even then, they had to make two trips to the library, one to borrow and one to return the journal. No wonder that several of the more senior academics said that they delegated these tasks to their research students. This is a rational deployment of the scarce and expensive resource of an academic's time. However, for libraries anxious to claim meaningful and costed roles (see Chapter 7), it would seem like an opportunity wasted. Many academic libraries already offer a photocopying service based on their own collections and, if supported by an appropriate budgetary structure, this could save institutions money by allowing academics to concentrate on value-added activities.

Mail services

A paper-based document access system such as *ILL–BLDSC* can rely heavily on mail services for the movement of requests and documents. This remains the case, even though more and more parts of the *ILL–BLDSC* system are being automated (such as ArtE-mail requesting by libraries and web-based ILL request forms at particular universities). The 'gaps' in automation, filled by physical mail systems, are clear from Fig. 5.1, which shows one arrangement for *ILL–BLDSC* within a British higher education institution.

We were able to infer, from FIDDO's fieldwork reported in Chapter 4, that direct requesting and delivery of documents reduced the delays in the system by about a half. However, this was only possible using the copyright-fee paid service, for which no copyright signature was required.

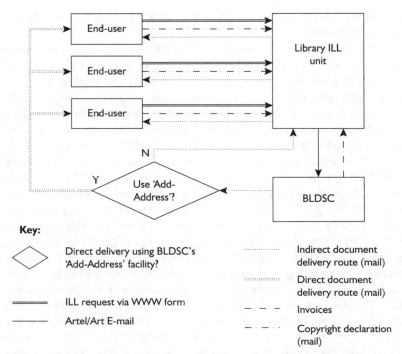

Figure 5.1. The *ILL–BLDSC* document access system, showing automated and non-automated (mail) linkages

Many libraries are currently working to develop a more direct 'fair-dealing' service for end-users wanting to request paper documents from the BLDSC. Clearly, the 'Add-Address' facility, wherein a delivery address can be included with each document request, is an important ingredient in such development work, since it eliminates at least one internal mail link in Fig. 5.1.

Desktop computers (work and home)

The equipment on a researcher's desk, whether at home or in the office, is a potentially weak link in the chain for electronic document access. The poor specification of some of this equipment even prevented some researchers from participating in the field trials. At other times they blamed the equipment for contributing to delays in navigating and downloading documents.

All the academics interviewed had access to their own office computer, and some additionally had their own computer at home, although this was not always networked. Most of these office machines were IBM-compatible PCs, but a significant proportion in geography departments were Macs, and some manufacturing engineers used Unix workstations. Post-graduate students were more likely to have to share computers, although some did have their own office machines.

The specifications of machines used by researchers varied and were dictated by the age of the machines; the computer market is such that one could usually tell the age of a desktop computer by its specification, and vice versa. Many of the more senior academics had computers that were no more than two years old; at the time of the trial this meant, for a PC, a Pentium II processor running at perhaps 200 MHz. However, perhaps half had machines older than this. Virtually all PhD students outside manufacturing engineering departments had access to much older machines, often up to eight years old (for example, basic 486 and even 386 PCs were still in use). Software was only available according to the constraints of the hardware, so that a significant number of those wanting to participate in the trials could not do so because their machines were not able to load either the Adobe Acrobat reader or a frames-capable version of an internet client. This was some three or four years after the HTML frames standard had been deployed.

Given the ages of the machines that we found in use, we were able to deduce that the academic departments we sampled seemed to be operating a replacement cycle for desktop computers of around eight years. Although the Dearing Report (National Committee of Inquiry into Higher Education, 1997) into British higher education did not recommend a figure, the submission of the Universities and Colleges Information Systems Association did suggest that an IT replacement cycle of four years should be the aim (UCISA, 1996). The position in the USA, as reported by Ringle (1997), was somewhat better than that found by FIDDO, with a norm of around five years.

Our work also confirmed that PhD and post-doctoral students, often the most active researchers in an institution, were also likely to be those with access to the oldest computers, although this was not necessarily the case in the manufacturing engineering departments.

Printing (work and home)

An indication of the importance of printing equipment can be gauged by noting that during the FIDDO trials researchers immediately printed out over 70 per cent of the documents that they downloaded from web-based systems. Printing equipment may be important, but is it adequate?

Most academics had an inkjet or similar printer in their offices, which they used for small *ad hoc* print jobs. Larger print jobs were delegated to a communal laser printer, often in a departmental office. Users with these arrangements experienced few printing problems. Some academics, and most post-graduate researchers, relied wholly on shared (networked) printers, usually laser printers. This arrangement caused more problems, either because of the inconvenience of the printer being some distance from the computer or, more frequently, because the slowness of the local network and printer (or the desktop machine running the printer driver) meant that printing out large files was neither reliable nor popular with others sharing the use of the printer. Some researchers supplemented the university equipment by using their own printer at home, or even by bringing it into the office. However, it is probably not acceptable that basic facilities such as printing should have to be provided out of researchers' salaries.

IT networks

From our interviews with researchers, there were only two types of occasion when the local campus network was mentioned. Firstly, given the subject of the interviews, researchers were very happy with increasing desktop access to library-based resources, especially the local OPAC and bibliographic databases. Secondly, they were deeply frustrated when the local network was insufficiently robust to do its job. This included not only printing out, but also accessing local and global web-based resources. Such occasions seemed to contribute significantly to any general sense of disillusion with a university already present in a researcher's viewpoint.

Chapter 4 described how local demands on researchers meant that some of them protected their research time by doing as much of it as possible at home. If network access was a part of this work then this meant that they relied on a modem connection and the support of the local computing services department. Researchers working at home tended to own better equipment than that supplied by the university, although it is unclear in the long term whether personal resources could (or should have to) improve on the eight-year replacement cycle currently achieved by universities.

Although not a focus of FIDDO's work, it is probably worth noting that if university research in a rich country such as the UK relies on personal ownership of computing equipment, how much more difficult must be the conditions of researchers in poorer regions of the world. We should, perhaps, ensure that our search for better document access, networked and electronic, is not at the expense of those already less advantaged.

Summary: infrastructure

Physical libraries rely on physical infrastructure. Although researchers high-lighted photocopying and ILL forms as the least satisfactory aspects of this, we concluded that mail systems were probably also having a detrimental effect on the standard of service offered by libraries. Electronic libraries rely on electronic infrastructure. Printing, as the equivalent of photo-copying in the electronic world, was an issue for researchers, as were the specifications and reliability of networks and desktop equipment. Hybrid libraries rely on both physical and electronic infrastructures, and on inte-gration between the two. This integration is an administrative and a budgetary issue (see Chapters 6 and 7), as well as a technical one. It is a matter of getting the right documents to the right people at the right time, and the right documents have to be in the right format and of the right quality. It is to these issues that we now turn.

Documents

End-users find some documents, like some document access systems, easier to use than others. Just as we discussed above the technical side of systems, in this section we are concerned with the technical side of the documents themselves. What makes a document easy to use? Our starting point was to ask researchers what they used documents for. We identified five types of document-based work task that researchers wanted to undertake.

- Selecting: in order to know that they needed to read a document further, researchers needed first to select it from the source in which it appeared: for example, a database or a web site.
- Scanning: researchers wanted to be able to scan the document quickly, identifying those sections that particularly interested them.
- Reading in detail: this was the classical view of the scholar's activity – quiet, reflective reading.
- Reviewing and interacting: researchers were reading with a purpose, so that they often needed to be able to interact with documents, for example, in the process of authoring documents of their own.
- Storing: documents may need to be consulted again and again, or they may not. Most researchers wanted to be able to store them just in case, and in a way that was easy and efficient. However, some did not want to replicate the work of the library, especially a hybrid library containing a mixture of print and electronic documents.

Our first question related to the format of documents. Did researchers prefer electronic or paper documents for these work tasks? What were their reasons? These questions formed a part of the field trials with various document access systems. Our second question related to the quality of documents. What made one paper document better than another for these work tasks? What made one electronic document better than another? We conducted a survey, based on paired comparisons (see Chapter 2), to answer the question with respect to paper document quality. Unfortunately, we did not have time to do the same with electronic documents, but some relevant issues did arise during the field-trial interviews with researchers.

Document format

It is widely known, and confirmed by research findings (SuperJournal, 1999), that people prefer to read in detail from paper. Some have assumed that this is because the technology (hardware and software) is not yet good enough (Davies, 1998). Others suspect that paper is just better (Dillon, 1992). However, reading in detail is only one task out of the five we identified for which documents are used. The preferences of researchers with respect to paper or electronic format depended on which of these was being discussed and, in particular, how and where the documents were being used. In addition, researchers mentioned certain particular document and user attributes that influenced their views.

Work method

How did researchers use documents in each of the work tasks described above? What impact did that have on their preferred document format? Researchers often described the ways they worked with documents as fairly fixed routines, and the document format was heavily embedded in those routines.

In terms of selecting, the vast majority of the researchers interviewed had used electronic databases of some sort to locate and select documents; this method seemed to have been generally accepted, although some did specifically mention browsing through journals. For selecting full-text documents, many researchers also preferred the electronic format. This was primarily due to the speed with which abstracts could be checked and, especially, the speed with which documents arrived with the researcher (see Chapter 4). Some researchers saw scanning, which overlapped to some extent with selecting, as being undertaken best with a paper copy because of the ease with which the physical document could be navigated (see 'document quality', below). However, others described scanning on the screen in terms of identifying sections for closer attention, for which only those sections would be printed out.

Although reading in detail was a task for which paper was always preferred, not all researchers mentioned it. Those that did emphasized the portability of paper as a means of controlling their working environment (see below). However, for some researchers in some subjects, the classic image of concentrated focused attention on a single text was not a major task in their working lives. These researchers were more likely to talk about interacting with perhaps multiple texts, or reviewing them. As with scanning (to which it was closely related), interacting was a task undertaken by researchers using both paper and electronic documents. Each was credited with offering the researcher flexibility. Paper documents allowed them to annotate and to view multiple texts easily, whereas electronic documents allowed copying and pasting into new documents. Hence, interactivity was a key attribute of documents as they were used, and one not limited to either format. In the distinct, final task of storage researchers again saw advantages with both paper and electronic documents. Some researchers expressed a general desire to hold documents physically, to be sure that they 'had' them, especially where they saw their local computing network as unreliable. Others cited the ease with which files could be stored, managed and searched as reasons for preferring electronic format. They disliked the increasing chore of managing their own collection of photocopied articles.

Work environment

Where do researchers work? In discussing their preferred document format, researchers noted that different work tasks are done in different places. Most researchers interviewed preferred to select and to scan documents in their offices, away from the potential interruptions of the library and yet within the well-networked world of campus. Reading in detail was carried out at home or while travelling (although one professor did note that people do not do nearly as much reading on trains as they think they do). Of those researchers who reported wanting to read in detail, all equated this with moving away from the computer.

> 'For me the computer is a functional source to do word processing or whatever. But when it comes to research, it is reflective, and when doing research I don't want to be reflective with a computer.'
>
> [Academic, Business School]

Those who did not report reading in detail, who were more concerned with interacting with the document, tended to see the computer as a working environment rather than as just a tool, even if they preferred paper to electronic documents to work with at the moment. Electronic documents were stored (within copyright) on machines in the office or at home, depending on the researcher's preference and habitual working location.

Document attributes

Researchers described both paper and electronic documents as having particular attributes in themselves that either helped or hindered the work tasks and methods. Paper documents could be either original journal volumes or photocopies or printouts. Although valued by some researchers for their resource discovery function, most saw original journal volumes as being rather like electronic documents in that they had to be processed in order to obtain workable (paper) documents. Original journal volumes had to be photocopied and virtually all researchers wanted the option of printing out electronic documents. One of the main disadvantages of electronic documents, as described by even those researchers who were otherwise very positive toward them, was that the reproduction of graphics could be poor or in a non-standard file type. This was especially important where photographic techniques were used in the presentation of research findings from techniques such as spectrometry or X-ray diffraction.

User attributes

Researchers claiming to prefer paper documents very frequently described themselves as old-fashioned, or even just 'old'! However, it would not be wise to take this too literally. Firstly, some of those claiming to be too old to use computers to their full potential were young PhD students.

> 'I am used to using things on paper. I suppose younger people would be more, just do everything on the computer but, well, it's a new thing for me.'
> [PhD Student, Manufacturing Engineering]

Researchers expressing a preference for paper tended to be quite defensive about it. Another young PhD student even claimed to be making a deliberate effort to change his mistaken and old-fashioned liking for paper.

> 'I think that people who have grown up with computers can read things quite comfortably off the screen but older people like myself have to print them out before they can read them. So I'm trying to train myself.'
> [PhD Student, Manufacturing Engineering]

Secondly, they were expressing these views to an interviewer who was bringing them news of an electronic document access system in which they had expressed an interest. Almost certainly, some of them were deliberately casting themselves as computer novices with respect to information systems because they felt that the interviewer knew more than they did.

It is probable that some researchers did feel defensive about preferring paper. They talked of being used to things, or of having routines that did not revolve around the computer. It is unfortunate that these preferences were commonly expressed in terms of a morally loaded phrase such as 'old-fashioned'. It may well be that paper is the best format for some researchers undertaking some work tasks; it is not a thing about which to be defensive.

Summary: document format

In the trials with the web-based systems *SearchBank* and *ProQuest Direct*, about 70 per cent of the documents downloaded were immediately printed out. This was despite the sometimes considerable problems with the local printing infrastructure, as described above. There would seem to be conclusive evidence that for most of the researchers sampled, most of the time, paper was necessary for at least some of the work tasks identified in this section. It may be that this will change, as technology becomes better suited to those tasks and, as is likely to happen, as those tasks become better suited to the technology (Ruhleder, 1995). It may also be that paper is integral to some types of scholarly work, and researchers may need to be encouraged to say this without fear of being accused of being 'old-fashioned'[1]. As Gimson (1995) has noted, 'the simplicity and directness of perception and physical manipulation of the page remain beyond our ability to emulate'.

Document quality: paper

If paper is likely to remain an important format for documents, then what qualities of paper documents make them more or less acceptable to users? We attempted to answer this question by using the paired comparison method described in Chapter 2. The results show how the work tasks identified above, along with the reading skills of researchers, interact with the attributes of documents to produce more or less usable texts.

Layout

Researchers noted that they used visual cues within documents, such as font sizes and styles of headings and text, to navigate effectively through

---

[1] Of course, some researchers need no encouragement in their support for paper, as any library manager who has tried to cancel a print journal subscription will testify!

them. Therefore, overall, they stated a preference for documents that offered a page image format and layout rather than a uniform, standardized format such as that of many documents then available from *SearchBank*. Researchers claimed that they could assume that significant expert effort had gone into ensuring that the 'original page images had the greatest visual and informational impact. They therefore saw their reading skills as complementing the skills of typographers and copy-editors in producing documents that 'worked'. Of course, replicating such typographically rich documents electronically, for example using PDF format, can result in large file sizes that are time consuming to download (see Chapter 4).

Print quality

Legibility, in terms of print quality, came out as the most important factor in researchers' preferences between documents. It can vary widely. On the criterion of text and graphic print quality, all of the researchers in the FIDDO study preferred photocopied articles from *ILL–BLDSC* to any other option, including laser-printed PDF documents. However, the other British Library option trialled, *BL inside*, was unanimously rejected by researchers due to the poor quality of the fax reproduction, especially when it came to graphics. Between these two extremes came the print-outs from PDF files, with laser-print preferred to inkjet. Although preferring BLDSC photocopies, researchers were, in general, fairly content with printout quality.

Size

The A3 size of photocopies from *ILL–BLDSC* let the system down in terms of document quality. Researchers preferred the smaller A4 documents that resulted from printouts or fax delivery in terms of their ease of handling and for storage and locating. A main reason given for this was that the title page of an A3 photocopied document was likely to be folded inside the document, thereby making it more difficult to identify when filed among other documents.

Summary: paper document quality

Clearly, the quality of the paper documents delivered by a document access system is only one criterion by which it should be judged. Nevertheless, documents have to be fit for the purposes described above as work tasks: selecting, scanning, reading in detail, interacting and storing. From our research, it would seem that the ideal paper document is a high-quality A4 photocopy with a clear title page at the front. Although neither constitute such ideal documents, BLDSC photocopies and laser-printed PDF files are the two closest to the ideal from those we reviewed. Of course, these are only available to those researchers with the appropriate infrastructure, and may be more costly (in terms of time and money) than other options.

Document quality: electronic

It would have been useful to have undertaken a paired comparison survey with electronic documents but we did not have time. However, researchers did make some comments in the field-trial interviews that bear reporting here. Firstly, they confirmed the widely reported finding (Dillon, Richardson and McKnight, 1990) that navigating through electronic text was difficult. Secondly, and relatedly, they noted that scholarly writing required the full referencing of any quotations used. Page numbers often form an important part of these references, and electronic formats that included them were preferred. The major disadvantage of PDF format was the size of the files (and hence the time to download them).

Summary: documents

Most researchers implied that both paper and electronic documents were useful to them, depending on what they were doing. Different styles of using documents, whether close attentive reading or the interactive manipulation of texts, seemed to be used by young and experienced researchers in all subject areas, and by the same researcher at different times. Therefore, we maintain that the situation is far too complex to assert that either paper or electronic is better for researchers. Several researchers noted that it was far easier for them to convert an electronic document to paper than vice versa. However, both the process and the result of printing out electronic documents have room for improvement.

Summary and conclusions

The physical infrastructure available to researchers is a combination of institutional and personally-owned equipment, along with university communication services such as internal mail and local area networks. This infrastructure acts as an interface between researchers and documents. Apart from its sheer efficiency, the key attributes of such an infrastructure are the degree to which it is integrated internally, and the degree to which it integrates with the ways in which researchers work. Documents have analogous attributes, being more or less easy to navigate, convenient as physical objects and well integrated with the working methods of researchers. Researchers are already operating in a hybrid world, using print and electronic infrastructures and documents according to the availability and perceived advantages of each. Improvements are possible in each of these, and all are probably necessary. Flexibility might be lost in any search for the universal ideal system.

PART THREE: LIBRARIES' CONTEXTS

Introduction to Part Three

Libraries are not just libraries

In introducing Part Two of this book, we discussed the researchers' *contexts of action* by noting that researchers are not just researchers. In the same way, libraries (providers of the information function) are not just libraries (physical collections). So far as full-text access is concerned, the information function can be described as managing the administration of legal, effective, efficient and equitable document access. This almost certainly does involve collections but, increasingly, it is likely to involve a great deal more. What, then, are the contexts of action for library managers?

Firstly, library managers have to administer document access systems locally. Chapter 6 explores the technical administration of document access systems and their integration into an information service. In terms of subscription-based services, there are authorization and authentication matters to be addressed. Pay-as-you-go systems have other technical issues, especially if they are based on Email as a carrier. There is the issue of management information: who monitors the use of these systems, and who gets to see the resulting data? There are also questions relating to the responsibility for initial and ongoing user support. Administering full-text access will, undoubtedly, be made much simpler as a result of the work of various eLib projects that are developing the hybrid library architecture (eLib, 2000). Currently, however, administering access to systems is not straightforward.

Secondly, a key role for the library is the accountable, efficient and effective allocation of the information budget. In addition, library managers

have to address issues of equity, both real and perceived, in the allocation of resources between the needs of client groups. The library manager
is often the arbiter in allocating scarce resources to support competing
constituencies (Jacobs and Morris, 1999a). Part One briefly introduced
discussions of various financial aspects of current systems. Chapter 7
extends those discussions to FIDDO's findings relating to existing and
new document access systems, in terms of pay-as-you-go vs. subscription
models, and central vs. devolved budgetary structures. Chapter 7 also
covers charging for document access systems via the library, and quasi-
financial solutions such as quotas.

A third context in which library managers work is that of the law.
In the UK, JISC initiatives, such as a joint working party with the Publishers
Association, have made considerable progress. Nevertheless, the situation
remains complex. Libraries are typically responsible for the legal implementation of document access systems. Library managers have generally
achieved a kind of 'accommodation' with current copyright legislation
as far as traditional, paper-based ILL is concerned. However the new
scenarios present new problems and responsibilities. These responsibilities extend to negotiating individual licences, the legal aspects of joining
consortia, privacy and, crucially, to some aspects of the local management
of intellectual property. Chapter 8 examines the evolving legal framework
for document delivery, and includes discussions of British and European
copyright legislation, the changing nature of 'fair dealing' in the electronic
environment, electronic signatures and digital object identifiers and
licensing initiatives.

The three contexts of action outlined above will be familiar to
practising academic library managers. In addition, many libraries in other
sectors are operating in similar circumstances. Administrative and
budgetary issues tend to be fairly universal and, although the legal context
may be slightly different in industrial libraries, many of the issues discussed
in Chapter 8 will also be of interest outside higher education. Although
sections of Part Four are specifically dedicated to libraries outside the UK
academic sector, much of Part Three will also be of interest to those
working in special and public libraries and information services.

CHAPTER SIX

The contexts of action of library managers: administrative

For an explanation of the technical terms used in this chapter, the reader should consult the glossary in Appendix C.

Introduction

Administering full-text access has never been straightforward. At its most basic, administering the local journal collection requires checking in of serials, binding, shelving and other maintenance. Similarly, administering mediated ILL includes checking requests for copyright issues, consulting the holdings of various possible sources and dealing with the mechanics of the request and delivery of the document. In addition, the technical infrastructure on which serials check-in and ILL departments depend has to be maintained, end-users often need help and guidance and data has to be collected on the use of ILL and, in an ideal world, local journal collections. These tasks have never been straightforward, but now each also has its counterpart with respect to newer document access systems.

    This chapter looks at some of the administrative issues involved in setting up and maintaining access to a number of document access systems, old and new, and they are grouped into four sections as follows:

- setup and authentication;
- infrastructure and skills;
- supporting the user;
- supporting the library manager.

In Part Two we described a series of field trials and other work with examples of traditional and new document access systems. Most of these were set up and administered by the FIDDO team and our experiences form the empirical background to this chapter. As noted in Chapter 2, most document access systems include, but do not wholly correspond to, recognized services or products. For example, end-users would require adequate computing and printing facilities in addition to the access to PDF files that is provided by many products. The document access systems included in this chapter are summarized in Table 2.1 in Chapter 2.

It is important to note that many of the newer systems used in FIDDO's work have been superseded, less than two years after the field work was undertaken. Such is the pace of change. However, we trialled the systems, not so much to assess the particular products, but to reveal the issues involved in the models of document access that they represented.

Setup and authentication

How easily can systems be set up? How easy is it to arrange and maintain authenticated access? Although it might seem pedantic, we include a brief review of these aspects of the traditional document access systems in this section as a baseline against which newer systems may be compared. Precedent can be a valuable aid in guiding future decisions.

As we noted in Chapter 2, setting up access to the *Local holdings* system involves checking in of serials, organizing their shelving and, if necessary, their binding and ensuring access to photocopying equipment. User authentication is hardly an issue, although some libraries have introduced card entry systems to restrict the use of local facilities to *bona fide* members of the university and authorized persons. Others, for example in the Sunderland area of the UK, have moved in the opposite direction[1]. Some libraries run photocopying services for remote users; a charge is made and the users again have to be *bona fide* members of the university.

[1]   In response to a British Government initiative for lifelong learning, all libraries (both academic and public) in the Sunderland area have open access to all users.

Setting up access to the *ILL–BLDSC* system involves establishing appropriate administrative, budgetary and technical links with the BLDSC, and creating and publicizing arrangements for local end-users to put in requests. Authentication is provided by the request form, which characteristically requires both a library ID number and a signed copyright declaration. Remote requesting is possible, by sending ILL forms to the library or, increasingly, through the use of web forms. The requirement for a physical signature on copyright declarations currently limits the value of the latter option.

This brief review of the set-up and authentication arrangements of traditional document access systems reminds us that there is no choice, for example, whether or not to have an authentication policy. There is only a choice of different systems, traditional and new, each with associated authentication issues and solutions. It is worth bearing this in mind when considering the newer systems, wherein these issues can appear much more obvious.

As explained in Part Two the FIDDO end-user field trials did not include *BL inside*. This meant that we did not have an opportunity to look at the local management facilities of *BL inside* – what was called the 'supervisor function'. This appeared to make the setting up and administration of end-users' access to the system relatively easy. However, we did set up our own access to *BL inside* in order to conduct the time trials reported in Chapter 4. For these, the system was accessed by a username and password specific to it (that is, not via ATHENS (ATHENS, 2000) or any other access management service). The use of username and password authentication

- allows straightforward access for users away from campus;
- allows for personalized services;
- makes access dependent upon the end-user remembering and keying in a username and password.

During all of the work with *ProQuest Direct* reported in Part Two, this system was also accessed with a username and password, although IP address authentication was an option. The passwords changed monthly, although this was not necessarily the case, and were sent to the FIDDO office to be distributed to end-users. They were long and meaningless strings of letters and numbers, difficult to remember and inconvenient to key in each time. Fortunately the *ProQuest Direct* server set a cookie each time it was accessed for the first time from a particular instance of a client, so that the end-users did not need to re-key their username each time. This approach only works if end-users have exclusive access to a computer or, more generally, if everyone having access to a particular instance of a web client is an authorized user of *ProQuest Direct*. In the case of the FIDDO trials, end-users were researchers who tended to have exclusive access to a computer, albeit sometimes a rather inadequate one (see Chapter 5). This approach to authentication meant that remote use was no different from accessing the system from a campus machine.

Authentication for *SearchBank* was handled by IP address. The parent company sent forms to each library participating in the FIDDO Project, asking for the IP domain of potential users, the IP address of any local proxy servers and details of any local preferences. Once this was completed, the local library's concern with administration was over, as long as off-campus access was not needed. If end-users wanted to use *SearchBank* from home (or elsewhere away from campus), then a different and less straightforward process was needed. Some of the end-users contacted by FIDDO in relation to the field trials said they did want to use *SearchBank* away from their offices, so we made an effort to arrange this. It involved setting up a Perl script and ASCII patron ID file on a local server so that *SearchBank* could access it. The local server had to be a CGI-capable environment, so that Windows or UNIX would have been acceptable. Unfortunately the server to which FIDDO had direct access during the trials was a Mac machine that did not support CGI. This meant that we had to negotiate with our local university computing services department, who were reluctant to put up an externally generated Perl script for reasons of security and maintainability. The script template was supplied by *SearchBank* but needed to be modified slightly, so that local CGI expertise would have been an advantage. As it was, *SearchBank* technical support performed this role. The patron ID file was merely a flat (ASCII) file, but it could have been a procedure called by the Perl script to consult, for example, student ID records. In the end, despite considerable help from the *SearchBank* technical support team, we could not set up off-campus access in time for the FIDDO field trials.

The *Geo–SL–BL* document access system linked a database with a document supplier, and user access and authentication were required for each. The structure of the system as we set it up for the field trials is

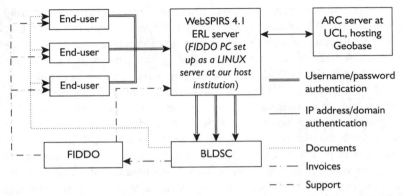

Figure 6.1. The *Geo–SL–BL* document access system as set up for the FIDDO end-user field trials

shown in Fig. 6.1. In discussing how we set up document access for end-users via *Geo–SL–BL*, we should bear in mind that SilverLinker, a central component of the system, was beta-release software that was at the time under active development by SilverPlatter Information. Our experiences probably reflected this but, for that very reason, revealed some of the issues involved in developing access and authentication arrangements. In terms of setting up the technical side of the system, we had to install a local web server with links to other systems (Fig. 6.1). The applications software (WebSPIRS) was available from SilverPlatter for use with most major server operating systems (NT, UNIX and so on). In fact, we had considerable problems setting up this server, due at least partially to FIDDO attempting to run the software on hardware that only just met the minimum specification set by SilverPlatter. As with *SearchBank*, we both needed and received considerable help from SilverPlatter's technical support team. If our experiences with *SearchBank* suggested that alternatives to IP domain authentication could involve local administrators in more work than they might imagine, then this was confirmed when we came to set up authentication for *Geo–SL–BL*. To search the database (Fig. 6.1), end-users during the field trials had first to log on to the local ERL web server (set up and maintained by FIDDO) using a username and password. (In the field trials these were the same for all end-users, but this is not usually the case.) These specified the databases to which the end-users had access: in this case, Geobase. The database was actually hosted on the ARC server at University College, London, (UCL) so that the IP addresses (or domain) of all end-users would usually have to be specified for access to that server. During the trial documents were ordered from the BLDSC, and the only way that this was possible was for FIDDO to open a 'parent' account with the BLDSC and then to ask them to set up a 'satellite' account for each end-user. This enabled the documents to be delivered to the end-user's address while the invoices and other liaison functions were between the BLDSC and FIDDO. This arrangement meant that end-users needed to key in a BLDSC username and password whenever they ordered documents. If authenticating campus use of *Geo–SL–BL* was not straightforward, then authenticating remote use would have been even less so, because IP domain authentication was a part of the overall system. We did not try it during the field trials.

It may be worth highlighting where we considered that the operation of *Geo–SL–BL* would have been different outside a trial situation. The first thing to note is that SilverLinker was designed to link between any of the databases hosted by SilverPlatter and a number of full-text sources, including local holdings, document delivery suppliers and publishers' servers. Hence, restricting it to one database and one supplier in the field trial meant that the setup and authentication were, if anything, simpler than might otherwise have been the case. In addition, it is not clear what arrangements could have been made with the BLDSC to enable SilverLinker to support document supply under the 'fair dealing' exemption in British copyright law (see Chapter 8). On the other hand, there were aspects of the field trial that a regular library operation would have found easier. For example, we had to set up and configure a dedicated server, whereas a library is likely to have server space ready to hand, along with relevant expertise.

In order for end-users to have access to *EiText* during the FIDDO field trials, their Email addresses had to be forwarded to Elsevier Engineering Information, Inc. to be authorized to order documents on the FIDDO trial account. Of course, this would not have been necessary if end-users had been paying for their own documents (see Chapter 7). The main problem associated with this approach was ensuring that Engineering Information always had a current listing of authorized users. We did this manually, but extending that method beyond a small trial environment would have required considerable and ongoing administrative effort. Since authorization was by Email address, and because such addresses were often accessible to users only from campus computers, remote use of the system was limited. This situation may change with easier remote access to campus network facilities, although such a change would depend on vendors and universities coming to an agreement on the technical and contractual bases for seamless, secure and easy-to-manage access to systems.

What are the lessons from the experiences described above? It is clear that there are wide variations between systems. Some systems place heavy demands on local libraries whereas others are relatively straightforward. Unfortunately, the relatively straightforward ones do not necessarily offer the best service to end-users, particularly those wanting to use the systems away from campus. It is on issues such as these that library managers can speak for end-user communities, ensuring that systems are designed from the outset with all users in mind, not just campus-based users or those with their own budgets!

Several groups, including the eLib project HEADLINE (HEADLINE, 2000), are looking at authentication issues, and it is clear from our experiences that their work will be valuable. Some building blocks are in place for electronic access, such as ATHENS and increasingly secure local network login procedures. In addition, alternatives to username, IP address and ATHENS-type authentication are being considered (Kelly and Lister, 1999). These alternatives include digital signatures, certificates and certification authorities. However, there are certainly commercial and legal, as well as technical, issues to be resolved before library managers can treat end-user authentication in the electronic world as a routine matter in the way that we do, perhaps, in the print world. Seamless access requires seamless authentication. In a hybrid library architecture, this means that separate authentication for resource discovery and for document access is now as unreasonable in the electronic world as it was when researchers consulted in the same library the printed versions of both Geographical Abstracts and the full text of an article. It is not just unreasonable for end-users; library managers have an interest in developing seamless access in order to reduce the administrative burden placed upon them.

In the meantime, we found that setting up access to, and user authentication for, several of the electronic document access systems required an infrastructure and skills that are not necessarily an everyday part of the library manager's tool-kit at the moment. These new skills and equipment needs are discussed in the following section.

Infrastructure and skills

Table 6.1 shows the results of a summary audit of the equipment, software and skills necessary to set up and administer the various document access systems. It excludes the necessities for budget allocation and management that are dealt with in Chapter 7, but includes the necessities for using the systems designed for unmediated end-user access. This is because we assumed that library managers would want to be able to use any system they were administering.

In thinking about the infrastructure and skills needed by the library to take advantage of electronic full-text resources we should not forget the considerable investment already made in traditional document access. So we start this section by reviewing very briefly the requirements of the document access systems *Local holdings* and *ILL–BLDSC*.

Administering the *Local holdings* system includes the serials check-in and cataloguing functions, which require access to the library system's electronic serials module or its equivalent. Administering a local collection requires significant library skills, although some of the routine work is obviously clerical. The *Local holdings* system also requires adequate photocopying facilities and enough staff with sufficient skills to maintain them. Payments for photocopying need to be administered.

Regarding *ILL–BLDSC*, the ILL module of library automation systems sold in the UK generally has BLDSC Artel/E-mail as a standard part of its configuration. The role of the university internal mail and other mail systems as infrastructures should not be ignored in *ILL–BLDSC*. Although Davies (1998) has noted that there is now less uncertainty in the job of the ILL librarian, 'with networked OPACs and union lists as well as the development of an exceedingly efficient and effective fee-based service by the BLDSC', he does not underestimate the skills of the ILL librarian. Experience is required in categorizing and selecting appropriate suppliers (for patents, documents and so on), and in making judgements about the circumstances in which to try each. These circumstances can vary according to many factors: for example, currency exchange rates and the past reliability of the supplier.

Table 6.1. The infrastructure, software and skills required to administer each document access system

System	Infrastructure	Software	Skills
Local holdings	Terminal/computer access to library automation system; telephone; photocopier	Serials checkin/ administration module	Collection administration
ILL–BLDSC	Terminal/computer access to BLDSC's Artel/ArtE-mail system; telephone; internal mail	Artel/ArtE-mail	End-user/supplier liaison; ILL administration
BL inside	Networked computer; fax machine; telephone	Web client; user ID database	End-user/supplier liaison; database administration
ProQuest Direct	Networked computer/printer; telephone; LAN	Web client; Adobe Acrobat reader; user ID database	End-user/supplier liaison; database administration
SearchBank	Networked computer/printer; LAN; telephone; web server for remote patron access	Web client; Adobe Acrobat reader; CGI/Perl script; remote user ID database	End-user/supplier liaison; database administration; CGI scripts; server administration
Geo–SL–BL	Networked computer; LAN; telephone; web server	Server OS (LINUX, NT, etc.); WebSPIRS web client	End-user/supplier liaison; server setup and administration
EiText	Networked computer with mailserver filespace for large files; printer; telephone; LAN	Attachments-capable Email software; Adobe Acrobat reader; user ID database	End-user/supplier liaison; mailserver administration; database administration

If the skills and equipment necessary to administer traditional document access are familiar to library managers, what about administering newer systems? Because we anticipated that the remaining five systems included in FIDDO's work would be unmediated, their administration was more 'behind-the-scenes' than that of ILL. FIDDO found that existing equipment and skills can make a necessary but, in themselves, insufficient contribution.

As noted above, *BL inside* included a 'supervisor function' that would simplify its administration. Even so, distributed username-based access would mean that library managers (or others) were having to maintain a user ID database. Equally, the FIDDO trials showed *ProQuest Direct* to be administratively straightforward, requiring little skill or equipment to manage. However, managing the changing usernames and passwords of a large patron base might require some knowledge of computing and/or database construction and maintenance. As far as equipment was concerned, *BL inside* required a fax machine, and *ProQuest Direct* required a networked computer/printer.

Facilitating remote access to *SearchBank* required non-trivial technical skills such as a knowledge of CGI scripts and local server architecture, as described above. In addition, it required access to a CGI-compatible server that was also accessible from outside the institution. The skills required then to link *SearchBank* authentication procedures to student and staff ID files would have been even more significant, although still well within the expected capability of local dedicated computer/systems staff.

Geo-SL-BL was a complex system that required proprietary web server software (WebSPIRS) to be downloaded from the SilverPlatter web site and installed on a dedicated local machine. This was a significant task and required skilled computing support including familiarity with the UNIX variant LINUX and web server configuration. A Windows NT server could have been used instead of LINUX. In addition, FIDDO staff had to liaise between local computing support, SilverPlatter technical support, UCL staff supporting the ARC server (hosting Geobase), and end-users of the system. Much of this liaison related to technical matters with which FIDDO staff had to be familiar.

EiText as trialled was basically an arrangement between the user and the supplier, so that little equipment and few skills were required to administer its use. Should the library be subsidizing use of the system then a database of authorized users would need to be maintained. In addition, some automatic financial control mechanism might be required (see Chapter 7). Like all the newer document access systems, *EiText* relied on general university computing facilities, along with the skills of those who maintain that infrastructure. In particular, documents were sent from

EiText as PDF Email attachments, which were sometimes quite large, so that one issue that did arise was the limited mailbox capacity of some researchers. If *EiText* were configured as a library-mediated system, then this would be a concern for local library managers.

All five of the network-based systems mentioned above required the maintenance of an adequate local computing infrastructure for users and administrators, including regular hardware, software and network upgrades. These are issues for local management policies – in particular, decisions over replacement cycles. They are also issues for suppliers, since their products will not be bought if they cannot be used. At the other end of the supply chain end-users, in this case researchers, rely on academic departments to provide industry-standard computing facilities where necessary. We found that this was certainly not always the case (see Chapter 5).

The two systems with perhaps the greatest potential for comprehensiveness, because they are essentially linking systems, are *Local holdings* and *Geo–SL–BL* (SilverLinker), although the British Library alone certainly has the potential to match them (see Chapter 3). However, since they are linking systems, the library skills required to manage them may be greater than for other systems that have fewer actors involved in their operation.

In summary, the different approaches to document access represented by the systems described above require a range of local computing and skills. For example, an administrator would have to be familiar with formats including Art-tel/ArtE-mail, Windows, World Wide Web, PDF, Email software, LINUX or Windows NT, CGI/Perl, and WebSPIRS and other proprietary software in order to set up, maintain and manage all the above access systems. Some of these formats and some of the skills in general are already present in libraries, but others are not. Convergence or collaboration between libraries and computing services departments may be one answer, but if the administration of document access is to remain a library role (as it surely should), then it cannot be the whole answer.

Supporting the user

Who, if anyone, should support the end-user? Certainly the document access systems trialled and administered by FIDDO made varying assumptions regarding this question. This in itself is not a problem so long as the local administrator and the end-user knows what to expect. However, in some newer models of document access the roles of product suppliers and local administrators are not yet settled. We identified some consequences of this during the FIDDO field trials. Again we start this section by describing the baseline situation as it generally exists with the more traditional models, and then move on to discuss newer systems.

It is difficult to imagine how anyone but the local library, helped by information provided by publishers and serials agents, could support the user of printed journal holdings. This support is, by now, embedded within general library routines such as user induction, reference and enquiry desks and photocopier maintenance. However, just because it may be difficult to identify a distinct set of library operations that could be attributed to the support of researchers using journal holdings, this does not mean that such support is provided for free.

More obvious, perhaps, is the support offered by the local library to users of the *ILL–BLDSC* system. There is usually an ILL desk in the library, staffed by dedicated and skilled librarians, where end-users can find out about the progress of their requests and whether they are likely to receive their document in time. Again, this support is considerably aided by the information provided by the supplier, in this case the BLDSC. As with journal holdings, the ILL system is so familiar to almost all in higher education that its support has been made a core library function, and users know where to find this support.

We trialled all of the newer document access systems in an unmediated configuration. That is to say, we gave users an introduction to each system and then asked them to use it to obtain the documents they needed, making it known that the FIDDO office was one option available to answer queries.

In general, *ProQuest Direct* and *SearchBank* generated the fewest queries reaching the FIDDO office[2]. The queries we did receive relating to *ProQuest Direct* tended to be either requests for us to contact the product supplier on technical matters, or questions about searching *ProQuest Direct*. Those relating to *SearchBank* also included users asking about accessing the system from home (see 'Setup and authentication'

---

[2]   We should beware of what Law (1997) has called the 'satisfied inept', or the end-user who is not asking for help even though he or she would benefit from it.

above). In both cases, follow-up interviews with end-users revealed that they had been aware of product help-desks but had been reluctant to use them. Some end-users had also contacted their local libraries for guidance, rather than the FIDDO office, which must be a positive comment on those libraries (or a negative one on FIDDO staff!). No end-users reported contacting their local computing services, although many of the queries that came through to the FIDDO office were technical. Clearly, this may have been due to the circumstances of the field trials, although those circumstances applied equally to more 'informational' queries on which libraries were consulted.

The pattern established in the field trials with *ProQuest Direct* and *SearchBank* was repeated and exaggerated in those with the other systems (*Geo–SL–BL* and *EiText*). Although the field trial circumstances of both of these systems were, perhaps, more artificial than those for *ProQuest Direct* and *SearchBank*, nevertheless we gained a strong impression that end-users were grateful to have the FIDDO office as a clearing-house for queries, rather than having to use product help-desks or some local services. We should point out that this is not a comment on the advice and support available from those places (which was often excellent, see 'Support for libraries', below), but a comment on user preferences and perceptions.

To summarize, end-users strongly identified journals and ILL with the library, and so expected support from the library. Newer systems, especially commercial products, had stronger brand identities and more obvious technical components. This meant that in administering field trials with the newer systems we found that users were not so sure whom to ask for help. They did not necessarily draw the same distinctions between service providers, such as libraries, computing services and product suppliers, as we did. Admittedly, this was in somewhat artificial field-trial circumstances, but we believe that the reasons for their indecision could be generalized. The unmediated configuration of the trial systems meant that end-users were left with the decision on whom to call when they needed help. They were unsure whether to call the unfamiliar (product help-desks), the familiar but perhaps daunting (computing services) or the familiar but perhaps sidelined (the library). In the event they often called FIDDO.

In 'real life', as well as in field trials, research has shown (Zeitlyn and Bex, 1997) that end-users want comprehensive help close-at-hand.

Ideally, they want to ask a knowledgeable colleague, someone who knows about their subject area, their working imperatives and methods, the products, the organizations and the technology. Such people are rare and busy and, in interviews with end-users, were rarely called 'librarians'. So who do they turn to next? If seamless access is one goal of the hybrid library, then surely seamless user support should be another?

Supporting the library manager

What support did the various product suppliers in each document access system offer to local library managers or, in the case of the trialled systems, to FIDDO? We noted above that end-users in the field trials tended to contact FIDDO rather than product help-desks. This meant that we were contacting those help-desks ourselves, and so gained some impression of their service quality. Furthermore, we asked the product suppliers for usage statistics that we could include in our research. A review of how the various systems fared on these counts reveals support for libraries that is, at best, patchy.

Traditionally, serials subscription agents and the BLDSC have both offered support to the local university library manager in the UK. Subscription agents have been invaluable in the chain of delivery, performing such integrative functions as single-point invoicing, flagging journal title changes, notifying library managers of new and discontinued titles, as well as supporting the attempts of library managers to make budgetary predictions. Such functions are unlikely to be less vital in the future. Similarly, the BLDSC offers customer (that is, library) support that has been described as 'friendly' and 'efficient' (British Library Bibliographic Services and Document Supply, 1999). Library staff interviewed as a part of FIDDO's work certainly agreed with these assessments. However, this type of support, valuable as it is, is only one part of the story. Another increasingly important need is for accurate and appropriate usage statistics. Measuring the use made of printed journals is notoriously difficult and, in any case, would probably be a job for local libraries. Statistics relating to ILLs, including those via the BLDSC, can often be collected using library housekeeping systems. The alternative would be to analyse BLDSC invoices or ILL request forms but as these are currently paper documents it would not be straightforward.

In using *BL inside* during the FIDDO time trials, we found that the British Library's customer (library) help-desk maintained its high standards. Furthermore, the supervisor function offers the potential for monitoring the use made of the system.

Administrative and technical support before and during the field trial with *ProQuest Direct* was rather unsatisfactory. Generally, we had to make several attempts, by telephone and Email, to make contact before a reply was received. *ProQuest Direct*'s parent company have noted that 1998, the year of FIDDO's fieldwork, was a year of considerable expansion for the system, and that it was likely that support structures did not keep pace with this expansion. In terms of usage statistics, they were never received despite promises. Statistics were supplied to regular subscribers, but appeared to be in paper form only rather than electronic, reducing their potential value to library managers. The parent company assured FIDDO that this was a temporary situation.

In terms of support for libraries, the contrast between *ProQuest Direct* and *SearchBank* was striking. Liaison with *SearchBank*'s London offices was easy, and the staff were always helpful and capable. The efforts to establish remote patron access (described above) tested fully the backup available from *SearchBank* to those administering the system locally, and it was found to be more than adequate. Statistics available from *SearchBank* were broken down by database, by journal title and by accessing URL. They were delivered promptly by Email every month.

The complex structure of the *Geo–SL–BL* system meant that support was required from the BLDSC, SilverPlatter Information and the database host ARC server support staff at UCL. As noted above, support from the BLDSC is generally helpful, competent and geared towards library managers as intermediaries. Customer service staff at the BLDSC adapted well to supporting the management of an end-user-oriented system, but the systems in place were not well suited to this role. SilverPlatter and UCL ARC support staff were very helpful, despite personnel changes through the field trial. As there were major technical problems getting the field trial underway, SilverPlatter staff in particular were called on intensively, and the support they gave was generally prompt, helpful and effective. Database usage statistics would have been available from the ARC server, but there was a specific technical problem that made this impossible at the time of the field trial. We were, therefore, unable to assess the extent to which such statistics would have detailed full-text access as well as database usage.

The merger between Engineering Information and Elsevier Science just before the field trial was due to start did, perhaps, have a detrimental effect on the level of support that was available from *EiText*. The change of personnel was unhelpful in setting up the field trial, especially as FIDDO's new contact was based in the USA. Administrative and technical support before and during the field trial was rather unsatisfactory. As with the other product with an American support contact *(ProQuest Direct)*, we had to make several attempts, by telephone and Email, to contact Engineering Information before a reply was received. In some cases this may have been due to technical difficulties with Email systems, but in most cases this was not the explanation. When we did get responses, their meaning was not always clear, and this made it difficult for us to advise end-users who were trialling *EiText*. Usage statistics relating to the field trial were not received from Engineering Information. In part this was because the initial proposal for researchers to use a web form, wherein each would need a username and password, was abandoned in favour of authorized users requesting via Email. Information received from Engineering Information came in the form of detailed invoices. These did contain all the information necessary for usage statistics to be extracted from them but they were in paper format so that such extraction would have been prohibitively time-consuming and labour-intensive. It is possible that Engineering Information's new European connection might in the future improve the support services offered to customers based in Europe.

In summary, the product suppliers evaluated by FIDDO during 1998 which at that time had a significant British base offered good support in terms of person-to-person contacts to resolve particular problems. Both of the more American-based systems *(ProQuest Direct* and *EiText)* offered less adequate support, although both were undergoing a period of some transition during the period in question. We are unsure whether the difference between the levels of support from American and British offices was a coincidence. If not, then it is not clear whether distance is the key factor, or the relative sizes of the British and American markets.

The provision of appropriate statistical feedback for library managers had not been prioritized by some systems. With increasing and justifiable calls for performance measurement and service accountability in terms of value for money, this is a major concern. Given the networked electronic nature of several of the systems in the FIDDO evaluations, we expected to be able to use extensive statistical data in our research. That this expectation was almost completely unrealized is disappointing, and indicates the work that needs to be done to ensure that this aspect of document access systems is adequate.

In general, traditional systems have set high standards in terms of supporting the local library. Networked systems have the potential to match these standards. Although it is early days yet, they are some way from realizing this potential.

Summary and conclusions

Although this chapter has included comments on specific systems, its aim has also been to raise and discuss issues more widely. These issues have included user authentication, local computing facilities, skill requirements, user support and library support from system suppliers. We have tried to emphasize that none of these is new. In many cases, traditional approaches have been very successful in addressing them. As newer systems are developed, the same issues re-emerge in new guises.

Few of the skills and issues described in this chapter appear to be settled in terms of who are the legitimate actors. Two main questions arise from FIDDO's experience of administering system trials.

1. Should a product supplier, the library, the computing services department (if distinct), or no one provide end-user support? If the answer is, 'It depends', then how is this to be explained to the end-user?
2. Who should collect and deploy statistics on the use of document access systems, and to whom should they pass them on?

Librarians have traditionally taken on the responsibilities, implicit in these two questions, for seamless user support and for performance measurement. Is there any *a priori* reason why this should not be the case in a hybrid library environment?

It will be clear to any practising library manager that these issues form part of wider contexts. In particular, FIDDO has considered money and the law. Usage statistics are valuable to product suppliers because they are market information; they are valuable to library managers for the same reason and because library managers are accountable for the information budget. User support is a vital role, partly because it includes advising users on how they can and cannot legally use documents and systems. The next two chapters take up these issues in more detail.

CHAPTER SEVEN

The contexts of action of library managers: budgetary

Introduction: transparency and budgetary structures

There is a maxim, reputedly American, that claims to guide those who want to know how organizations work. It simply says, 'follow the money'. This chapter aims to do just that, with the help of a series of interviews with senior library staff, as described in Chapter 2. The focus is on budgetary arrangements within British higher education, so that the wider economics of scholarly document access are only briefly mentioned. The latter have been exhaustively reviewed by Halliday and Oppenheim (1999).

Financial considerations have rarely been as high on the higher education research agenda as they are now. There has been a general movement to devolve responsibility and budgets to cost centres within higher education institutions (Baker, 1997). For example, a British report (J.M. Consulting Ltd., 1999) has put forward proposals, currently being implemented, that call for all research costs to be made explicit, or 'transparent'. There are ongoing moves for libraries to be able to cost their services and even to use such costs to organize quasi-market arrangements within institutions. Full-text document access, whether by subscription or on a pay-as-you-go basis, is an obvious target for such initiatives.

In this spirit, if we think of document access as a market-type arrangement, then we must look at the characteristics of the markets and of the products. In FIDDO's universe, the markets were higher education institutions. These clearly vary in the size of their information budget but, in terms of budgetary arrangements, their principal characteristics are the extent and ways in which the information budget is centralized or devolved. FIDDO looked at a fairly typical range of document access systems, which might be understood as the products in this approach. There are more or less expensive options but, in terms of their financial arrangements, the main feature is whether they are charged on a subscription or a pay-as-you-go basis. If we think in these terms, then we have a two-by-two matrix of possibilities as shown in Table 7.1.

The first part of this chapter is organized according to the matrix in Table 7.1, and is based on the interviews with senior library staff described fully in Chapter 2. Rounding off this chapter is a brief review of how transparency fits in with our findings.

Of course, there is a range of possibilities between centralized and devolved budgets. For example, a part of the information budget might be allocated to cost headings within the library with more or less departmental liaison. However, the characterizations of 'centralized' and 'devolved' are useful shorthand for trends that practising library managers will understand. The whole issue of budgetary devolution in academic libraries has been reviewed by Lyon *et al.* (1998).

A further caveat to mention is that subscription and pay-as-you-go systems are often not solely differentiated by the charging regime. Certainly, the *ILL–BLDSC* document access system results in the private provision of documents to individuals, as compared with library subscriptions, which typically result in a collective resource available to the whole user community. The licensing arrangements of copyright fee paid

Table 7.1. Document access within higher education; the possible budgetary arrangements (with examples)

Information budget structure ⇒ Centralized		Devolved
System charging basis ⇓		
Subscription	Central library journal subscriptions	Departmental subscriptions to subject-based products
Pay-as-you-go	ILL via the central library	Departmental budgetary arrangements supporting access to document delivery

document delivery services also restrict the collective use of the documents supplied, although often not as severely as the 'fair-dealing' exemption in British copyright legislation on which the *ILL–BLDSC* system is based (see Chapter 8). The question of whether the library caters for individual users, communities or for a single user community is addressed in Chapter 9.

Subscription charging

Centralized budgets

This is the traditional view of the library and perhaps the one with which the library managers interviewed were most comfortable. Most of the administrative tasks associated with this model have been incorporated into the operations and structure of the library or information unit. The one issue that has emerged in the electronic world is authentication. This was discussed in the previous chapter in terms of administration, but it is also a budgetary issue when the licensing conditions of products put a high price on access that was, in the print world, inseparable from the journal on the shelf. An example would be reference use by researchers from other institutions. In Chapter 3 we saw that combining the largely print journal subscriptions of a number of academic libraries produced a resource with a high level of coverage. Such combinations of electronic subscriptions would probably be prohibitively expensive. One approach to this and other issues has been to pursue consortial licensing, the obvious example in the UK being the National Electronic Site Licence Initiative (NESLI, 2000), supported by the Joint Information Systems Committee (JISC) of the Higher Education Funding Councils. It is likely that the future role for libraries in terms of subscription services will be increasingly as institutional representatives in such consortia. Purchasing consortia are already common in the USA, and Gammon (1998) notes that they can control price increases and influence library expenditures. Another advantage cited for consortia is that they can benefit smaller libraries, although one UK library manager interviewed by FIDDO foresaw the opposite:

'. . . it could put suppliers in competition with each other, and publishers, and therefore there might be certain price advantages and probably a consortium of libraries getting together for price deals. I suppose in that case the small institutions could lose out because they don't have the clout . . .'

[ILL librarian]

There is little evidence as yet for this effect in the new British consortia.

We should point out that neither the traditional subscription-based system (journals), nor any electronic equivalent, is wholly costed on subscriptions. This is because they involve sometimes substantial photo-copying or printing costs in order to be used fully by researchers (see Chapter 5). Such costs are obviously pay-as-you-go.

Devolved budgets

Interviews with library managers indicated that subscription charges become more complex in a devolved environment. However, those inter-viewed were expressing opinion rather than experience, since none of them worked in a situation where academic departments usually took out subscriptions to a large number of journals or full-text online services. Furthermore, only library managers were interviewed, and it is possible to argue that they have a vested interest in centralized budgets. The prece-dent of print journal subscriptions certainly led some of them to question the possibility of devolved payment for subscription-based electronic services.

'I would probably expect the library to pay because, if I have understood it completely, it's almost the equivalent of having a copy on your shelves that you've paid a subscription for and the user then has access to it. Therefore it is a central facility.'

[Subject Librarian]

Despite the potential vested interest of library managers, the issues they raised in relation to subscription charging/devolved budgets were valid and need to be addressed. Firstly, agreement to subscribe (or to become a part of a consortium) has to be obtained from all the relevant budget holders. Where the potential for inequity might exist in consortia of libraries, how much more would this be the case if academic depart-ments were the consortia members? Secondly, arrangements still have to be made for authentication, but in a devolved environment these may have to include links with each relevant budget holder. Thirdly, the problem arises as to how the costs of subscription are to be divided up. Clearly, use is one possible criterion, but this relies on comprehensive usage statistics being available and, as the previous chapter made clear, this is by no means always the case even in the electronic world. The inter-related problems of equity, authentication and budgetary responsibility were summed up by one library manager discussing an electronic subscription.

> 'It might depend on how that was regulated throughout the University. Some departments may want six simultaneous users, others may not be prepared to pay for any at all. I mean departmental funds for document delivery seem variable.'
>
> [ILL Librarian]

Variability in departmental funds, if applied to subscription services over time, could, in David Baker's words, 'play havoc with those areas of library activity which require a degree of continuation in their funding' (Baker, 1997).

Pay-as-you-go charging

Centralized budgets

Pay-as-you-go charging has been a significant feature of libraries in the UK since before the British Library Lending Division was established in the 1960s. However, widely publicized developments such as internet commerce and electronic document delivery have ensured that pay-as-you-go charging is an increasingly realistic option.

Precedent is a powerful driver in the library world. Certainly, in our interviews we found that library managers were basing decisions about how to manage hypothetical scenarios on the closest examples they knew. Since pay-as-you-go document access via the BLDSC (*ILL–BLDSC*) is currently so dominant within British higher education, it is probably worth reviewing briefly how this is managed financially, before looking in more detail at how two common approaches might fare in managing electronic pay-as-you-go access.

Most documents supplied by the BLDSC to the British academic community are photocopies provided under the 'fair dealing for research or private study' exemption in UK copyright legislation (HMSO, 1988). Under the law, libraries are obliged to make a charge for such documents. The actual charges imposed by libraries have been surveyed by Clinton (1995, 1999). The emphasis of this charge within libraries varies; some see it solely as a cost recovery exercise, others more as a demand management tool, and still others as a painful necessity. In most cases, British academic libraries do not pass on to either individual researchers or their departments the full costs, including local administration, of ordering documents from the BLDSC (Coopers and Lybrand, 1989, unpublished data; Chambers, 1996). Because of this, and since, as one library manager put it, '*the issue fundamentally is one of financial control*', many universities, including all of those participating in the FIDDO research, use quasi-budgetary methods of restricting demand. The library managers interviewed highlighted two of these – quotas and routing requests via intermediaries. Each of these imposes non-financial costs on the user. In the case of quotas, as noted in Chapter 1, this cost is the loss of opportunity to request another document. In the case of routing requests, it is the inconvenience of not having direct end-user requesting from the desktop.

Quotas

Quotas are a quasi-devolutionary response by libraries to a pay-as-you-go pricing environment for access to remote documents, typically ILLs. Their use varied across the institutions surveyed by FIDDO, depending partly on the level and type of devolved budgetary structure in place. In one university library a budget was internally allocated to departments who then allocated a quota to students. In three others quotas were allocated by the library to individuals. In the last university quotas were allocated by budget-holding departments to students. Quotas could be combined with budgetary arrangements, so that a certain number of requests were either subsidized by the library or 'free', after which they had to be paid for at a higher rate (typically equivalent to the price of one BLDSC voucher per request).

The use of quotas by libraries was seen as multi-functional – to control the ILL budget while maintaining a visible role for the library and library funds. However, this itself could be problematical.

'. . . they do find the system of quotas and charges confusing. I think staff find it confusing I'm not happy to admit that. But you may say 'why don't you charge, why do you have quotas and then costs?' It was because we wanted to promote the idea that we would still subsidize some of the costs.'

[Subject Librarian]

The library managers interviewed saw a continuing role for quota systems. Indeed, they saw an increasing need for quotas as end-user access became more prevalent, with the potential for a loss of budgetary control. However, they also felt that quotas should become easier to manage and enforce in a more electronic environment.

'It might be easier for us in a way to find out how many things they've [users] got on order at any one time. Because at the moment, using [BLDSC] they can do it but they have to run a job, so it might be easier in some ways.'

[Subject Librarian]

Several library managers anticipated the development of some kind of counting or metering software that could monitor automatically the document requests of users and relate those requests either to budgets or quotas. This view should probably be seen as a part of a general expectation by library managers that better management information will be a key advantage of new electronic document delivery systems. Chapter 6 indicated that this may not necessarily be the case in the near future.

Routing requests

As part of their role to ensure the fair distribution of the information budget in a pay-as-you-go environment, some libraries working with FIDDO had a policy of routing all ILL requests via a library subject specialist or ILL staff in order to screen out 'excessive' or 'unnecessary' requests. Less overt routing of requests is possible. For example, many libraries will not accept ILL requests from students without a confirmatory signature from a member of academic staff. This involvement of academic staff could be seen as quasi-devolution. Another example of demand management by the covert routing of requests is the requirement for the requester's signature on the copyright declaration for each 'fair dealing' document from the BLDSC. The signature is not required for that purpose; nevertheless it does serve that purpose because the library is, *de facto*, the campus body charged with copyright. A physical signature associated with each request has to be deposited with the library. Apart from demand management, another purpose served by such measures is that, like quotas, they allow the library to be seen as an essential part of the institution's information landscape.

> 'What we don't want, and it comes back to the point I was saying about the library being perceived as the information provider, we don't want to write ourselves out of the loop.'
>
> [Subject Librarian]

However, many users of the *ILL–BLDSC* system feel that the way this is done at the moment is one of the very worst aspects of their access to documents. The BIODOC study noted that an increase in the number of requests was partially related to 'the ease with which material could be requested' (Bevan et al., 1998). Certainly, several researchers interviewed by FIDDO commented on the inconvenience of filling in ILL forms.

The future of full-text access is widely agreed to include end-user ordering and receipt of documents. Surely, routing requests is anathema to this model? The library managers interviewed during the FIDDO Project did see the two requirements for a signature (copyright and to restrict students' use of ILL) being complicated by electronic pay-as-you-go systems. They noted that the lack of an acceptable electronic copyright signature had the potential to limit the value of the British copyright exemption. They also noted that, even if electronic authorization were acceptable, students could be excluded.

> 'We get an Email request, we Email Doctor X to ask if student Y can have this – it's never going to work. This is the difficulty with authorization and students would definitely lose out.'
>
> [Subject Librarian]

Although difficult, library managers saw the facility to route requests for remote documents via the library as an important part of any document access system (such as *ILL–BLDSC*) that supported the library function. Some commented on how they saw the kind of metering software noted above supporting the intermediary role of libraries between the user and the document supply function, without being seen to suppress demand arbitrarily. Such software might also bear some relation to copyright and licence management functions, reinforcing further the role of the library.

To summarize, pay-as-you-go systems present libraries with significant challenges if they are to continue allocating the information budget equitably, accountably and efficiently, and in a way that does not threaten spending on the collection or other collective resources. Current practices, such as the use of quotas, will probably only work in the hybrid environment if better management control systems are available (Arkin, 1998). Some suppliers have recognized this (*BL inside*'s supervisor function is an example), but would perhaps customer library initiatives also be appropriate to a local management problem? Otherwise libraries may have no option but to offer the document delivery budget to departments. As Webster (1997a) noted, 'we may move rapidly from an access vs. holdings debate to an 'access vs. bypass' problem'.

Devolved budgets

The library managers we interviewed were dubious about the abilities of academic departments to manage an information budget. They claimed that these departments:

- do not have the administrative infrastructure to carry out an information role efficiently, effectively and equitably;
- do not have the information expertise to assess and evaluate different sources;
- may not have information provision as a high priority, especially for undergraduates;
- may view the library as the information provider of last resort, and so pass users back to the library when departmental funds run out;
- generally seem to administer devolved budgets by appointing gatekeepers who can then exert considerable influence over their colleagues.

Library managers in one university known to FIDDO, wherein the ILL budget had been devolved to departments, claimed that:

- there was, allegedly, a thriving black market in ILL credits in at least one department;
- inequitable inter-departmental variations existed in ILL provision:

'[T]here are discrepancies which we are certainly very unhappy about, because a lot of departments will give final year undergrads a quota, which is fair enough, [but] some departments won't even give postgrads a quota. There is one department which we have discovered that a lecturer is paying for their postgrads to get ILLs out of their own pocket.'

[Subject Librarian]

We noted above that these were the views of library managers with, perhaps, a vested interest in retaining the information budget. However, the points they raised need to be addressed. We also noted above that document access systems operating pay-as-you-go charging regimes require effective financial management systems at the local level, and that this requirement increases with electronic systems. It was not clear from the interviews with library managers how they saw such systems being integrated effectively within and across departments, should the relevant budget be devolved. This apparent problem might be an obstacle to the tendency towards devolution in a pay-as-you-go environment.

But what about transparency?

It is clear that the library managers interviewed by FIDDO did not want the information budget to be devolved to departments, or even to end-users. This is understandable; institutional influence is often related to control over budgets. The issues they raised regarding authentication, equity, accountability and financial management need to be addressed, and it may be that they are the best people to do it. However, what about transparency? The point of allowing resource allocation choices to be made close to the resource generation (teaching and research) units of a university is that it promotes transparent accountability between income and expenditure. Although a laudable principle, it is not the only one. The consequences of its application need to be borne in mind. Moves toward larger licensing consortia for subscription services and smaller micro-transactions for pay-as-you-go document delivery mean that the demands of transparency may conflict with other laudable principles, such as effectiveness, efficiency and equity.

FIDDO has consistently been biased toward the end-user perspective. In Part Two we described three contexts of action for end-users and, in discussing effectiveness, efficiency and equity, we refer to them again. The effectiveness of document access is analogous to managing that access to achieve the best possible coverage (see Chapter 3). The efficiency of document access is analogous to managing that access to minimize the time costs for end-users (see Chapter 4). Equity of document access does not map so easily onto a context of action, but it certainly includes ensuring the maintenance of an adequate and integrated technical infrastructure (see Chapter 5). However, it also includes the maintenance of an adequate and integrated budgetary infrastructure.

Effectiveness

The influence of budgetary arrangements on the effectiveness of document access is substantial. Subscription charging regimes only represent value for money when used for core material, however that is defined. The wide scatter of user requirements in higher education means that many of them are best satisfied using pay-as-you-go options. However, we have seen in this chapter that local budgetary structures and the absence of adequate management control tools can lead to difficulties in managing pay-as-you-go options from a central budget. Equally, subscriptions to core material are problematical when undertaken from devolved budgets. In the UK, the Transparency Review of Research has recommended that 'institutions should calculate costs of teaching, research and other activities at departmental level, and by research sponsor type, both for internal management purposes, and to satisfy needs of sponsors and others.' (J.M. Consulting Ltd., 1999). Since the effectiveness of information support depends on the appropriate charging regime being adopted for different user requirements, then strict adherence to a departmental transparency requirement may in some cases impede such effectiveness.

Efficiency

Costs in terms of delays and the time that researchers have to dedicate to acquiring documents are measures of inefficiencies in any document access system. These costs are related to the products and infrastructure components in such systems; for example, time costs are often incurred as a result of an inadequate technical infrastructure. Support units, both within and outside higher education, can reduce their costs by spending less on the maintenance of this infrastructure, effectively passing these costs (in the form of delays and so on) on to academic researchers and their departments. It is not clear whether this is transparent accounting. In terms of providing an account of the allocation of public funds then it probably is; in terms of providing incentives for best practice then it may not be. The value of an institution-wide perspective of these costs is clear.

Equity

In the interviews the library managers commonly asserted that devolved budgets could lead to inequitable results, in that some end-users may have better access to documents than others. Clearly, the more the academic departments buy in support services, the more necessary it is for their accounting procedures to be transparent. Some library managers already complain that information services are allocated inequitably among departments, and among end-users within departments. By 'inequitable', they mean that access decisions are made not according to need but according to ability to pay or position within an organizational hierarchy. Whether these are acceptable or transparent criteria by which to allocate information services is questionable.

Summary and conclusions

Budgetary structures within higher education institutions are inter-related with the charging regimes of document access systems. Libraries have been happiest with centralized budgets buying in subscription-based access, such as print journals. However, the wide scatter of user requirements, not to mention the 'serials crisis', means that there is an important place for accessing documents on an *ad hoc*, pay-as-you-go basis. Such systems need to be controlled effectively if they are not to consume a disproportionate amount of the information budget. The instant desktop access promised by electronic systems will exacerbate this need, but such systems may eventually offer better management tools than are currently available in order to satisfy it. Usage data from online subscription full-text services, whether licensed by an institution or a consortium, will also be a high priority for library managers. We can only agree with Chowdhury and Chowdhury (1999), who have identified management and payment structures and techniques as being key priorities for future digital library research.

Calls for budgets to be devolved to cost centres, such as academic departments, and away from central services, such as libraries, have been made on the bases of accountability and transparency. Such devolution worried the library managers interviewed as a part of the FIDDO Project on grounds of effectiveness, efficiency and, perhaps especially, equity.

Direct end-user access to pay-as-you-go document access, paid for by devolved budgets, was viewed by these library managers as unlike a library service. There were two ways in which they made this point:

1. 'I think who actually pays for [the documents] is much less clear for this because this is something which the users will have access to over the web, without any need for the library to be involved at all. So it could, well, just be like, as it were, phoning up for a pizza, with no library involvement whatsoever.'

    [ILL Librarian]

2. 'This whole issue of direct end-user access sounds fine from the user's point of view, but if it's institutional money that supports [it], then we really do need to ensure that it's an institutional benefit rather than an individual benefit that results.'

    [Head Librarian]

Libraries provide a service to individuals, to user communities and, often, to a wider community (see Chapter 9). The last would include, but not be limited to, an archive function. Pizzas are not generally a collective resource and they are not archived. Document access based solely on this model does not constitute a library service, even though it may allow for easy and transparent cost accounting and, as noted in Chapter 1, satisfy some expectations of some current users.

CHAPTER EIGHT

Copyright and document access management

Introduction

A contemplation of document access management cannot be regarded as complete without a consideration of copyright matters. The raw material that is the staple of information and library management – recorded information – represents valuable intellectual capital that, in most instances, carries a price that is normally payable to someone. Feather (1994) has put it very well: '. . . our society has created a chain of supply in which the dissemination of the printed word can be achieved only by the exchange of money'.

The background

It is probably fair to say that the typical busy library manager is not preoccupied with copyright on a day-to-day basis, and wants (and needs) to know only enough to ensure that the organization and its clients keep well away from litigation. Nonetheless, a basic background knowledge of copyright legalities is necessary to place the various document access options and scenarios into context. Increasingly, licences, contracts and agreements specify and bind clients into conditions regarding the use of copyright material. So a basic outline of the situation is presented here. It should be appreciated that to understand the detail there is really no substitute for consulting the appropriate legislation (HMSO, 1988) or one of the several useful guides available (Wall, Oppenheim and Rosenblatt, 1994; JISC, 1998a; Wall, 1998; Cornish, 1999).

What is copyright?

Copyright is a property right conferred on someone who creates an original work regardless of its technical or literary merit. Copyright confers upon the owner an exclusive right to exploit the work. In the UK, copyright is governed by the Copyright, Designs and Patents Act 1988 as modified by later Statutory Instruments and Directives from the European Union.

In the UK copyright subsists in:

1. original literary, dramatic, musical or artistic works (including computer programs and code, tables and compilations which extend to the content of databases);
2. sound recordings, films (including video recordings), broadcasts or cable programmes (including online databases);
3. typographical arrangements of printed material.

Copyright subsists in a work whether or not the material is 'published' in the conventional sense; it simply has to be recorded somehow and, after creating the material, no special procedure is required to secure copyright in the UK. However, for convenience and clarity and to ensure copyright in an international context in many jurisdictions beyond the UK, the creator's name, the date of creation and a © symbol are added to a work. Copyright does not last for ever but it normally extends to 70 years beyond the death of the creator. Copyright in typographical arrangement of printed works lasts for 25 years. The copyright in typographical work can be particularly significant for document access since text material that may well be out of the author's copyright – for example, in historical and literary research – may have been reissued in a publisher's edition very recently and the typography will remain protected. Keying in and distributing widely a text of a Shakespeare sonnet is quite legal; photocopying or scanning a Penguin edition of the same sonnet without permission certainly is not!

Generally, the original owner of copyright in a work is the person who created it: the author, artist, playwright, composer or similar individual. Computer-generated works are the copyright of whoever performed the necessary arrangements for producing them. Very importantly in the UK, an employer is normally regarded as the owner of copyright in work produced by an employee. This can have a significant influence on the creation of material in the academic context. Unless an institution chooses otherwise, it can lay claim to the copyright of material produced as part of its activities. In many instances, institutions encourage scholarly publishing by relinquishing this right of ownership in selected works to their employees.

Copyright, as a property right, can be transferred by sale, gift or even bequest. It may also be 'shared' or held jointly, if the owner so determines, with another party. Therefore, the holder of copyright may not always be the original creator. In many (perhaps the majority) of cases in academic publishing, the author gives away the copyright in exchange for seeing his or her work published. Still further, in some instances authors (or their sponsoring organizations) are asked to pay page charges for getting into print – an incentive for not being too wordy! In recent times, however, sentiment against simply giving away copyright material to commercial publishers has hardened in some academic quarters, the argument being: 'Why give away intellectual capital, simply to buy it back again packaged in expensive scholarly journals?'.

It was noted above how copyright confers upon the owner an exclusive right to exploit the work; however this is true only up to a point. Legislation prescribes certain limited concessions to users of copyright material in the form of 'permitted acts' that can be undertaken by others without infringing copyright. These include copying as part of writing a criticism or review, reporting news and current events and the incidental inclusion of material in an artistic or audio-visual production.

In the scholarly research context, perhaps the important permitted act is 'fair dealing', which describes a means by which a restricted amount of copying, for research or private study, may be made of literary, dramatic, musical or artistic works. With regard to books and periodicals, the making of *single* copies of *limited* portions of texts for 'the purpose of research or private study' is permitted. Limited portions are normally regarded as being one article from any periodical issue, or up to five per cent of a book. It should be noted that a discrete item appearing in a book, such as a table, diagram or illustration, may be regarded as a complete work for the purpose of making this assessment. The academic community, and researchers in particular, are able to exercise these concessions to advantage.

Special concessions are prescribed for education and libraries. In the educational environment, some copying is permitted while people are under instruction, and short extracts may be put into anthologies designed for teaching. In addition, copyright is not generally infringed if material is used to set or answer examinations. Some interpret the concession to include material used extensively for assessed coursework.

Helpful concessions apply to what are called 'prescribed libraries'. These are generally non-profit making ones, and those in the academic sector certainly fall into this category. They are permitted to make what amount to fair dealing copies for others, provided that certain conditions, including not making multiple copies for several individuals, are met. Prescribed libraries may also make 'replacement' copies to protect or preserve originals, or to restore damaged or lost items where it is not reasonably practical to buy items for that purpose. They may also furnish fair dealing copies through interlibrary loan to other libraries.

Fair dealing and similar concessions intentionally limit the scope and amount of copying. The production of multiple copies of copyright items, say, for a group of researchers or for one researcher to distribute to others, is not permitted. (It was observed earlier how researchers do many things with documents other than read them: storing and indexing them and, significantly, passing them, or copies of them, to colleagues.) Neither is multiple copying for classroom use or for wholesale distribution to students in a department permitted. Document access and supply that relies on fair dealing and similar concessions has, therefore, to keep within a narrow path to ensure that it is legal activity.

Moreover, there is much conjecture surrounding what can be done electronically in this context. It is not clear whether fair dealing extends to electrocopying, electronic replication by scanning or re-keying and distribution of such material. In strict terms, more than one digital 'copy' resides in a system through which material is being transmitted. For some time debate has also raged regarding the role of the fax in document access and delivery, the argument being that at some stage more than one copy is extant for the fax process to work. These may sound like spurious technical arguments on a par with 'angels on pinheads' discourses, but to a publishing community uncertain and wary of the impact of the new technology, they serve to stave off what may be regarded as threats to the commercial future.

Copyright does not stand still, not least because the enabling technology to duplicate material is evolving and new ways of using (and misusing) copyright material are emerging. The European Union has been active in drafting legislation recently and there is a distinct possibility that more stringent regulation of use of material and a drastic curtailment of fair dealing may be introduced. The changes in the European Parliament brought about by elections, coupled with the appointment of a 'new' Commission in 1999, have delayed the development of new legislation. Deliberations in the World Intellectual Property Organization (WIPO) also have an influence on the future of copyright globally. The outlook is far from clear – or encouraging for those who have become reliant on the relative freedom to use material for individual study and research. A recent initiative that might offer some encouragement, however, is that from the Association of Learned and Professional Society Publishers (ALPSP, 2000a). A 'Licence to Publish' (ALPSP, 2000b), developed by the ALPSP, offers an alternative to authors passing the copyright for published articles to publishers (Patel, 2000). This licence would appear to allow the authors of published articles to make those articles available in limited ways via the Internet. It is too early as yet to assess the likely impact of such a development.

Licensing schemes

From the users' perspective, any reduction in the concessions embodied in law threatens to restrict severely the use of copyright material and diminish its value for academic purposes. Seeking permission from each copyright owner on each and every occasion is both cumbersome and unrealistic. To introduce some flexibility into the situation, several licensing schemes have been created. These are derived from the legislation, which incorporated several incentives to the creation of appropriate licences.

One of the most prominent in the UK is that devised through the Copyright Licensing Agency (CLA), a body that was formed to represent publishers' interests. For universities the licence has been negotiated between the CLA and the Committee of Vice-Chancellors and Principals (CVCP), and it can be described as being oriented towards learners rather than researchers. Participating institutions acquire a licence on payment of a fee based on a per-capita calculation determined by student (but, interestingly, not staff) numbers. The licence allows for *ad hoc* copying of limited extracts from books (up to five per cent or one chapter) and periodicals (up to a single article from an issue), and for these copies to be distributed in quantities appropriate for student use, or for research and administration purposes. Systematic provision of material to learners in study packs attracts additional fee payments, which are based on the number of copyright items and the quantity distributed. Any study pack copied under these arrangements may be supplied to staff and students of the university at a price set to recoup the cost of production. Recently, the CLA has recognized the need for the licence to embrace electronic copying. It should be noted that not all publishers are signatories to the CLA and some publishers do not include *all* of their output. Thus, one may discover that some important scholarly journals are excluded.

The Newspaper Licensing Agency operates a similar scheme of licensing for a relatively broad range of newspapers, but by no means all. The focus again is on facilitating the use of material for administration and in the learning situation, and electronic copying is also covered by payment of an additional fee.

Other licensing schemes exist for specialized material such as British Ordnance Survey maps and British Standards Institution specifications, and there are similar schemes for other media that are outside the remit of this book. Again, these schemes permit copying and related practices beyond that which would normally be permissible in the legislation.

Where the provisions of general legislation, or the conditions of licensing, do not permit the use of copyright material in an appropriate way, then specific permission from a copyright owner has to be obtained. In a sense the royalty levies paid in document access are a form of 'buying' this permission; the pricing structure reflects the levels of fees that document delivery agencies have previously negotiated with copyright holders. In other instances, where subscription-based access to a whole range of documents is involved, the conditions of use, including downloading and copying, will be incorporated into a contract agreement that 'licenses' the activity.

Management practicalities

The various scenarios for document access already described in Chapter 2 embody a complex mix of copyright issues. The models that are currently being operated and being developed incorporate a range of tariffs relating to the cost of buying access to intellectual capital, and the work of FIDDO has demonstrated how complex the task of optimizing delivery strategies can become. It is appropriate to try to disentangle, as far as possible, the issue of copyright in these considerations.

In some models of document access and delivery the participants in the chain of delivery rely on concessions in the copyright legislation, such as fair dealing or the library concessions, to operate from day to day, particularly where paper is the medium and photocopies are distributed. One of the 'traditional' routes of document access in the UK, the acquisition of photocopies from the BLDSC, relies on fair dealing as a mechanism through which, in response to an appropriate signed declaration, material is supplied to an individual through the library. The material thus provided may not be further copied or passed on, or indeed used for any reasons beyond the permitted acts – otherwise the declaration is invalidated. In circumstances where the concessions cannot be applied to acquiring copies, the provision of 'copyright cleared' material has been introduced. Here, a 'clearance fee' is levied as an addition to the normal costs of document access. Other agencies that provide photocopies or fax copies, many of which operate on a commercial basis, levy a copyright fee and attach conditions regarding the use and re-use of documents.

Where digital text is concerned, the concessions in legislation play a lesser part. Users and vendors have had to reach an accommodation as to what can be done and how, and for what payment. There is normally some kind of levy to be paid for the use of copyright material. Arrangements span a range of commercial expediencies from pay-as-you-go (each document is supplied with a copyright charge that may vary from publisher to publisher, and even from document to document) to a subscription-based system where there is unlimited copying or a quota on copying. Either way, there is a considerable extra burden of copyright fees to be paid by someone. Moreover, commercial document access providers working with publishers – the copyright owners – are in some sense in a sellers' market; if one wants the product in this convenient fashion then one must pay what is asked. Competition between vendors is a mechanism that promises some price stability and/or enhancements to terms of service, but the market does not appear to have matured sufficiently so far for that state of affairs to come about. Furthermore, and inevitably, vendors and copyright owners with different business plans are driven by different priorities, policies and agendas and indeed differing perceptions of the value of their copyright. Thus, the tariffs and conditions offered by various vendors were found by FIDDO to vary greatly (see, for example, Appendix A), and the situation does not appear to be changing.

In the UK the NESLI service, which features a variety of options for electronic text subscription to journal collections, offers an example where there is a diversity of deals available, incorporating different access and copying/printing/downloading regimes from the different participating publishers.

In considering the options between various routes for access an important question arises, particularly for anyone having to fund the endeavour. If most of the material is required on an individual basis for specific researchers/scholars who require material for research or private study, then why pay a copyright fee for something that amounts to 'fair dealing'? It can be argued that a high premium is being paid for convenience and speed of supply. As noted in the previous chapter, some library managers, accustomed to deploying funds for material that can be used collectively as part of a common and re-usable resource – the library collection, express unease at a situation where the library is effectively providing and paying with scarce resources for what amounts to individual article supply.

Sometimes conflicts arise in the juxtaposition of modern technology and conventional practice. Thus it may be possible to acquire electronic documents very rapidly but the law and the system demand that a signature be obtained from a client end-user to confirm that the material is required for fair dealing. And the signature must be 'real'! This causes delay in document access and reflects badly on the library providing a service. There is currently a strong reluctance to accept electronic signatures as legally valid and acceptable, although there are signs that things will change as new methods of verification are developed and security measures are refined and become more sophisticated. The EU is also working to develop a framework in which electronic signatures can be legally acceptable (European Communities, 2000). Another impetus for change is the growth in volume and profitability of electronic commerce.

For the library manager concerned to work within the legal framework and to offer a service of quality there are many considerations and a great deal of work is entailed. The conditions prescribed by the various vendors need to be made known and observed. There may be some emphasis on documentation and record keeping, although much of this may be incorporated into the system. A further obligation, though it is debatable how far it extends, is the need to ensure that copyright is observed by those to whom documents are supplied through the library as 'agent'. To what extent can the library assume and carry responsibility for what end-users may or may not do with electronic documents, supplied under licence, that are easily replicated and distributed? It is not a new issue, but it is one that is brought into sharper focus as document access arrangements become jeopardized through infringement of contract conditions. Where, in some scenarios, document transactions become increasingly devolved and by-pass the library, how far then does the almost traditional role of the library as 'guardian' of copyright extend?

The mechanics of acquiring and distributing documents pose logistical difficulties, especially where several delivery options or systems co-exist. The electronic copy management systems being developed offer methods of streamlining activity, as do the digital object identifiers, which enable clearer identification of items and smoother administration of transactions.

Some philosophical issues

The business of an information and library service fundamentally involves pairing information with users. Optimally, the information provided to the user matches exactly what he or she needs and it is delivered in the appropriate format as cost-effectively as possible.

The books, periodicals, papers and even other media such as audio and video recordings, photographs and computer software, which are used for research, teaching and administration, embody intellectual property normally protected by copyright. A significant component of information and library management thus entails managing intellectual capital in whatever format it is disseminated.

The relationships between creators, users and the several interme-diaries in the information chain are ones where this intellectual capital is severally given away, loaned or bought. Copyright, once a mechanism to provide a monopoly for publishers while simultaneously monitoring and regulating what they disseminated, has matured into a complex legal code linking the world of ideas to the world of commerce with the almost inevitable financial transactions somewhere in the system.

In the not so distant past, providing document access meant literally that: access to a document. The scholar might travel to a library to see a document, or in some cases it could be made available by borrowing it from another institution's library. Note-taking was the customary method of extracting all or any of its content. With regard to copyright, few real problems were created in the scholarly environment. The advent of the electrostatic photocopier altered the situation somewhat since copies became so much easier, quicker and cleaner to make. It was far easier to infringe copyright and copyright owners became very aware of the potential of the new technology, with a resultant hardening of attitudes towards 'freeloading' users. Digital technology makes things even worse because the technology enables perfect copies to made time and time again and they can be distributed swiftly, easily and widely over networks. The copyright owners again see the potential for misuse and, at the same time, are alert to ways of creating additional income streams through digitized document products.

At some stage of the proceedings, whether buying a book, paying a journal subscription, performing a credit card debit for an electronic document or even submitting a prepaid voucher to the BLDSC, some currency is flowing. If the dissemination of information is to be sustained, whatever the conduit, there will be attendant overheads and, in many cases, the risks of taking on those overheads will have to be balanced by the promise of returns for those engaged in the process. In an earlier age Dr Johnson asserted with some force, 'no man but a blockhead ever wrote, except for money' (Boswell, 1953). In these times publishers and booksellers are undoubtedly sustained by turnover and profits, though men and women may sometimes write for other motives. Modern academics may not write for money but there is certainly a 'virtual' reward perceived in publishing (if only the respect of one's peers) and the regular UK Research Assessment Exercises, which take publishing practice very much into account, do translate, however tenuously, into funding gains (or losses).

However there is another dimension to the issue, and it is applied over a whole range of intellectual property. It is the argument that reasonable access to information is needed to nurture further creativity and invention, and that if this is limited too greatly then future scholarship will be stifled. It is a principle embodied in concepts such as fair dealing. The advent of sophisticated technology for replicating and distributing material has raised anxieties about the extent to which fair dealing can be reasonably maintained and developed. The unfortunate consequence of these two imperatives (commerce and access to information) is the greater polarization of sectors that would be better engaged in forming alliances to disseminate information for the ultimate benefit of society. The ambivalence in the relationship between owners and users of copyright has been evident for some time. Helge Sonneland, in describing the function of copyright, says succinctly: '. . . [it] answers the question: how best to reconcile the partly shared, partly contradictory interests of authors who give expression to ideas, publishers who disseminate ideas and members of the public who use ideas' (Sonneland, 1997).

Such is the volume and complexity of information and transfer mechanisms that many intermediaries, such as publishers, booksellers, software houses, database vendors, network services and document suppliers to name but a few, are involved in the process nowadays in order to make it work effectively and efficiently. Without a sound financial basis for these endeavours (whether through commerce or state subsidy) then, again, they would be hard to sustain. In some way or another the infrastructure that enables the transfer of information, whether print-based or electronic, has to be funded.

The debate about copyright often revolves around the notion of why, how, when and by whom the financial underpinning of the dissemination process should be achieved. The situation is exacerbated by the fact that information and library services, as heavy users of this intellectual capital, have less and less money to contribute in real terms even if they wished to do so. In addition, the way in which IT enables use to be measured (and thus costed and billed) has given a new dimension to the situation. In the public library sector even loans are measured on a statistical sampling basis and authors are compensated through the Public Lending Right. Access to electronic documents could readily be metered and charged out in the academic environment.

Conclusion

The FIDDO Project revealed several anxieties and misgivings among library managers about certain aspects of copyright and related issues. They stemmed from an awareness that copyright was a cost issue and that there were attendant complexities in managing the options. It could be expected that librarians would pay more heed to these issues than researchers who, if not entirely oblivious, are less preoccupied with the detail of law and more concerned with using the information expediently.

Respecting intellectual property rights is, however, central to nurturing effective global scholarly communication, particularly in the electronic age. Copyright performs a crucial role in the information supply chain, linking authors (a generalization for all creators) with readers (a generalization for all users). It can be argued that without copyright protection it would be difficult to sustain a creative base.

A working consensus is needed between owners and users of copyright material that facilitates the easy use of information while at the same time making the costs reasonably predictable and affordable. The crucial issue is, perhaps, not whether or how copyright should be observed, but rather the imperative of providing the user community, including libraries, with sufficient resources in these straitened times to enable adequate and sustainable document access to be a reality.

PART FOUR: LIBRARY MANAGEMENT

Introduction to Part Four

Parts Two and Three of this book have focused mainly on the findings of the empirical work undertaken by the eLib project FIDDO. The aim of the three chapters in Part Four is to take these findings and discuss their relevance for three groups of people: academic librarians, other librarians and those conducting research and development work in the field of full-text document access.

FIDDO, and the whole of the eLib Programme, has been funded through the UK Higher Education Funding Councils. Therefore, the principal audience for our work consists of British academic librarians. Chapter 9 is an update and an extension of the FIDDO summary report to eLib: 'Document delivery in a dynamic hybrid environment' (FIDDO, 1999a). It includes a number of *Key Points* from FIDDO's research. After outlining the Key Points in Chapter 9, we look at how strategic and organizational issues relate to FIDDO's findings. What organizational structures are appropriate for document access in fast-changing times? We refer back to the Key Points in the remainder of Chapter 9, and in Chapters 10 and 11.

Chapter 10 broadens the picture further. We have noted throughout the book that there are many ways in which higher education in the UK is not unique in terms of the issues of full-text access. Many industrial, commercial, legal and public information units are faced with similar circumstances, including constrained funding, technological change and demanding end-users. In Chapter 10, we take FIDDO's Key Points from Chapter 9 and assess the extent and ways in which they are relevant to workplace and public libraries and information services.

The final chapter, Chapter 11, seeks to examine what is at stake in document access. To do this, we look at FIDDO's Key Points in the context of the research and development agenda. This includes developments such as the eLib phase three (hybrid library) projects (eLib, 2000) and a JISC/Publishers Association pilot project (JISC and the Publishers Association, 1999) for the supply of electronic documents, complementing inter-library loan. These projects were either planned or ongoing at the time of writing. In addition, we look briefly at international developments, in North America and Australia. What is the research agenda? What might usefully be added to it?

CHAPTER NINE

FIDDO and academic library management

Introduction

This chapter relates FIDDO's research findings to the literature and practice of academic library management. We attempt to distill the key findings in each of Chapters 2–8 and relate them to the management of academic libraries. One of FIDDO's deliverables, as a research project, was a set of guidelines for academic library managers (FIDDO, 1999a), and these have been included as Appendix D. We asked a number of practising library managers to evaluate these guidelines and, although they were positive overall, they did suggest ways in which the guidelines could be improved. The Key Points in the first part of this chapter represent a thorough revision and updating of them.

The Key Points are then discussed in the context of two principal aspects of management: strategy and organization. Strategic academic library management is concerned with the development and deployment of an information strategy, often including an information technology strategy and an information systems strategy. The organizational side of academic library management is represented in this chapter by a discussion of the implications of FIDDO's research for the debate over 'convergence'. Hence, the chapter is divided into three sections: Key Points from the research; strategic issues: information strategy; and organizational issues: convergence.

Key Points from the research

Definitions

Budd and Harloe, as library managers, have stated that '[i]n the era of electronic access there is a need for a new vocabulary for describing what it is that we do, a vocabulary that focuses on content and transcends the very static dichotomy of 'ownership and access"' (Budd and Harloe, 1997). The UK eLib Programme (eLib, 2000) has perhaps been more productive of such a vocabulary than most other initiatives. At the risk of adding to an already long list of neologisms, in Chapter 2 we defined a **document access system** as any means by which an end-user obtains a paper copy of a document. We wanted an expression that allowed us to compare the functionality and performance of both print and electronic technologies in terms of full-text access. We used this definition as one basis for structuring our research, and we have found it robust and generative of insights. It has enabled us to look at products and services from the end-user perspective – in the jargon, a customer focus. This, then, is our first Key Point.

1. **Comparing print and electronic resources on a level playing field can be difficult. FIDDO developed the idea of the** *document access system* **as a way of describing an end-user perspective on full-text services. All the systems and procedures with which an end-user interacts between requesting and receiving a paper copy of a document go to make up a document access system. A traditional example of a document access system is a library holding printed journals coupled with photocopying facilities. No document access system will cover all of an end-user's needs, so that the goal for the 'hybrid' library service is to provide seamless access** *across* **systems.**

As already noted, eLib projects have supplied us with several new terms for considering the evolving information chain. One of the most useful of these, the 'hybrid library', was used in Key Point 1. The hybrid library was an important organizing term in the MODELS workshops noted in Chapter 2. As it has generally been used, the term hybrid library has referred to the seamless availability of resources regardless of whether they are paper-based or electronic. Since hybrid library has become so widely used, we feel that it is important to expand the definition or else we run the risk of having the direction of the library profession determined solely by technological considerations. As the eLib Programme Director Chris Rusbridge has said, 'It's not the technology, stupid, it's the people.' (Rusbridge, 1999). The second Key Point reflects this imperative.

2. **Some writers have described 'hybrid' libraries as bringing together paper-based and electronic resources. Our research has suggested that this is only a start. There are several other dimensions to consider apart from the format of the material. These include central/devolved budgetary structures, subscription/pay-as-you-go charging regimes and mediated/ unmediated requesting and delivery. Seamless access for end-users needs to be seamless across all of these dimensions as well as between paper-based and electronic resources.**

Chapters 3 and 4 were concerned with two of the most important features of document access systems from an end-user's perspective: coverage and time. Conceptually, these features are perhaps fairly simple; 'coverage' reflects the extent to which end-users can access the required documents and 'time' is how long they need to spend to do so. However, real end-users work in contexts (what we have called contexts of action), such as their discipline and their local department. Coverage and time are strongly mediated by these contexts. Therefore we found it useful to draw a distinction between the **actual** coverage of a document access system, which could be measured by standard methodologies, and the **effective** coverage of a document access system, which was the coverage of the system as perceived by real end-users in context. So although we could (and did) use experimental techniques to measure the **actual** time necessary to use document access systems, the contexts of end-users meant that they saw the systems in terms of **effective** time. Clearly, actual and effective features can be strongly related, but we found the distinction useful in assessing how different systems worked in the real world. This gives rise to the third Key Point.

3. The *actual* coverage of document access systems is only half
    the story. User requirements are for *effective* coverage, or
    coverage that they can use easily in their work contexts. The
    actual and effective coverage of traditional paper-based docu-
    ment access systems currently far outstrips that of electronic
    resources. The actual/effective distinction also holds for the
    time necessary to use document access systems. Electronic
    systems are, in general, superior to paper-based systems in
    terms of both actual and effective time.

The unit of analysis

In our work we attempted to be open-minded about the most appropriate level of analysis. So far as end-users were concerned, we included
academic researchers in chosen disciplines in specific departments in
particular universities. We found evidence that the work of individual
researchers crosses such boundaries (Chapter 3, and see Hamaker, 1996).
We therefore concluded that one appropriate level of analysis was the
individual. All of the universities included in FIDDO's work had fairly
centralized management structures; none had information budgets wholly
devolved to departments, although the degree of centralization still varied
considerably (Chapter 7). Perhaps as a partial consequence of this, we
concluded that the institution was the most appropriate aggregation of
academic researchers so far as document access was concerned, although
we also found potential for even higher-level aggregation. The issues of
resource sharing and library consortia are relevant here (Joint Funding
Councils' Library Review Group, 1995; Kingma, 1997; Hughes, 1999).

The systems we looked at also varied. From the work discussed in
Chapter 7 we found that the most important distinction, so far as library
managers were concerned, was not between print and electronic, but
between pay-as-you-go and subscription-based systems (see Key Point 2).
As a result of discussions with library managers and researchers, we
concluded that there was a meaningful link between the unit of analysis
(individual or institution) and the charging regime of document access
systems.

We inferred that library managers had to think in terms of both
the individually assigned, pay-as-you-go approach and subscription
services geared toward a user community. We discussed in Chapter 6 the

importance and difficulties associated with management information relating to these. However, we found a marked lack of management tools and techniques in use for each, especially relating to electronic systems. Such tools need to be both quick and effective; the MA/HEM decision support tool (MA/HEM, 1999), developed as an eLib project, was not used by library managers because of the time required to gather the necessary information. The work of Kingma (1996) is also relevant here. These issues therefore generate the next five Key Points.

4. **Users' requirements in terms of coverage are complex. They cross disciplinary boundaries, and the extent to which this is important varies between different groups of users. Their requirements are also not necessarily determined by their departmental affiliation, even if their department is itself interdisciplinary. For this reason, it is difficult to make assessments of users' requirements that are based on institutional structures such as departments. Indeed, such assessments are likely to lead to an inaccurate view of demand and an inefficient use of library resources. Devolved budgets may be little help here. It is better to assess users' requirements at the level of either the individual researcher or the institution (or an even larger unit). However, management techniques and tools are underdeveloped in this area.**

5. **If users' requirements are individual, then pay-as-you-go charging regimes also disaggregate the supply of documents. Moves towards pay-as-you-go individual article supply are backed up by management initiatives that emphasize transparent accounting, by the economic pressures of the 'serials crisis' and by the possibilities of using micro-charging via the Internet. However, pay-as-you-go individual article supply, rather than subscription-based approaches, makes the central information function difficult. Again, management techniques and tools are underdeveloped in this area.**

6. **If users' requirements are institutional or even more aggregated, then subscription-based regimes also bundle the supply of documents. The management of subscription-based supply is also changing, though in the opposite direction to that of pay-as-you-go. Economies of scale are driving**

subscriptions to electronic resources up from the level of the library to that of the consortium. This may be in the form of national site licensing for networked resources. **FIDDO** also found potential for more conventional resource-sharing among libraries.

7.   The management of individual article supply to individual end-users is somewhat different from the management of subscriptions for a user community. Appropriate library management mechanisms that allow for seamless access, regardless of payment mechanism and document format, are not yet established for either, and need to be developed for both.

8.   Library managers typically divide users' requirements into those that are best addressed by subscription-based systems, such as journal subscriptions, and those that are best addressed by individual article supply. This decision is an economic one, and is based on the idea of a 'core' of titles that are frequently used. However, library managers rarely have had adequate information to make this decision, the basis of which is profoundly altered by changes in the nature of both subscriptions and pay-as-you-go document access.

Paper-based systems

Although we found that other considerations were at least as important as whether a document access system was paper-based or electronic, there were issues that related specifically to systems as a consequence of the document format. The delays in the traditional paper-based systems, discussed in Chapter 4, were uppermost in the minds of researchers, despite the views of many professionals (Hanson, 1999) that waiting a few days is no great hardship. Since some quantitative research (Weaver-Meyers and Stolt, 1996) supports the latter view, we can only assume that low user expectations are at work. The concerns of researchers with system delays were not limited to ILL, but also extended to local journal holdings.

9.   **In the UK, paper-based individual article supply is dominated by ILL via the BLDSC. Researchers typically wait up to a week**

for documents using this system. This performance could be improved by reviewing ILL procedures. In particular, the library and/or the university internal mail are currently sources of major delay, nearly doubling the potential response time. In addition, the necessity to visit a library means that researchers often 'batch' document requests, further slowing the process. It is clear why researchers prefer direct desktop ordering and receipt of documents. It is likely that this will become the minimum standard level of service, despite the legal and administrative difficulties with such an approach.

10. If desktop access becomes the minimum standard service for individual article supply, then why should researchers at universities with substantial collections be penalized by being made to visit the library each time they want an article from that collection? The waste inherent in a system that demands that highly-paid researchers queue with under-graduates for photocopiers is surely unacceptable. Seamless access should mean that end-users receive comparable levels of service regardless of the physical location of articles that they require.

Electronic systems

As noted above, there were issues that related specifically to systems as a consequence of the document format. For more electronic systems, these issues did not include 'time' because they were typically, though not always, quicker than paper-based systems. However, while researchers could take the operation and infrastructure of traditional systems for granted, this was not the case with electronic systems. Chapters 5 and 6 specified a number of areas where both academic researchers and library managers felt that electronic systems were not yet living up to their potential in terms of support, authentication, infrastructure and management information.

11. Support for users of electronic systems is not well inte-grated and, in general, users are unsure of the boundaries between different spheres of responsibility. For example, it

is often difficult for a user to decide whether their question relates to local technical facilities, to a particular product or to their information skills (Zeitlyn, David and Bex, 1999). Researchers want to ask a knowledgeable colleague or the nearest equivalent; they want a distributed support structure. Barry has noted that 'librarians will have to go out into the organization' (Barry, 1996). User support needs to be centrally co-ordinated but increasingly distributed in delivery.

12.   Researchers, and other users, are increasingly working away from campus. Access in this case often requires special authentication procedures. Complex authentication procedures have been shown to be a significant disincentive to use (SuperJournal, 1999). Remote use therefore must be included in the design specification of electronic systems and of their administration (Leggate, 1998).

13.   Electronic systems need an adequate technical infrastructure. This infrastructure is likely to remain a moving target, as systems are upgraded to take advantage of technological developments and market conditions. In terms of management, the requirement is not necessarily always to have the latest equipment, but rather for user and institutional equipment replacement cycles to be compatible with industry standards.

14.   Electronic systems offer the potential, not yet fully realized, for improved management information. Ideally, this information should be appropriate to the needs of library managers, configurable and in electronic format. National or international standards for management information/performance indicators may be necessary.

Contextual issues

FIDDO's brief was limited to issues relating directly to academic library management. Nevertheless, we did touch on wider issues such as the law (Chapter 8) and funding. While we did not have an opportunity to pursue these issues in any great depth, we did identify them as important areas for future research.

15. Regarding British copyright, 'fair-dealing' or an equivalent is essential to document supply in higher education in the UK. Whereas publishers fear that networked resources will rob them of control over their intellectual property, libraries and users fear that this issue might be used to abandon fair dealing. The JISC and the Publishers Association are (at the time of writing) setting up a pilot individual article supply scheme that may offer a way forward (see Chapter 11).

16. Just as market researchers are interested in why customers behave as they do, so FIDDO has been interested in why researchers use the scholarly literature as they do. Chapter 7 started with the maxim 'follow the money', and research practice is heavily influenced by the conditions imposed by grant-awarding bodies. This in turn influences how research should be supported by, for example, libraries. FIDDO has not had an opportunity to look at the impact of research funding regimes on libraries, but we feel that this would be valuable. For example, what effect would any move away from formula funding towards short-term project funding have on scholarly communication patterns, or on libraries? How do publication-based research funding regimes, such as the UK Research Assessment Exercise, impact on libraries? (See Chapter 11.)

Strategic issues: Information Strategy

Introduction

The evolution of information strategies in British higher education has been described by Brindley (1998). She notes the strong and continuing influence of national reports, such as the Follett (Joint Funding Councils' Libraries Review Group, 1993) and Dearing (National Committee of Inquiry into Higher Education, 1997) Reports, and of the Funding Councils in the form of the JISC. The JISC has published guidelines regarding the development of information strategies in higher education (JISC, 1995; JISC, 1998b). As they relate to research, these guidelines (JISC, 1998b: Executive Briefing) are concerned with:

- 'the balance of investment to be made between local, regional and national facilities and the uses of databases, processing capacity and research material;
- the encouragement of, and mechanisms for, working across disciplinary boundaries to capitalize on the institution's relative strengths;
- the use of online network facilities within the institution, with other institutions and with national facilities (e.g. for super computing, research equipment, and databases).'

These three areas of concern might be reduced to two: the vertical and horizontal integration of information. Vertical integration is the extent to which information is integrated between individual, local, regional and national (and international) levels. Horizontal integration is the extent to which information is seamless across disciplines. If we follow this path, then the research aspects of an information strategy could be considered under a two-by-two matrix structure. The picture is slightly complicated by including the level of the individual researcher, which obviously implies no vertical or horizontal integration at all. The matrix is shown in Table 9.1, with each cell representing one possible unit of analysis.

Relation to the Key Points

There is clearly a relationship between Table 9.1 and Key Points 4 and 11, which are also concerned with the unit of analysis. In Key Point 4, we noted that the demand characteristics of researchers in higher education are interdisciplinary. If we divide document access systems into those aspects that limit coverage, such as journal subscriptions or full-text web databases, and those that do not, such as photocopiers and printers, then the former need to be assessed at either an individual or an institutional

Table 9.1. The dimensions of an institutional information strategy

Vertical integration ⇒	None	Low	High
Horizontal integration ⇓			
None	Individual researcher		
Low		Department	Discipline
High		Institution	Academic community

(or even inter-institutional) level – or referring to Table 9.1, with either a high level of vertical integration or none at all. It is more difficult to make the assessment at the level of the department, which means that it is difficult for libraries to make full-text document access available to user communities (compared with either a user community or individual users).

If the assessment is made at the institutional level, then we can say that the library is contributing to a service for a user community rather than for a collection of individual users. This is certainly the approach favoured by Friend (1999), who then notes that for libraries 'traditional control may be replaced by greater influence in a broad-based information strategy'. Information functions, such as systematic archiving and a facility for users to browse, are possible within this framework. However, Key Point 6 notes that this is only straightforward within a subscription-charging regime, rather than pay-as-you-go. Information strategies (and accounting structures), whether at the institutional or the academic community level, need to reflect this.

If the assessment is made at the individual level, then it might bypass libraries altogether. FIDDO found evidence that certain document access arrangements had an increasing potential to operate at this level, outside the scope of institutional managers (Key Point 5). Clearly, this has always been the case to some extent; academics have always taken out their own private subscriptions to journals, for example. However, micro-charging Internet technology is now opening up the possibility that more comprehensive information provision will be available outside the formal structures of higher education. It is possible for libraries to operate within this pay-as-you-go framework, and to serve a collection of individual users rather than a user community. Unfortunately, in doing so they may become wholly reactive, abandoning collective functions such as systematic archiving and the facility for users to browse. If such functions are to be maintained, then information strategies will need to state explicitly how this is to be achieved.

The 1998 JISC guidelines suggest that an information strategy is especially important where devolved budgets have the potential to lead to fragmentation of the academic community. The library managers we interviewed were able to point to practical examples of the kind of fragmentation noted in the JISC document (see Chapter 7). The central co-ordinating role of a strategy is vital where devolved budgets allow departments to organize their own document access. Even where information and other budgets are not devolved, document access is affected by the more-or-less co-ordinated decisions of academic departments about the equipment available to researchers (Key Point 13). However, this may be more an issue for the institutional IT strategy than the information strategy *per se*.

There are forces pulling the information function simultaneously downward towards the department, or even to the individual, and upward towards the consortium (Key Point 4). The resulting tension is clear in the 'next steps' advocated by the JISC guidelines. The Funding Council urges institutions 'to decide that an Information Strategy . . . would be a valuable process to undertake (and not simply because the Funding Council says that it would)' (JISC, 1998b: Executive Briefing). FIDDO found areas where vertical integration is necessary, such as in the development of standards for management information and performance indicators (Key Points 8 and 14). Work underway under the European Commission's Telematics for Libraries Programme (EQUINOX, 2000) and elsewhere (Tuck, 1998) reflects this need . Other examples of new voluntary vertical integration are resource sharing, such as LAMDA, and consortial negotiating agreements, such as NESLI (Key Point 6). The future of existing examples, such as the BLDSC, is unclear at the time of writing (Key Point 9, and see Chapter 11).

So far we have not been concerned with discipline-specific issues. The preceding issues are those wherein horizontal integration is assumed to be high, perhaps because they emerge from cross-disciplinary bodies (libraries, the JISC and even FIDDO itself). If information issues remain within disciplines, however, then information strategies must address the different ways of working of those disciplines. There is evidence that some institutions are addressing this structurally, using subject support teams, without this approach necessarily being a reflection of an institutional strategy (Day and Edwards, 1998). FIDDO found that user support requirements suggest an approach that is vertically integrated but discipline- or department-specific (Key Point 11).

In summary, there are important links and tensions between the following dimensions of document access:

- subscription and pay-as-you-go charging;
- central and devolved budgets;
- libraries serving a user community or individual users;

- document access systems, user support for those systems and technical support for those systems.

Institutional (and other) information strategies will increasingly need to address these links and tensions if the information function is to be co-ordinated.

Organizational issues: convergence

The trend in the UK toward converging library and computing services shows no sign of slowing (Law, 1998). Such convergence is often associated with the development of an institutional information strategy, although not necessarily as the formal outcome of such a development. Information strategies drive convergence by emphasizing the need to take an institution-wide view of information. In Chapter 7 we noted one benefit of such a broad view, relating to issues of equity in document access, but there are many others.

Co-operation between support services is a good thing. To the extent that convergence fosters this co-operation, it too is a good thing. Several of FIDDO's Key Points would suggest that convergence has the potential to improve service to end-users. In particular, one rationale for convergence is said to be to develop seamless user support regardless of the format of the material required by researchers. Key Point 11 suggested that such user support should be organized along subject-based lines, and many of the new converged services have subject-based teams focusing on user support (Sykes, 1998). However, computing and library workers on the ground can find it difficult to take a holistic view of user support, even when they are formally organized into subject teams (Walton and Edwards, 1997). This is especially likely where convergence is inspired more by institutional politics than by users' needs.

Convergence addresses one dimension of the hybrid library – that of document format, since it brings together those responsible for the infrastructure allowing print and electronic resources to be used effectively. To this extent, Pinfield (1998) is right when he notes that the eLib vision of the hybrid library 'may be viewed as convergence in action'. Seamless support for print and electronic resources is likely to become increasingly important as the remote use of information resources increases (Key Point 12). However, as Simmonds (1996, unpublished data) has stated, 'the theory of convergence is rooted in a faith in the transformational potency of informational technology'.

Throughout the FIDDO research we have been faced with the everyday realities of library managers and academic researchers who are looking beyond the technology towards professional, financial and other issues. We have listed some of these as institutional budgetary structures, charging regimes for remote resources and mediation in information provision (Key Point 2). Convergence does not necessarily address these other dimensions of the hybrid library, since organizational structure is only tangentially relevant to them.

Concluding remarks

Let us then summarize the main points of this chapter.

* Hybrid libraries provide seamless access to, and support for, a number of document access systems. Such systems include not only products and services but also the technical, administrative and budgetary infrastructures necessary for them to work.
* Document access systems can be assessed in terms of their coverage and speed, but these are subjective (effective) as well as objective (actual) features of systems.
* Libraries serve individual users and user communities. The distinction between these two groups is related to that between pay-as-you-go and subscription-charging regimes.
* Significant improvements are possible within the current paper-based document access systems.
* Significant improvements are possible within electronic document access systems.
* Contextual issues, such as copyright and research funding regimes, affect document access.
* An institution's information strategy can be analysed according to how it is concerned with the vertical and horizontal integration of information; FIDDO's findings are relevant to such integrations.
* Organizational convergence can be effective in addressing some, but not all, of the issues of document access.

It is clear that in the UK there is much at stake in full-text document access. The stakeholders (researchers, library managers, publishers, suppliers and others) are finding their roles changed, and are also re-positioning themselves. Technology is certainly one factor in these changes, but the hybrid library is not solely a technological institution. Economic, legal, professional, academic and other factors are also important. Nor is technology solely a driver of change; it is also the result of change. The technology that is produced to support document access will be the product of the work of the very stakeholders whose roles will be changed by that work.

CHAPTER TEN

Implications outside academic research

Introduction

The FIDDO Project was funded to investigate document access options that support research within higher education. In Chapter 9 we discussed the Project's findings as they relate to that activity. However, the concepts that we ended up using, such as 'document access system' and 'effective coverage', are sufficiently general to make the FIDDO findings relevant beyond academic research. In this chapter we broaden our focus, firstly to consider FIDDO's findings in relation to teaching and learning within higher education and, secondly, to move outside the university altogether and to consider them in relation to workplace information services and public libraries. We refer to FIDDO's findings in terms of the Key Points described in the first part of Chapter 9.

The first section, on teaching and learning in higher education, draws both on research work in the area and on the experience of the authors as practitioners. The second section, broadening the focus to workplace information services and public libraries, draws on an evaluation of the Key Points by practitioners in these fields.

Teaching and learning

Chapter 1 detailed ongoing changes in British higher education that have already been rapid and far-reaching, and the future seems to offer no let-up. Teaching and learning in particular have been altered substantially over the past 20 years. The most obvious change has been from an elite to a mass higher education system (Creaser and Murphy, 1999). The sheer number of students in higher education has forced lecturers, administrators and support staff to re-evaluate their roles, functions and methods. There have also been other drivers of change. The funding of teaching and learning in higher education in the UK has become increasingly focused on the number of students taught and, in contrast to the research arena, there is no direct relation between funds allocated and the *quality* of teaching and learning[1]. The latter is systematically assessed, but funds do not follow directly the results of the assessment. However, the assessment has indirectly affected approaches to teaching and learning, with academic departments keen to achieve a high standing in order to attract the best (or the most) students. One means by which such high standing has been sought has been the use of new technology in innovative ways. In terms of library support certainly there has been no lack of new technology to use, and no lack of research and development projects investigating its use (Halliday, 1997; Ramsden et al., 1998; ACORN, 2000).

Of particular interest to FIDDO is a perceived shift toward student-centred learning, resource-based learning and distance learning as models of the student experience (Telford, 1995). These models have at least two things in common: they emphasize independent activity on the part of the student, and they introduce academic-style research as a learning technique. Both of these features make the activities of students more like those of academic researchers, not just when the students are writing a final thesis or dissertation, but throughout their programmes of study.

FIDDO's Key Points (see Chapter 9) were generated in part by investigations into the information requirements of academic researchers, including PhD students. Inasmuch as the experience of 'taught' students now includes significant elements of 'research', then the Key Points are directly relevant. In addition, several of the Key Points have some relevance to information support for conventional lecture/seminar/ tutorial-based pedagogy. Indeed, some have argued that these various pedagogical models are converging (Tait and Mills, 1999).

---

[1] A report (Higher Education Funding Council for England, 1999) notes that the 'dominating influence' of the Research Assessment Exercise in the UK inhibits innovation in the use of new technology for teaching and learning.

We should note that many students, especially undergraduates, continue to rely more on books than on the journal articles or conference papers that were the focus of FIDDO's study. Therefore, a principal concern of theirs might be that emerging document access systems may take library resources away from already overstretched monograph collections. The remainder of this section excludes any major consideration of monographs, as did FIDDO as a whole.

We assessed the requirements of researchers in terms of three 'contexts of action': their discipline, their local department and the physical aspects of their environment (Chapters 3–5). In Chapter 2 we noted that different end-users would have different contexts of action. What then would be the contexts of action of students? We identified three that corresponded in some ways to those of researchers.

1.   The programmes of study undertaken by students stand between those students and the disciplines proper. The *content* of the programmes of study, therefore, stands in the same relation to students as the *discipline* does to academic researchers (see Chapter 3); it is a context of action.

2.   The local non-research demands on academic researchers consist of teaching and administration, which we have called the *departmental* context of action (see Chapter 4). For students, these demands are made by the *administrative arrangements* of the *modules that make up the* programmes of study. Examples of these administrative arrangements would be assessment deadlines or weekly reading requirements.

3.   The dimensions of the *physical environment* of students, in terms of the technical infrastructure and information artefacts available to them, are similar to those of academic researchers (see Chapter 5). However, the particulars of this environment may vary. For example, students may have different access to computing equipment than academic researchers.

The information content of programmes of study might be represented by the reading lists of the modules making up the study programmes. In contrast to the requirements of academic researchers, those of students are often at least partially documented in such reading lists. In the experience of many lecturers, students rarely go beyond the reading list in order to fulfil module assignments; they tend not to consider it essential. Allied to this is the fact that reading lists have become central to the planning of many programmes of study by both teaching and library staff. Library managers tend to assume that, overall, they can take the reading lists to be representative of the content of modules, and there- fore of the resource requirements of students taking these modules. So, whereas researchers' information needs tend to be interdisciplinary (Key Point 4), those of students on a particular programme are, at least potentially, predictable and discrete. Of course, reading lists need to reach the library in good time!

Greater numbers of students without proportional increases in the numbers of teaching staff have tended to lead to bigger classes that, in turn, have often brought extreme peaks of demand on library resources. Libraries have tried to cope with this in three ways, by buying multiple copies, shortening loan periods (sometimes drastically) and looking into electronic solutions. Multiple copy provision is limited by cash and shelf-space. Shortening loan periods reduces the 'effective' coverage (Key Point 3) of collections by making them less user-friendly. (Their 'actual' coverage, as judged by a comparison of the collection with reading lists, is independent of peaks in demand.) Electronic reserve collections, such as that developed by Project ACORN (ACORN, 2000), have been piloted but for a variety of reasons they are not a complete solution. Significant work continues in this area (eLib, 2000; SITEBUILDER, 2000).

FIDDO's Key Point 3 also noted a distinction between the 'actual' and the 'effective' time required to use a document access system. In the case of students the distinction is based on the administration, rather than the content, of individual programme modules (see above). Where assign- ment deadlines are short, as is common, then even apparently trivial delays in accessing documents can be unacceptable.

The technical environment of taught students varies (Key Point 13). The computing and printing equipment available to them within an acad- emic department is often of a higher specification (that is, newer – see Chapter 6) than that of the department's academics and, especially, than that of its more junior researchers. This means that taught students who have ready access to campus can have a good technical infrastruc- ture supporting their use of those information resources that are networked to the department. In addition, richer students with their own high-specification computers, living in networked halls of residence, may well have a far superior technical infrastructure at their disposal than most others in higher education. However, this rosy picture hides some important problems. Firstly, not all universities can afford sufficient high-specification equipment for students. Secondly, not all students have ready access to campus. Some mature students, part-time students and distance learners may find a technical infrastructure that is restricted to campus virtually useless. Thirdly, technical and legal restrictions may prevent information resources being networked away from campus, even though that is where many students need access to them. Again, we are not only referring to distance learners here; part-time and mature students undertaking 'standard' courses may also need to work away from campus facilities. FIDDO noted that remote use needs to be designed into electronic systems for researchers (Key Point 12). Authentication procedures that rely on the physical location of the user are increasingly anachronistic in a networked world.

During FIDDO we have been careful to remember that computing infrastructure is only part of the story. Paper-based document access systems, still vital for students, also rely on a technical infrastructure. In this case the infrastructure is made up of photocopiers and mail systems rather than printers and cables. In Key Points 9 and 10 we noted that, like the electronic infrastructure, the paper-oriented infrastructure should be made more appropriate to the needs of those for whom a visit to the library is difficult or inconvenient.

In Key Point 8 we made an economic link between the idea of a 'core' of literature and document access available on a subscription basis, rather than pay-as-you-go. The nature of student demand (intermittent peaks) makes reading list material neither core nor peripheral; it falls between the two categories and so is not conveniently paid for by either subscription or pay-as-you-go. Of course, we are talking about library payments here. Passing on access charges, either directly or in terms of travel to other libraries (Key Point 6), to students is another issue entirely. Reproduction costs (photocopying, printing) are regularly passed on to students, but libraries do strive to maintain access 'free at the point of use'.

If there are major technical and economic questions, then the related legal questions are surely no less important. Whereas researchers in the UK have relied on the 'fair dealing' exemption in British copyright law (Key Point 15), the legal and licensing positions with regard to reserve collections and study packs have been less straightforward. Electronic reserve collections have tended to pay copyright fees for documents. They have therefore needed elaborate copyright management systems to keep track of the use made of electronic documents, and to monitor concomitant payments. Commercial alternatives to this locally managed, pay-as-you-go approach are available, such as ProQuest's SITEBUILDER, but they tend to have limited coverage.

In her review of electronic reserve collections, Kingston (1998) notes that service development needs to take account of the support and training needs of users. Given the far more open access policy adopted recently by British higher education as a whole, library managers are likely to be faced with a highly diverse user base. FIDDO noted that technical, product and information support for researchers needs to be as seamless as the systems themselves (Key Point 11). It is unlikely that the diverse student population will be less demanding than this. Indeed, those working independently, away from campus and perhaps without informal peer support, are likely to need systems that are both well supported and easy to use (Key Point 2). Even campus-based users may not have the information skills, confidence and support that has perhaps previously been assumed.

In summary, things are changing. Document access systems that may have been suited to serving the needs of a relatively small number of 18 year-old, campus-based, full-time students whose first language was English may not serve the needs of a larger and more diverse user base. Certainly, it is possible to see a number of technical fixes to the various challenges thrown up by recent changes in teaching and learning. However, most of the fundamental challenges are not technical. We have been able to use FIDDO's findings to illuminate some of the basic issues involved in addressing them.

Workplace information services

Workplace information services and libraries are as diverse as workplaces themselves. For example, they range from being one part of the job description of a single person to large and sophisticated library services. While it would be impossible to evaluate FIDDO's Key Points (see Chapter 9) from the perspective of every type of workplace information service, we wanted to have as broad a view as possible. Taking our lead from an extensive survey of workplace libraries and information services (Spiller, Creaser and Murphy, 1998), we divided workplaces into nine sectors:

1.   Government departments
2.   Government organizations (non-departmental)
3.   Voluntary agencies
4.   Professional, trade and learned associations
5.   Legal organizations
6.   Commercial and financial companies
7.   Energy organizations
8.   Pharmaceutical companies
9.   Management and information consultants

We asked for feedback on the FIDDO Key Points from each of these sectors, and the six replies we received form the basis for most of what follows. However, before summarizing the relevance of the Key Points for workplace libraries, it is worth noting some of the relevant findings of the Library and Information Statistical Unit (LISU) survey from which the above sectors were taken.

Findings from the LISU survey

The findings in this section are taken from Spiller, Creaser and Murphy (1998), and refer to the nine sectors noted above.

The median number of journal subscriptions varied across sectors from two to 15. Around 90 per cent of subscriptions were in print format, rather than CD-ROM or online. In no sector did a majority of workplace libraries report subscribing to a decreasing number of journals. This probably contrasts with academic libraries.

'Interlending' (for photocopies) was practised by most libraries in all sectors. The most popular sources of photocopies were peer organizations and the BLDSC. The most frequent requesters were libraries in the pharmaceutical and government department sectors. There were no clues as to an explanation for this in figures for library size or size of user base, since libraries in other sectors appeared to have similar profiles for these variables. However, both government department and pharmaceutical libraries had relatively low median numbers of journal subscriptions

(5.5 and 4 respectively). These can be compared with the numbers for sectors such as law (15) and finance (10.5) whose interlending figures were much lower than those for government department and pharmaceutical libraries. The suggestion could be made, on this evidence, that pharmaceutical and government department libraries were operating a more 'just-in-time' approach to document access than libraries in the law and finance sectors.

Desktop access to reference CD-ROMs and databases was available in some libraries in all sectors, and in most or all libraries in every sector except voluntary agencies. However, on average, perhaps a half of workplace libraries reported no desktop access to reference CD-ROMs and databases. The picture was somewhat better for desktop Internet access, with all sectors reporting a relatively low proportion of libraries as having no desktop access at all. Apart from the figure quoted above relating to electronic journal subscriptions, there were no findings concerning electronic full-text document access.

Feedback on the FIDDO *Key Points*

We sent FIDDO's Key Points to a library manager in a representative library in each of the sectors outlined above, and asked for comments on how, if at all, the Key Points related to the operation of workplace libraries. Although we followed the LISU typology in our methodology, analysis of the six detailed replies we received indicated that workplace libraries might be divided into two broad types:

Type 1: libraries and information centres serving a particular site or organization, their relationship with their users being defined in terms of supporting the goals of the site or organization as a whole. These libraries were, therefore, concerned to supply all the explicit and implicit information needs of a discrete group of users;

Type 2: libraries and information services serving a particular trade, profession or subject area, their relationship with their users being defined in more or less market terms, even if particular transactions might not appear market-based. These libraries were, therefore, concerned to provide an information service at a price that the market could bear, satisfying explicit user demand. Comprehensiveness in any subject area was not essential, although it might be a selling point of the service.

Clearly, these are idealized, and the real libraries contacting FIDDO did not fit them exactly. Nevertheless, we think this simple typology is useful in discussing how FIDDO's Key Points relate to workplace libraries.

Both types of library reported general moves toward the provision of full-text documents in electronic format. User expectations were leading the way in several cases. Barriers to the wider use of electronic documents included cost, copyright, skill and equipment limitations.

Type 1 libraries

Type 1 libraries received a budget from their parent organization for all front-line services including document access. Where FIDDO's research had to address the considerable potential complications of devolved budgeting (Key Points 2, 4 and 5), neither this nor cross-charging were widespread in the Type 1 libraries contacted by FIDDO. However, one library manager did note that notional costing of documents might be used by senior management in an organization to bring home to library users the true costs of acquiring information.

Current, pay-as-you-go, paper document access was mediated (Key Point 2), monitored and loosely controlled by simple management information routines. These had proved to be adequate so far, although one library manager did express a concern about the effectiveness of such methods in an electronic environment (Key Points 5 and 14). Just as important to some were control mechanisms to ensure that libraries were not paying twice for documents, for example by ordering material already held. However, at least one library manager noted that she did not even check ILL requests, assuming it to be more efficient simply to pass them on to the library's preferred suppliers. A supplier has confirmed that this is the case in more than one workplace library. Clearly, whether or not it is efficient to check ILL requests depends on a number of issues, including the size of the local collection and the searching behaviour of the local users.

All Type 1 libraries that contacted FIDDO recognized the bottleneck in the paper document supply system described in Key Point 9. The technical feasibility and potential benefits of desktop requesting and delivery meant that, as in the academic sector, there was some impatience expressed with the bureaucratic and expensive implications of copyright legislation and publishers' licences. All Type 1 library managers noted that these features of the information landscape had the most profound effects on the service that they were able to offer.

Three other features were shared by all Type 1 libraries that contacted FIDDO. Firstly, none recognized the consortial approach to subscriptions described in Key Point 6, certainly because of the nature of the commercial environment in which they operated. Secondly, none confirmed that the remote use and hence the authentication of document access systems (Key Point 12) was a significant issue. Thirdly, they all noted that they relied for IT support on a separate department within the parent organization. This last point led to some problems, including the apparently low position of libraries on the priority list of some IT departments and, as suggested in Key Point 11, confusion among end-users over the respective responsibilities of the library and the IT department.

Looking into the future, the managers of Type 1 libraries foresaw the information role becoming less one of mediation and supplying documents to end-users, although 'difficult' requests would always need expert advice. Instead, these managers envisaged information workers as having roles in selecting subscription resources, alerting end-users to their existence and training them in their use. Pay-as-you-go options were noticeably absent from this vision.

Type 2 libraries

The Type 2 libraries that contacted FIDDO received a general revenue stream from membership fees, but they also charged for photocopied articles. Hence, in terms of their users they were operating a pay-as-you-go system, and the library managers concerned noted the consequent accounting issues. One of these libraries sought to be a 'clearinghouse' while the other aimed to be one of a number of options that a user might try. This difference in the business plans of the two libraries had a significant impact on their views of FIDDO's Key Points. For example, in terms of Key Point 6, only the library that sought to provide a comprehensive service noted that there was scope for consortial subscription arrangements. A second example was that of catalogue access. Web catalogues had made a major difference to the operation of both libraries, with a decrease in the number of mediated searches as users took advantage of the ease of use of the web. However, whereas the 'clearinghouse' allowed anyone access to their web catalogue, seeing it as an interface with other services, the other library viewed access to their catalogue as a membership benefit, and a password was required. This obviously led to the two libraries differing in whether or not remote authentication was an issue (Key Point 12). The difference is likely to be reduced if both libraries market electronic full text, since copyright holders will insist on proper protection for their material.

Copyright was a major issue for Type 2 libraries (Key Point 15). Neither of them saw current licences as a basis for a commercial service, principally because of their expense. As one library manager put it, 'we felt the market would not bear the pricing levels imposed under the CLA licensing scheme'. The licence fees of individual publishers were also criticized as unrealistic. However, operating under the 'fair dealing' exemption in British copyright law is only available for paper copies and requires signed copyright declarations to be provided by users. Although Type 2 library managers considered that they had minimized delays in their service, they did confirm the view of academic librarians that mail systems and copyright forms do slow down the paper-based system (Key Point 9). They were also keen for reasonable arrangements to be put in place quickly in the electronic world. The various legal and commercial arrangements in place for licensed, fair-dealing, locally held and electronic material meant that one library manager considered that differentials in service were inevitable, and that users did not necessarily understand these differentials (Key Point 10).

Both Type 2 libraries used management information to a greater extent that Type 1 libraries, and had higher expectations of it in the future (Key Point 14). Their more market-like relationships with their users explained this, since they needed to ensure cost effectiveness.

Summary: workplace libraries

Although Type 1 and Type 2 libraries differ from each other, and each differs from academic libraries (which themselves vary), the overlap in important issues is notable. These points of overlap can be summarized as:

- copyright regulations;
- copyright fees;
- technology;
- management information;
- financial accounting.

These issues have been addressed during the FIDDO research project, and the development projects described in the next chapter should make progress in easing current difficulties for all stakeholders in the academics' research information chain. Workplace libraries, too, should benefit from this work.

Public libraries

Public libraries differ fundamentally from both academic and workplace libraries. Whereas the latter usually function in support of the goals of a parent institution or profession, public libraries have a civic responsibility to provide services to anyone residing within a particular area. Since geography is the only defining feature of the users of public libraries, the demands of these users have the potential to be substantial and diverse. Nevertheless, when compared with the users of academic and workplace libraries, certain generalizations can be made. Perhaps the most important of these, with respect to the FIDDO research, is that users of public libraries (with one exception described below) seem to be much less interested in article-length documents than are groups of academics or professionals. Public library users are more concerned with books, audiovisual resources, community information and the reference function in all its manifestations. Nevertheless, some of FIDDO's Key Points have relevance for public library management.

One group of public library users does tend to be interested in scholarly articles, and that is higher education students. Some students use public libraries to request ILLs because of restrictions placed on their use of the ILL service of their university. Prowse (1999b) undertook a survey of public library authorities in which he asked them to estimate the number or proportion of ILL requests they received from students. The results, although not conclusive, do suggest that there is considerable use of public libraries for this purpose. Apart from the load on public libraries, this should also concern academic libraries because it is another example of 'access' arrangements bypassing them.

Until recently, public libraries could have been seen as the Cinderella of the British library world, being even more under-resourced than other libraries. While the under-resourcing continues, the central role of public libraries in the information age has at least (and at last) been recognized by policy makers (Department for Culture, Media and Sport, 1998; Library and Information Commission, 1997; 1998). Characterizations of public library users are changing, with renewed emphases being placed on life-long learning, social inclusion and economic development. No longer are users merely 'customers'. FIDDO suggested that the incentives of academic researchers were relevant to their use of libraries (Key Point 16). Similarly, these new characterizations of public library users imply new incentives and, consequently, new roles for the library. For life-long learning the public library has to be the 'university on the corner'. For social inclusion the public library has to be a 'community information network'. For economic development the public library has to provide value-added services. Of course, these new demands from users come in addition to current demands, not as substitutes for them. To complement national policy initiatives, it may be that 'bottom-up' research is also neces-sary into exactly how people want to use public libraries in these new and exciting ways (Key Point 16).

In looking at document access within higher education, FIDDO noted the issue of the unit of analysis (Key Points 4–7). This was an impor-tant factor in assessing the requirements of the user community, communities or individual users. There are direct parallels here with the public library function. At the community level the public library has a role in supporting community information networks (Yu, Dempsey and Ormes, 1999) that can promote social inclusion and democratic participation. Within the policy agenda attention has also been given to user communi-ties. For example, *Building the new library network* (Library and Information Commission, 1998) emphasizes the need to provide content that reflects the UK's multicultural and multilingual society. Finally, the individual library user's needs are attended to, both at the reference desk and in terms of management initiatives promoting a 'customer focus'.

FIDDO related the unit of analysis to purchasing (or licensing) arrangements. That is, we suggested (Key Points 5–6) that user require-ments that were best assessed at the level of the community were also best addressed by subscription or even consortial arrangements. Conversely, user requirements that could only be assessed on an individual basis were best left to pay-as-you-go arrangements. Although public libraries do not generally subscribe to a large number of journals (the main subscriptions in question throughout FIDDO), their users do have other requirements that are best assessed at the level of the community. These are, perhaps, focused on the technologies that facilitate the library service and this is where consortial arrangements are found (EARL, 2000; Froud, 1999). If FIDDO found that not all academic researchers had access to adequate computing equipment (Key Point 13) then the position of British public library users is worse (Batt, 1998). It is likely that the ultimate consortium – Government – will need to be involved in bridging the gap between current provision and that envisaged (Library and Information Commission, 1998).

Two other 'technical' issues from *Building the new library network* (Library and Information Commission, 1998) relate to FIDDO's findings. Firstly, current proposals suggest that first line technical support (Key Point 11) will be provided by trained library staff, backed up by maintenance contracts with outside suppliers. It is reassuring that the split between technical and information-oriented user support that is prevalent in higher education is not to be repeated in public libraries. Secondly, authentication and ease of use issues (Key Point 12) are being specifically addressed, as is remote access.

In summary, the issues raised during FIDDO's research, although more directly relevant to academic and workplace libraries, do have parallels within the world of public libraries.

Implications outside academic research: summary

This chapter has presented FIDDO's findings outside their primary intended context of academic research. It has taken relevant Key Points from Chapter 9 and discussed them in the contexts of teaching and learning, workplace libraries and public libraries. These contexts proved to be progressively less and less like academic research; many of FIDDO's Key Points as stated were substantively relevant to teaching and learning, but only analogously relevant to public libraries. However, in all of these contexts, FIDDO's user focus was generative of insights. In particular, it became apparent that a multi-layered approach to assessing user requirements and a seamless approach to addressing those user requirements were both needed in academic, workplace and public library services.

CHAPTER ELEVEN

The document access research and development agenda

So what of the future of document access? What can the FIDDO results say about the research and development agenda, both in the UK and more widely? This chapter aims to relate the key findings from the FIDDO Project, detailed in Chapter 9, to national and international initiatives. We recommend, therefore, that readers read this chapter in conjunction with the Key Points outlined in Chapter 9.

Funding issues

As far as we are aware there is no research being undertaken into the effects of academic research funding regimes on researchers' information needs and, therefore, on library provision (Key Point 16). In the UK the four-yearly Research Assessment Exercise (RAE) has placed research funding firmly in the context of publication. Academic departments are rated, at least partially, by the quality and quantity of the publications produced by the academics therein. Funding then follows these ratings. The Funding Councils have sponsored research into the effects of this approach on academic behaviour and scholarly communication in general (Higher Education Funding Council for England, 1997), concluding that overall the RAE is benign in this respect. However, the lack of research into the effects of funding decisions on information provision is worrying, especially if pressure persists within higher education for 'transparent accounting' (see Chapter 7). Transparent accounting is likely to relate library budgets even more closely to the results of the RAE, and the consequences are surely worth attention (Friend, 1999). This is especially the case after the Anderson Report (Joint Funding Council's Library Review, 1995) suggested inter-library collaboration as a means to support academic research. Such collaboration may prove impossible to co-ordinate if library budgets are increasingly tied into the results of local funding considerations.

There have been reports that the RAE is to be revised or even replaced with a system more closely linking university research with innovation and industry (Thomson, 1999). The subject areas included in the FIDDO Project – business, geography and manufacturing engineering – include substantial near-market research agendas. However, the researchers interviewed in 1998 as a part of the FIDDO field trials generally discussed their document access in terms of the research cycle outlined in Chapter 3, rather than in overtly market terms. There were exceptions, with some researchers occasionally using independent funds from outside the academic world to bypass the collective resource of the library, but these exceptions were relatively rare. However, the balance between RAE-associated income from funding councils and income from research grants and contracts has been slowly shifting in favour of the latter (Noble, 1996; 1998; 1999). Any further move in this direction might have even more profound implications for campus libraries than the RAE, which, at least, operates mainly within the scholarly world. These implications would need to be investigated.

Other issues

In terms of research and development into the practicalities of document access, there are several initiatives underway in the UK that promise progress. These include the eLib phase three hybrid library projects (eLib, 2000) called, rather exotically, AGORA, BUILDER, HEADLINE, HYLIFE and MALIBU. Another JISC initiative in this area is a pilot electronic 'inter-library loans' project (JISC and the Publishers Association, 1999). Internationally, there have been many projects and developments relevant to the future of document access for academic researchers. FIDDO has maintained a list of these on its web site, now maintained by Aslib (Aslib, 2000). For the purposes of this chapter, we briefly look at just two: the NAILDD project in the USA and KINETICA in Australia.

The developments themselves are well documented elsewhere; we have not tried to summarize them here. Instead, we have tried to relate them to FIDDO's Key Points from Chapter 9.

eLib phase three: hybrid libraries

Phase three (hybrid libraries) of the UK Electronic Libraries Programme (see Chapter 1, and Rusbridge, 1998) was based largely on two earlier eLib projects, MODELS (MODELS, 2000) and EDDIS (Larbey, 1997). It was these projects that emphasized the hybrid library as supporting seamless user access across formats. As noted in Chapter 2, MODELS developed a schematic information architecture that has served as the blueprint for several of the phase three projects, most notably AGORA. The projects themselves have been summarized by their project managers (Pinfield et al., 1998), and the following list gives a brief description. (More details can be found on their web sites, see Appendix C.)

* AGORA is developing a hybrid library management system in order to integrate the functions of resource discovery, location, request and delivery.
* BUILDER aims to build a working model of the hybrid library in a number of subject areas, focusing on service integration, authentication, database (metadata) management, digitization and organizational and cultural change.
* HEADLINE is also building exemplars of hybrid library systems, and focuses on authentication issues.
* HYLIFE is a broad project, both in terms of participants and focus, developing hybrid library interfaces and looking at user, management and evaluation issues.
* MALIBU is developing institutional models for the management and organization of hybrid library services.

Relation to FIDDO's Key Points

The first thing to note about these projects is that their orientation mirrors the integration of the MODELS Information Architecture described in Chapter 2 – that is, seamless functionality from resource discovery to delivery. For example, the AGORA project (AGORA, 1997) is explicitly developing the hybrid library management systems that form the central parts of the MODELS Information Architecture. Another example is the MALIBU project, which has developed high-level user-oriented functional models of the hybrid library that include everything from resource discovery to the publication of papers based on the resources discovered (Wissenburg, 1999). This contrasts with FIDDO's focus on full-text document access (Key Point 1), integrated from supplier to user and including *all* aspects of that chain, but excluding activities outside full-text access. Both approaches emphasize the need for management, budgetary and user support systems to be implemented seamlessly across the paper–electronic spectrum.

The MALIBU project, in emphasizing both management and users, certainly echoes FIDDO's agenda. The MALIBU project proposal (MALIBU, 1997) specifically includes sections concerned with both 'organization and management of services' and 'delivery of resources [to users]'. The former includes a concern with library–IT support convergence within higher education institutions, which was highlighted in Chapter 9, while the latter stresses the technical and infrastructure contexts of users that were discussed in Chapter 5 and Key Point 13. The HYLIFE and BUILDER projects, too, are user-focused, although they are concentrating on cultural as much as technical or managerial issues. HYLIFE has identified the needs of remote users as particularly and increasingly relevant to the work of those building hybrid libraries (Wynne and Edwards, 1999). FIDDO's Key Point 12 suggests that this is especially relevant to the work of HEADLINE on authentication systems.

One important aspect of the hybrid library that is apparently omitted from the design of all the eLib phase three (hybrid library) projects is the existing document delivery infrastructure in the UK, principally the BLDSC[1] but also LAMDA (LAMDA, 2000). FIDDO has consistently found (Morris and Blagg, 1998) that the BLDSC is, and is likely to remain, an overwhelmingly important part of what the eLib projects call the 'information landscape' (AGORA, 1997) in the UK (Key Point 9). This is

---

[1]   The eLib phase three (hybrid libraries) project AGORA includes the BLDSC as a 'prototype service provider', but not as a formal partner. The BLDSC is actively involved in the eLib phase three (clumps) project RIDINGS, although this is concerned more with resource discovery than the seamless access focus of the eLib (hybrid libraries) projects.

despite recent small increases in the level of requests unsatisfied by the BLDSC (Creaser and Murphy, 1999; Parry, 1997; Smith, 1997). If the BLDSC is likely to be a key part of the future of document access, then so are the resource sharing initiatives such as LAMDA that are part of the vision of the Anderson Report (Joint Funding Councils' Library Review, 1995) for the support for academic research. The eLib phase three projects can only be distanced from academic library practice in the UK by excluding these existing stakeholders. Of course, the BLDSC is only likely to remain a key feature of document access if it is not forced to compete solely on publishers' terms.

JISC/Publishers Association pilot project: electronic inter-library loans

In July 1999 the JISC and the Publishers Association in the UK published a joint request for proposals (RfP) for a pilot project for the supply of electronic documents, complementing inter-library loan. The pilot project's principal features were described in the RfP (JISC and the Publishers Association, 1999):

'The pilot project would provide an alternative to inter-library loan for the supply of electronic copies of journal articles, whether these are retained in electronic or only in print form. The route for supply would be from the server of the publisher of the journal article via a clearing-house service at a standard price similar to what libraries currently pay for an inter-library loan request ... The clearing-house service [would]: receive electronic requests from libraries; establish whether or not electronic delivery is available (and, if not, redirect the request to the normal paper-to-paper system); identify the source of the article; request the article from the publisher or other supplier; transmit the text to the user (via the library if necessary); notify the library of delivery; invoice the library; and distribute an agreed proportion of the income to the publisher.'

The immediate background to this initiative was a series of consensus discussions undertaken in a working party set up between the JISC and the Publishers Association to investigate the future of the concept of ILL in the electronic environment. Its financial justification was described in terms of the anticipated substantial reduction in marginal costs in the electronic environment. This, it was argued, would enable the ILL process to provide a revenue income stream to publishers where none exists in the paper-to-paper system, or even in paper-to-electronic-to-paper systems such as LAMDA. This revenue stream would be possible while providing an electronic service to higher education at approximately the same price as the current paper-to-paper service.

In January 2000, the decision was announced to accept a joint proposal submitted by ingenta Ltd. in partnership with the University of Lancaster. The former is a company active in the aggregation and distribution of electronic scholarly information, and the latter has developed ILL management systems in use in many British university libraries.

Relation to FIDDO's Key Points

So, what can be said about this pilot project from FIDDO's findings? Certainly such a project represents the core of a new document access system (Key Point 1). However, there are several issues left undefined in the proposal, and these relate others of FIDDO's Key Points.

Firstly, the end-user was not mentioned in the RfP, and there was some ambiguity in the companion project evaluation RfP as to whether end-users would be stakeholders in the project at all. Consequently, excluded from the proposal was any mention of support for the end-user (Key Point 11), either in terms of equipment (printers and so on) or in terms of help facilities. Clearly, it could be argued that this is a local issue (Key Point 13), but FIDDO's findings suggest that such support will be a critical success factor for the proposed system.

Secondly, and relatedly, requests were described in the RfP as coming from libraries, with no mention of the end-user as a requester. Presumably the RfP anticipated individual libraries setting up local arrangements for the receipt, checking and forwarding of requests, although the inclusion of the University of Lancaster in the successful consortium might suggest that some of this work could be done by the new system. The work would certainly be necessary if end-users were to enjoy desktop ordering (Key Points 9 and 12). An important and non-trivial part of this system would be a facility for checking local holdings (and other subscriptions) in case the requested document was available from these sources. On these issues, it is only to be hoped that the pilot scheme integrates thoroughly with systems developed within eLib phase three.

The need for appropriate statistical information was stated in the proposal, and this is welcome (Key Point 14). Researchers at the Centre for Research in Library and Information Management (CERLIM) have been developing standards for management information and performance indicators (Wynne and Brophy, 1998), following on from the work of the Joint Funding Councils (Joint Funding Councils' *ad hoc* Group on Performance Indicators for Libraries, 1995). There is clearly potential for the proposed system to work within this framework, especially as it is to be evaluated by the Lancaster Information Management Consultancy led by Professor Brophy.

In terms of budgetary issues the proposed system would be, like ILL, a pay-as-you-go system. We noted in Chapter 7 that institutions have developed ways of managing mediated ILL but that tools and techniques for managing unmediated or electronic document delivery are not yet in place (Key Point 5). There may be potential for the proposed system to be extended to include such tools and techniques; we certainly hope that this is the case. However, it may have been better for the proposal to have included specifically a requirement for a management tool such as *BL inside*'s 'supervisor function'.

Many of the points noted above might be described as 'technical'. However, there are more fundamental issues at stake and these may be summarized as copyright (Key Point 15), resource sharing (Key Point 6) and the existing document access systems (Key Points 9 and 10).

Although the RfP was unclear, it appeared that the proposed system would not be based on the 'library privilege' exemption in British copyright law (see Chapter 8 and Key Point 15). One reason why library managers in the UK have been keen to retain some form of analogous exemption in the electronic environment is that publishers have traditionally charged substantial and variable fees for licensed copies. The BLDSC service, based on the library privilege exemption, makes costs to libraries affordable and predictable. The RfP implied that charges for documents obtained via the proposed pilot system should match this affordability and predictability, so removing the financial need for the library privilege exemption. On a practical level, it is not clear whether this would be sustainable as the pilot is widened to include publishers whose charges for licensed copies have, until now, been significantly higher than the cost of a BLDSC voucher. At a more fundamental level, as noted in Chapter 8, there are major moves in Europe that threaten to remove or reduce exemptions to copyright legislation, and a cynic could argue that the proposed scheme might encourage such moves. However, there are at least two differences between the proposed system, being licence-based, and arrangements based on the library privilege exemption. Firstly, the library privilege exemption can only be revoked by Parliament, whereas licences are finite so that their terms can be renegotiated on expiry. Whether this is a threat (insecurity) or an opportunity (flexibility) for libraries is unclear. Secondly, the library privilege allows any qualifying library to share its resources with any other; licences do not.

FIDDO found that there was scope for resource sharing between academic libraries (Key Point 6), a finding supported by the success of LAMDA (LAMDA, 2000). If successful, the proposed system would (by definition) supplant such activity and so might effectively end the long tradition of libraries sharing resources, especially now that subscription access to electronic scholarly information is also licensed (via NESLI (NESLI, 2000) in the UK) rather than being bought by libraries in printed volumes. It is to be hoped that those with overall responsibility for the evaluation of the pilot system believe in the continued value of inter-library resource sharing.

Perhaps the most obvious example of inter-library resource sharing in the UK and throughout the world is the BLDSC. However, just as with the eLib phase three (hybrid library) projects, the JISC/Publishers Association RfP did not include the BLDSC, or even the ex-JISC-funded service LAMDA, in its vision of a future ILL system – except perhaps as safety nets. The companion project evaluation RfP not only apparently excluded end-users as stakeholders in the main project (see above), but also seemed to exclude those who dominate the existing market-place. There must be major question marks over the ability of what the RfP calls 'the conventional inter-library loan system for non-returnable items' to continue operating if publishers can cherry-pick requests. Of course, this argument was initially used against LAMDA, a not-for-profit organization, but how much more pertinent is it to a system whose principal operators (ingenta Ltd. and commercial publishers) have shareholders to satisfy?

We found that the coverage of paper-based systems, such as the BLDSC and university library holdings, far exceeds that of current electronic systems (Chapter 3). A common prediction among professionals (Crawford and Gorman, 1995) that this would remain the case for some time shows few signs of being contradicted. We found that paper-based systems have substantial potential for improvement (Key Points 9 and 10), especially in those tasks that take place within universities. We have noted that it is often these local arrangements, rather than those of document suppliers, that limit document access – whether paper or electronic (Key Point 13).

We understand that publishers might be keen to stop genuine ILL, since they see it as reducing their income. However, it is surely short-sighted for publicly-funded development work to ignore the special status of the BLDSC in the UK. The exclusion from the design of electronic alternatives to ILL of the decades of skill and experience in document delivery available at the BLDSC must be counter-productive. If it is symptomatic of an attempt to marginalize the BLDSC, then this should ring alarm bells within higher education in the UK and beyond. There is a substantial risk to information provision world-wide if the BLDSC, a key player, is marginalized in its home market.

The NAILDD Project and the ISO 10160/1 ILL Protocol

The Association of Research Libraries (ARL) in the USA has been actively trying to improve the processes whereby ILL is undertaken in that country. One initiative in this vein has been the North American Inter-library Loan and Document Delivery (NAILDD) Project (NAILDD, 2000). This was set up to promote improvements in ILL processes in North America (Jackson, 1999) and, among other things, it sponsored the 'Inter-library loan and document delivery performance measures study' (Jackson, 1998) noted in Chapter 1. The NAILDD Project has also become a major contributor to the discussions around the development of an international standard for ILL messaging: ISO 10160/1. Discussions continue on the implementation of the standard under the auspices of an implementors' group, IPIG, that emerged from the NAILDD project (IPIG, 2000). At the time of writing, it is not totally clear whether the ISO protocol, an alternative derived from the widespread Z39.50 search and retrieve standard or neither will become the most commonly accepted.

The existence in the UK of the BLDSC can make British library managers complacent. The lack of a comparable central facility anywhere else in the world (Cornish, 1998) means that standards are, perhaps, an even more key issue outside than within the UK. However, the international clientele of the BLDSC, along with indigenous challenges to its role (see above), mean that international standards do impact on UK services.

A recent survey by the International Federation of Library Associations (IFLA) (Gould, 1999) found that librarians were increasingly using Email for ILL requesting and that much of it complied with standards such as the ISO protocol (although there was still a need for IFLA guidelines on 'free form' Email requests). So far as the BLDSC is concerned (Key Point 9), a decision has been made not to migrate their existing 'ART' standard to the ISO protocol. Instead, the Centre is developing a gateway between ISO 10160/1 and ART (Davidson et al., 1999).

Although ostensibly a matter of rather narrow interest, standards are key development tools for those working to create new document access systems. The ISO 10160/1 and Z39.50 item-order standards are both geared toward library-mediated ILL systems. Hence, they are both contributions to the management of individual article supply (Key Point 7). In order to be useful for desktop ordering and receipt (Key Point 9), the standards would need to be embedded in the hybrid library broker such as that, for example, being developed by the eLib project AGORA. AGORA is implementing the ISO protocol. However, because the standards are not designed to support desktop ordering and receipt, let alone remote document access (Key Point 12), authentication and authorization are excluded from them. Work on these issues will need to be compatible with international ILL messaging standards if the hybrid library is to be seamless. Regarding management information and performance indicators (Key Point 14), comprehensive implementation of the ISO 10160/1 protocol would go some way to allowing comparative statistics to be available.

From the above, it appears that the North American standards development agenda is strongly influenced by a library-to-library paradigm of document supply. While initiatives in the UK must incorporate international standards if they are to support moves toward seamless access for the end-user, such seamlessness might be jeopardized if specific national contexts are ignored.

Australian initiatives: Kinetica

In contrast to the UK, which has no comprehensive national catalogue but rather a national document delivery resource (the BLDSC), Australian inter-lending is decentralized but has access to a physical national union catalogue (Sood, 1998). There has been a succession of projects that have sought to build on the Australian Bibliographic Network and thereby improve inter-lending processes. These projects, noted in Chapter 1, have been reviewed by Wells and Amos (1999) and references to them can be found in a review of document delivery web sites (Jacobs, Chambers and Morris, 1999). They have culminated in an infrastructure and a service called Kinetica (KINETICA, 2000), hosted by the National Library. The Kinetica Document Delivery Service (KDDS) uses Fretwell Downing's OLIB VDX system, and enables inter-lending to be structured and easily managed. Local, university and state libraries have access via Kinetica to a number of Z39.50 target databases including the national union catalogue. Since the system has implemented the ISO 10160/1 protocol, any request can then be managed throughout its lifecycle. This has a number of advantages. For example, local libraries can monitor the state of particular requests.

Kinetica is a linking system, like SilverPlatter's SilverLinker system trialled by FIDDO. However, unlike SilverLinker, it is designed to offer specific support for resource sharing between ordinary (that is, not necessarily national or deposit) libraries. FIDDO has found potential for such resource sharing in the UK (Key Point 6), although the situations in the UK and Australia are very different. The consequences of these differences would need to be borne in mind if further moves toward a resource-sharing model were to be proposed.

FIDDO found a need for a consistent approach to management information and performance indicators (Key Point 14). The KDDS offers an opportunity in Australia to achieve this consistency, and statistical reporting facilities are being built into the system.

On the question of desktop ordering and receipt of documents (Key Point 9), the KDDS is not yet set up with this in mind. However, this is more to do with the business plans of participating libraries, and that Kinetica is still in its infancy, rather than it being a firm national position. End-user access to the KDDS is anticipated eventually.

Finally, Kinetica builds on national strengths (the pre-existing Australian National Bibliographic Network and the Australian legal context) in a way that British developments seem to be avoiding. As noted above, JISC-funded initiatives in the UK seem to exclude the most effective inter-lending resource in the UK (Key Point 9), if not the world: the BLDSC.

Kinetica appears to be an approach to document access that both addresses the key findings of the FIDDO project and is appropriate to the national context in which it has been developed.

Concluding remarks: the research and development agenda

The international research and development agenda, insofar as it includes moves toward standards-compliant, linking infrastructures such as Kinetica, is certainly in tune with FIDDO's key findings. Seamless access across the paper–electronic divide is definitely on the agenda. However, we have found little evidence of work designed to integrate the subscription and pay-as-you-go charging regimes (Key Points 5–8) faced by library managers. Such management tools and techniques are likely to become increasingly important. MA/HEM (MA/HEM, 1999) is certainly a start but, as noted in Chapter 9, it was too time-consuming to use. In addition, the relationships need to be investigated between centralized and devolved information budgets, research funding mechanisms and library support for academics and researchers.

Of course, more fundamental questions are being asked about the future of scholarly communication, by Harnad and others (American Scientist September Forum, 2000). While FIDDO has not been able to address these, some of the solutions being proposed are potentially revolutionary. Halliday and Oppenheim (1999) have included some of them in their review of the economics of the digital library.

So far as the current British research and development agenda is concerned, while there are promising developments, the apparent exclusion of the BLDSC from many of them is problematical. Developers in the UK would surely do better to follow the Australian example and, taking a leaf from the collection developer's handbook, 'build to strength'.

The FIDDO project, being focused on document access within higher education in the UK, has been able to offer to library managers two levels of support. The first level of support, for the duration of the Project, was the making available of up-to-date information on document supply, including the list of document suppliers shown in Appendix A and at the relocated FIDDO web site (Aslib, 2000). The contents of the second level of support will, we hope, have longer term relevance. These are our attempts, documented in this book, to identify the critical document access issues for libraries that are supporting academic research. We have developed an approach, including a structured methodology, that offers an integrated view of issues that are perhaps marginalized in other parts of the research and development agenda. Having cleared this view, we hope that these very practical issues can now be addressed more success-fully by the library and information profession.

References

ACORN (2000) *web site*: acorn.lboro.ac.uk/

AGORA (1997) Project proposal. *web site*:
hosted.ukoln.ac.uk/agora/documents/proposal/proposal.html

AGORA (2000) *web site*: hosted.ukoln.ac.uk/agora/

ALPSP (2000a) *web site*: www.alpsp.org.uk/

ALPSP (2000b) *Licence to Publish*. Available at www.alpsp.org.uk/grantli.pdf

American Scientist September Forum (2000) *Freeing the refereed journal literature through online self-archiving*. Available at
amsci-forum.amsci.org/archives/september98-forum.html

Arkin, E. (1998) User-initiated interlibrary loan. *Interlending and Document Supply*, **26**(3), 119–122

ARL (2000) *ARL statistics and measurement program, supply and demand in ARL libraries, 1986–97*. Available at www.arl.org/stats/arlstat/1998t3.html

Aslib (2000) *Aslib/FIDDO web site*: www.aslib.co.uk/fiddo

Aslib Electronic Journals (2000) *web site*: www.aslib.co.uk/pubs/ejournals.html

Association of Research Libraries (1998) *ARL statistics and measurement program, supply and demand in ARL libraries, 1986–97*. Available at
www.arl.org/stats/arlstat/1998t3.html

ATHENS (2000) *web site*: www.athens.ac.uk

Baker, D. (1997) (ed.) Resource management: the context. In *Resource management in academic libraries*. London: Library Association

Barry, C. (1996) The digital library: the needs of our users. Paper presented at the *International Summer School on the Digital Library*, August 1996, Tilburg University

Batt, C. (1998) *Information technology in public libraries*. London: Library Association

Bevan, S.J. *et al*. (1998) BIODOC – The transition from research project to fully fledged service. *Serials*, **11**(2), 152–162

Blackwell (2000) *Electronic Journal Navigator web site*: navigator.blackwell.co.uk

Boswell, J. (1953) *Boswell's life of Johnson*. Oxford: Oxford University Press

Brindley, L. (1998) Information strategies. In *Managing the electronic library*, eds. T. Hanson and J. Day. London: Bowker-Saur

British Library Bibliographic Services and Document Supply (1999) *Facts and figures*. Available at www.bl.uk/services/bsds/dsc/pdf_files/factnfig.pdf

Brook, D.F. and Powell, A. (1994) ESCO 1995 serial price projections. *Serials Review*, **20**(3), 85–94

Brookes, B.C. (1969) Bradford's Law and the bibliography of science. *Nature*, **224**, 953–956

Budd, J.M. and Harloe, B.M. (1997) Collection development and scholarly communication in the 21st century: from collection management to content management. In *Collection management for the 21st century*, ed. G.E. Gorman and R.H. Miller. Westport, Conneticut: Greenwood Press

BUILDER (2000) *web site*: builder.bham.ac.uk/

CAIRNS (2000) *web site*: cairns.lib.gla.ac.uk/

Cambridge University Press (2000) *Cambridge Journals Online web site*: www.journals.cup.org/

Chambers, J. (1996) Determining the cost of an interlibrary loan in North American research libraries: initial study. *Proceedings of the 62nd IFLA General Conference, August 1996.* Available at www.ifla.org/IV/ifla62/62-chamj.htm

Chowdhury, G.G. and Chowdhury, S. (1999) Digital library research: major issues and trends. *Journal of Documentation,* **55**(4), 409–448

Clinton, P. (1995) Charging users for remote document supply in UK university libraries. *Interlending and Document Supply,* **23**(4), 14–19

Clinton, P. (1999) Charging users for interlibrary loans in UK university libraries – a new survey. *Interlending and Document Supply,* **27**(1), 17–29

Cornish, G.P. (1996) Resourcing academic libraries – is IT the answer? Electronic document delivery services. *New Review of Academic Librarianship,* **2**, 83–90

Cornish, G.P. (1998) The book stops here: barriers to international interlending and document supply. In *Interlending and document supply: resource sharing possibilities and barriers; Proceedings of the 5th Interlending and Document Supply International Conference, Aarhus, Denmark, August 1997,* eds. S. Gould and D. Johnson, pp 89–98 Boston Spa: IFLA Offices for UAP and International Lending

Cornish, G.P. (1999) *Copyright: interpreting the law for libraries, archives and information services* 3rd edn. London: Library Association

Crawford, W. and Gorman, M. (1995) *Future libraries: dreams, madness and reality.* Chicago: American Library Association

Creaser, C. and Murphy, A. (1999) *LISU Annual library statistics 1999.* Loughborough: Library and Information Statistics Unit, Loughborough University

Crotteau, M. (1997) Support for biological research by an academic library: a journal citation study. *Science and Technology Libraries,* **17**(1), 67–68

Dade, P. (1997) Electronic information and document delivery: final report on the pilot trial of the Uncover database. *Vine,* **103**, 43–45

David, H.A. (1988) *The method of paired comparisons.* London: Griffin

Davidson, E. et al. (1999) *Building an ISO ILL interface to the request processing system (BIIIRPS). BLDSC ISO ILL/ART Gateway ISO ILL Profile: version 2.09.* Available at www.bl.uk/is/profile.doc

Davies, C. (1997) Organizational influences on the university electronic library. *Information Processing and Management*. **33**(3), 377–392

Davies, C. (1998) Future user issues for the networked multimedia electronic library. In: *Elinor: electronic library project,* ed. A. Ramsden, pp. 106–130. London: Bowker-Saur

Davies, J.E. (1998) Strategic issues in managing information and document supply in academic libraries. *Library Management,* **19**(5), 318–326

Day, J. and Edwards, C. (1998) Overview: managing change. In *Managing the electronic library,* eds. T. Hanson and J. Day, pp. 129–152. London: Bowker-Saur

Deegan, M. (1998) The electronic library in teaching and research. In *Managing the electronic library,* eds. T. Hanson and J. Day, pp. 3–24. London: Bowker-Saur

Dempsey, L. (1999) The network and the library: working in a new shared space: infrastructure and institutions. *The Electronic Library,* **17**(4), 207–211

Dempsey, L., Russell, R. and Murray, R. (1999) A Utopian place of criticism? Brokering access to network information. *Journal of Documentation,* **55**(1), 33–70

Department for Culture, Media and Sport (1998) *'New library: the people's network'* – the Government's response. Cm 3887. London: HMSO

Department for Education and Employment (1988) *The Learning Age: a renaissance for a new Britain.* Available at www.lifelonglearning.co.uk/greenpaper/index.htm

Department for Education and Employment (2000a) *Higher education for the 21st century: Change in higher education.* Available at www.dfee.gov.uk/highed/index.htm

Department for Education and Employment (2000b) *Investing in excellence – guide to the structure and financing of the education and employment sectors: higher education.* Available at www.dfee.gov.uk/invest/guide/

Dillon, A. (1992) Reading from paper versus screens: a critical review of the empirical literature. *Ergonomics,* **35**(10), 1297–1326

Dillon, A. (1994) *Designing electronic text: ergonomic aspects of human information usage.* London: Taylor and Francis

Dillon, A., Richardson, J. and McKnight, C. (1990) Navigation in hypertext: a critical review of the concept. In *INTERACT '90*, eds. D. Daiper *et al.* Amsterdam: North Holland

EARL (2000) *Consortium for Public Library Networking web site:* www.earl.org.uk

EBSCO (2000) *web site:* www.ebsco.com

ECHO (2000a) *DALI web site:* www.echo.lu/libraries/en/projects/dali.html

ECHO (2000b) *FASTDOC web site:* www.echo.lu/libraries/en/projects/fastdoc.html

eLib (2000) *Electronic Libraries Programme web site:* www.ukoln.ac.uk/services/elib/

Engineering Information Inc (Ei) (2000) *web site:* www.ei.org

EQUINOX (2000) *web site:* equinox.dcu.ie/

European Communities (2000) Directive 1999/93/EC of the European Parliament and of the Councils of 13 December 1999 on a Community framework for electronic signatures. *Official Journal of the European Communities*, **Part L13** (19 January), 12–19

EU Telematics for Libraries Programme (2000) *web site:* www.echo.lu/libraries/en/libraries.html

Evans, J., Bevan, S.J. and Harrington, J. (1996) BIODOC: access versus holdings in a university library. *Interlending and Document Supply*, **24**(4), 5–11

Faxon (2000) *E-Journal Services web site:* www.faxon.com/html/it_ejsvc.html

Feather, J.P. (1994) *The Information Society: a study of continuity and change.* London: Library Association

FIDDO (1999a) *Document delivery in a dynamic hybrid environment.* Final report to Electronic Libraries Programme

FIDDO (1999b) *Methodology toolkit.* Available at www.lboro.ac.uk/departments/dis/fiddo/toolkit.htm

FIDDO (2000) *web site*: www.lboro.ac.uk/departments/dis/fiddo/fiddo.html

Friend, F.J. (1999) Changing the financial model for libraries. *Serials*, **12**(1), 7–11

Froud, R. (1999) The benefit of Foursite: a public library consortium for library management systems. *Program*, **33**(1), 1–14

Gammon, J.A. (1998) Consortial purchasing: the US experience with electronic products. *Serials*, **11**(2), 109–114

Gardner, T., Miller, P. and Russell, R. (1999) *The MIA logical architecture version 0.3*. Available at www.ukoln.ac.uk/dlis/models/requirements/arch/

Gimson, R. (1995) Electronic paper – can it be real? *Aslib Proceedings*, **47**(6), 139–143

Glaser, B.G. and Strauss, A.L. (1967) *The discovery of grounded theory: strategies for qualitative research*. New York: Aldine de Gruyter

Goffman, W. and Warren, K.S. (1969) Dispersion of papers among journals based on a mathematical analysis of two diverse medical literatures. *Nature*, **221**, 1205–1207

Gould, S. (1999) *Universal availability of publications core programme: IFLA guidelines for sending ILL requests by email*. Available at www.ifla.org/VI/2/p3/g-ill.htm

Halliday, L. (ed.) (1997) *The impact of on-demand publishing and electronic reserve on students, teaching and libraries in higher education in the UK*. London: Library Information Technology Centre, South Bank University

Halliday, L. and Oppenheim, C. (1999) *Economic models for the digital library: Final report*. Available at www.ukoln.ac.uk/services/elib/papers/ukoln/emod-diglib/final-report.pdf

Hamaker, C.A. (1996) Designing serial collections for the 21st century. *Journal of Library Administration*, **24**(1/2), 35–46

Hanson, T. (1999) Investing in document delivery services: management perspectives. In *Proceedings of a Conference on Document Delivery Beyond 2000*, British Library, September 1998, eds. A. Morris, N. Jacobs and J.E. Davies, pp 12–22 London: Taylor Graham

HEADLINE (2000) *web site*: www.headline.ac.uk

Higginbotham, B.B. and Bowdoin, S. (1994) *Access versus assets: a comprehensive guide to resource sharing for academic libraries*. Chicago: American Library Association

Higher Education Funding Council for England (1997) *The impact of the 1992 Research Assessment Exercise on higher education institutions in England*. Available at www.niss.ac.uk/education/hefce/pub97/m6_97.html

Higher Education Funding Council for England (1999) *Communications and information technology materials for learning and teaching in UK higher and further education*. Available at www.niss.ac.uk/education/hefce/pub99/99_60.html

HMSO (1988) *Copyright, Designs and Patents Act, 1988*. London: HMSO

Hughes, C.A. (1999) Resource sharing. In *Librarianship and information work worldwide 1999*, eds. G. Mackenzie and P. Sturges. London: Bowker-Saur

HYLIFE (2000) *web site*: hylife.unn.ac.uk

IEEE (2000) *web site*: www.ieee.org/

Infotrac (2000) *web site*: www.galegroup.com

Infotrieve (2000) *web site*: www.info@infotrieve.com

Ingenta (2000) *web site*: www.ingenta.com

Instant Library Limited (2000) *web site*: www.instant-library.com/

Institute for Scientific Information (2000) *web site*: www.isinet.com

IPIG (2000) *web site*: www.arl.org/access/naildd/ipig/ipig.shtml

J.M. Consulting Ltd. (1999) *Transparency review of research*. Report to the Joint Costing and Pricing Steering Group. Available at www.bris.ac.uk/JCPSG/transpar/index.htm

Jackson, M. (1998) *Measuring the performance of interlibrary loan operations*. Washington, DC: American Library Association

Jackson, M.E. (1999) The implications of standards implementation: interfacing between library, supplier and other systems. In *Proceedings of a Conference on Document Delivery Beyond 2000*, British Library, London, September 1998, eds. A. Morris, N. Jacobs and J.E. Davies, pp. 173–180. London: Taylor Graham

Jacobs, N., Chambers, J. and Morris, A. (1999) Document delivery websites. *Interlending and Document Supply*, **27**(2), 65–70

Jacobs, N. and Morris, A. (1999a) Negotiating the digital library: document delivery. *Education for Information*, **17**(2), 135–144

Jacobs, N. and Morris, A (1999b) Winners and losers in an 'access' world: accounts from end users. In *Proceedings of a Conference on Document Delivery Beyond 2000*, British Library, London, September 1998, eds. A. Morris, N. Jacobs and J.E. Davies, pp. 64–74. London: Taylor Graham

Jacobs, N., Woodfield, J. and Morris, A. (in press) Using local citation data to relate the use of journal articles by academic researchers to the coverage of full-text document access systems. *Journal of Documentation*, **56**(5)

JISC (1995) *Guidelines for developing an information strategy.* Available at www.jisc.ac.uk/pub/infstrat/

JISC (1998a) *Copyright guidelines for JISC and TLTP Projects.* London: JISC/TLTP. Also available at www.ukoln.ac.uk/services/elib/papers/other/jisc-tltp/jisc.pdf

JISC (1998b) *Guidelines for developing an information strategy – the sequel.* Available at www.jisc.ac.uk/pub98/guide_seq/

JISC (2000) *web site*: www.jisc.ac.uk/

JISC and the Publishers Association (1999) *Request for proposals: pilot project for the supply of electronic documents, complementing 'inter-library loan'.* Available at www.jisc.ac.uk/pub99/jp-edd-mainrfp.html

Joint Funding Councils' ad hoc Group on Performance Indicators for Libraries (1995) *The effective academic library.* Bristol: Higher Education Funding Council for England

Joint Funding Councils' Libraries Review Group (1993) *Report (The Follett Report).* Bristol: Higher Education Funding Council for England. Available at www.ukoln.ac.uk/services/papers/follett/report/

Joint Funding Councils' Library Review Group (1995) *Report of the Group on a national/regional strategy for library provision for researchers (The Anderson Report)*. Bristol: Higher Education Funding Council for England. Available at www.ukoln.ac.uk/services/elib/papers/other/anderson/

Kelly, B. and Lister, P. (1999) Open authentication systems for the web. Submitted to *Vine*, **112**. Draft available from: www.ukoln.ac.uk/web-focus/articles/vine-112/

KINETICA (2000) *web site*: www.nla.gov.au/kinetica/

Kingma, B.R. (1996) *The economics of access versus ownership: the costs and benefits of access to scholarly articles via interlibrary loan and journal subscriptions*. New York: Haworth Press

Kingma, B.R. (1997) Interlibrary loan and resource sharing: the economics of the SUNY Express Consortium. *Library Trends*, **45**(3), 518–530

Kingston, P. (1998) Managing electronic reserve collections. In *Managing the Electronic Library*, eds. T. Hanson and J. Day, pp. 567–586. London: Bowker-Saur

Kling, R. (1991) Computers and social transformations. *Science, Technology and Human Values*, **16**(3), 342–367

LAMDA (2000) *web site*: lamdaweb.mcc.ac.uk/

Larbey, D. (1997) Project EDDIS: an approach to integrating document delivery, location, request and supply. *Interlending and Document Supply*, **25**(3), 96–102

Larby, D. (1999) Management information requirements and the potential of document delivery systems to fulfil them. In *Proceedings of a Conference on Document Delivery Beyond 2000;* British Library, London, September 1998, eds. A. Morris, N. Jacobs and J.E. Davies, pp. 163–172. London: Taylor Graham

Law, D. (1997) Parlour games: the real nature of the Internet. Paper presented at the *UKSG/NAG Conference, Spiders or Flies: managing electronic information in libraries*, Oxfordshire, May 1997. Published in *Serials*, **10**(2), 195–201. Also available at uksg.lboro.ac.uk/law.htm

Law, D. (1998) Convergence of academic support services. In *Managing the electronic library*, eds. T. Hanson and J. Day, pp 49–62. London: Bowker-Saur

Leggate, P. (1998) Acquiring electronic products in the hybrid library: prices, licences, platforms and users. *Serials*, **11**(2), 103–108

Library and Information Commission (1997) *New library: the people's network*. London: Library and Information Commission

Library and Information Commission (1998) *Building the new library network*. London: Library and Information Commission

Line, M.B. (1974) Draft definitions: information and library needs, wants, demands and uses. *Aslib Proceedings*, **26**(2), 87

Line, M.B. (1985) Use of citation data for periodicals control in libraries: a response to Broadus. *College and Research Libraries*, **46**(1), 36–37

Lyon, E. et al. (1998) *Impact of devolved budgeting on library and information services in universities in the UK*. British Library Research and Innovation Report 138. Boston Spa: British Library

M25Link (2000) *web site*: www.M25lib.ac.uk/M25link/

McDougall, A.F. (1989) Academic library co-operation and document supply: possibilities and considerations of cost effectiveness. *Journal of Librarianship*, **21**(3), 186–199

MA/HEM (1999) *Methodology for access/holdings economic modelling final report*. Available at www.ukoln.ac.uk/services/elib/papers/other/ma-hem/

MALIBU (1997) *Project proposal*. Available at www.kcl.ac.uk/humanities/cch/malibu/background/bid.pdf

MALIBU (2000) *web site*: www.kcl.ac.uk/humanities/cch/malibu/

MCB (2000) *web site*: www.mcb.co.uk/

MODELS (2000) *web site*: www.ukoln.ac.uk/dlis/models/

Morris, A. and Blagg, E. (1998) Current document delivery practices in UK academic libraries. *Library Management*, **19**(4), 271–280

Morris, A., Woodfield, J. and Davies, J. E. (1999) Experimental evaluation of selected electronic document delivery systems. *Journal of Library and Information Science*, **31**(3), 135–144

Murray, R., Smith, N. and Pettman, I. (1999) The UNIverse project: a review of progress up to the demonstration phase. *New Library World*, **100**(1149), 153–159

NAILDD (2000) *web site*: www.arl.org/access/

National Committee of Inquiry into Higher Education (1997) *Report (The Dearing Report)*. Available at www.ncl.ac.uk/ncihe/index.htm

NESLI (2000) *web site*: www.nesli.ac.uk/

Newton-Ingham et al. (1999) *AGORA Hybrid Library Management System Release 1 Specification, version 1.3*. Available at hosted.ukoln.ac.uk/agora/documents/documents.html

Noble (1996) *Noble's higher education financial yearbook 1996*. Edinburgh: Noble Financial Publishing

Noble (1998) *Noble's higher education financial yearbook 1998*. Edinburgh: Noble Financial Publishing

Noble (1999) *Noble's higher education financial yearbook 1999*. Edinburgh: Noble Financial Publishing

Parry, D. (1997) Why requests fail. *Interlending and Document Supply*, **25**(4), 147–156

Pat Wressel and Associates (eds.) (1997) *Library service provision for researchers: proceedings of the Anderson Report Seminar organised by the Library and Information Co-operation Council and the Standing Conference of National and University Libraries, Cranfield University, 10 and 11 December 1996*. Bruton: Library and Information Co-operation Council

Patel, K. (2000) Rethink on copyright. *Times Higher Education Supplement*, **1420**, 28 January 2000, p. 6

Pinfield, S. (1998) Building a hybrid library. *Taking Stock: Libraries and the Book Trade*, **7**(1), 11–14

Pinfield, S. et al. (1998) Realizing the hybrid library. *New Review of Information Networking*, **4**, 3–21. Also published in *D-Lib Magazine*, (10), 1998. Available at mirrored.ukoln.ac.uk/lis-journals/dlib/dlib/dlib/october98/10contents.html

Price, S.P., Morris, A. and Davies, J.E. (1996) An overview of electronic document request and delivery research. *The Electronic Library*, **14**(5), 435–448

ProQuest (Direct) (2000) *web site*: www.bellhowell.infolearning.com

Prowse, S.W. (1998) Trends and developments in interlending and document delivery in the UK in 1997. *Interlending and Document Supply*, **26**(2), 83–92

Prowse, S.W. (1999a) A review of interlending in the UK in 1999. *Interlending and Document Supply*, **27**(2), 80–88

Prowse, S.W. (1999b) *The FIL survey on the use of public libraries for inter-library loans by students in higher education.* Manchester: Forum for Interlending

Ramsden, A. *et al.* (1998) *ELINOR: electronic library project.* British Library Research and Innovation Report 22. London: Bowker-Saur

RIDING (2000) *web site*: www.shef.ac.uk/~riding/

Ringle, M.D. (1997) Forecasting financial priorities for technology. *Cause/Effect*, **20**(3). Also available at www.educause.niss.ac.uk/ir/library/html/cem9736.html

RLG (2000) *web site*: www.rlg.org/

Ruhleder, K. (1995) Reconstructing artifacts, reconstructing work: from textual edition to online databank. *Science, Technology and Human Values*, **20**(1), 39–64

Rusbridge, C. (1998) Towards the hybrid library. *D-Lib Magazine*, (7/8). Available at http://mirrored.ukoln.ac.uk/lis-journals/dlib/dlib/dlib/july98/rusbridge/07rusbridge.html

Rusbridge, C. (1999) Reported in the *HyLife Newsletter*, **2**(July) 1999

Russell, R. and Dempsey, L. (1998) *A distributed national electronic resource?* MODELS workshop 6 report, 5–6 February 1998. Bath: UKOLN, University of Bath

Rutstein, J.S., DeMiller, A.L. and Fuseler, E.A. (1993) Ownership versus access: shifting perspectives for libraries. In *Advances in Librarianship*, ed. I.P. Godden, Vol. 17, pp. 33–60. San Diego: Academic Press

ScienceDirect (2000) *web site*: sciencedirect.com

SEREN (2000) *web site*: seren.newi.ac.uk/user/seren/

SilverPlatter (2000) *web site*: www.silverplatter.com

SITEBUILDER (2000) *web site*:
www.bellhowell.infolearning.com/hp/Support/Sitebuilder/

Smith, M. (1997) Letter to the editor: why requests fail. *Interlending and Document Supply*, **25**(4), 183

Snyder, C.A. and Fox, J.W. (1997) *Libraries and other academic support services for distance learning*. London: JAI Press

Sonneland, H. (1997) Introduction to Copyright. In *Copyright Issues in Libraries: global concerns, local solutions. Proceedings of a conference sponsored by the IFLA Office for Universal Availability of Publications and International Lending, August 1996*, ed. J. Watkins, pp. 3–14. Boston Spa: IFLA Offices for UAP and International Lending

Sood, C. (1998) Interlending and document supply infrastructure developments in Australia. In *Interlending and Document Supply: resource sharing possibilities and barriers. Proceedings of the 5th Interlending and Document Supply International Conference, Aarhus, Denmark, August 1997*, eds. S. Gould and D. Johnson, pp. 57–64. Boston Spa: IFLA Offices for UAP and International Lending

Spiller, D., Creaser, C. and Murphy, A. (1998) *Libraries in the workplace. LISU Occasional Paper no. 20*. Loughborough: Library and Information Statistics Unit, Loughborough University

SuperJournal (1999) *Summary of SuperJournal findings*. Available at
www.superjournal.ac.uk/sj

Sykes, P. (1998) Case study: converged working at Liverpool John Moores University. In *Managing the electronic library*, eds. T. Hanson and J. Day. London: Bowker-Saur

Tait, A. and Mills, R. (eds.) (1999) *The convergence of distance and conventional education: patterns of flexibility for the individual learner. Routledge studies in distance education*. London: Routledge

Tavistock Institute (1998) *Synthesis of eLib Project 1998 annual reports*. Available at www.ukoln.ac.uk/services/elib/papers/elib-synth/ah152meld.pdf

Taylor, S. (1999) Document delivery in practice: the LAMDA project. In *Proceedings of a Conference on Document Delivery Beyond 2000, British Library, London, September 1998*, eds. A. Morris, N. Jacobs and J.E. Davies, pp. 102–107. London: Taylor Graham

Telford, A. (1995) Mixed-mode delivery: the best of both worlds. In *Flexible learning strategies in higher and further education*, ed. D. Thomas, pp.164–175. London: Cassell

Thomson, A. (1999) RAE faces axe in DTI review. *Times Higher Education Supplement*, **1408**, 29 October 1999, p. 1

Tuck, J. (1998) Performance and measurement in academic research libraries. *Liber Quarterly*, **8**(4), 389–400

UCISA (1996) *UCISA's Submission to the Dearing Inquiry into Higher Education*. Available at www.ucisa.ac.uk/docs/reports/dee45.htm

UMI (1999) *web site*: www.umi.com

Uncover (2000) *web site*: uncweb.carl.org

UNIverse (2000) *web site*: www.fdgroup.co.uk/research/universe/

Unwin, L., Stephens K. and Bolton, N. (1998) *The role of the library in distance learning: a study of postgraduate students, course providers and librarians in the UK*. London: Bowker-Saur

Vickers, S. (1994) Recent developments at the British Library Document Supply Centre. *Vine*, **95**, 7–11

Wall, R.A. (1998) *Copyright made easier* 2nd edn. London: Aslib

Wall, R.A., Oppenheim, C. and Rosenblatt, H. (1994) *The Aslib guide to copyright* (loose-leaf publication, 1994–). London: Aslib

Walton, G and Edwards, C. (1997) Strategic management of the electronic library. In *Libraries for the new millennium*, ed. D. Raitt. London: Library Association

Weaver-Meyers, P.L. and Stolt, W.A. (1996) Delivery speed, timeliness and satisfaction: patrons' perceptions about ILL service. *Journal of Library Administration*, **23**(1/2), 23–42

Webster, K. (1997) *End-user requirements of document delivery services*. Paper presented at the *Focused Investigation of Document Delivery Options (FIDDO), Issues in Document Delivery Project Workshop*, Department of Information Science, Loughborough University, UK, February 1997. Available at www.lboro.ac.uk/departments/dis/fiddo/fiddo.html

Webster, K. (1997) Research collections. In *Resource Management in Academic Libraries*, ed. D. Baker. London: Library Association

Wells, A. and Amos, H. (1999) What a librarian should look for in a document access system: developing a new resource sharing infrastructure in Australia. In *Proceedings of a conference on Document Delivery Beyond 2000, British Library, London, September 1998*, eds. A. Morris, N. Jacobs and J.E. Davies, pp. 150–162. London: Taylor Graham

White, H.D. and McCain, K.W. (1989) Bibliometrics. *Annual Review of Information Science and Technology*, **24**, 119–186

Williams, F. (1997) Electronic Document Delivery: a review and comparison of different services. *Ariadne*, (11). Available at www.ariadne.ac.uk/issue11/edd/

Wissenburg, A. (1999) *MALIBU Hybrid Library Models; version 1*. Available at www.kcl.ac.uk/humanities/cch/malibu/reports/modv1.htm

Wynne, P. and Brophy, P. (1998) Performance measurement and management information for the electronic library. In *Proceedings of the 2nd Northumbria International Conference on Performance Measurement in Libraries and Information Services*, ed. Pat Wressell & Associates. Newcastle upon Tyne: Information North

Wynne, P. and Edwards, C. (1999) The HyLiFe Project. Developing the hybrid library: matching delivery with expectations. In *Proceedings of Internet Librarian & Libtech International '99*, eds. C. Nixon and H. Dengler, pp. 128–133. Medford, New Jersey: Information Today

Yu, L., Dempsey, L. and Ormes, S. (1999) Community networking: development, potentials and implications for public libraries. *Journal of Librarianship and Information Science*, **31**(2), 71–83

Zeitlyn, D. and Bex, J. (1997) Cultural and technical networks: a qualitative approach. *Education for Information*, **15**(4), 351–361

Zeitlyn, D., David, M. and Bex, J. (1999) *Knowledge lost in information: patterns of use and non-use of networked bibliographic resources.* British Library Research and Innovation Centre Research Report no. RIC/G/313. London: Office for Humanities Communication

APPENDIX A

Document delivery suppliers

Information is as provided by suppliers contacted by the FIDDO project during December 1999. No responsibility can be accepted for errors or omissions.

A regularly-maintained and extended version of this list is available at: www.aslib.co.uk/fiddo

Name of Service	Coverage	Delivery time	Charges	URL
Access/Information, Inc.	All subject areas	Next-day delivery for local, faxed or Emailed items. 72 hours non-local. International courier service	Consult supplier. Back copyright charges are payable.	www.access-information.com/
Action Court Services, Inc.	Research and retrieval of documents in all courts nationwide (USA)	Approximately five day turnaround in California and 7–10 days out of state. Rushes within 24–48 hours	A flat rate fees for research (different prices in different courts) plus additional fee for copies.	www.actioncourt.com
ADONIS	Biomedical, pharmaceutical and chemical	Less than five minutes	ADONIS Document Delivery Service: NLG36 000 p.a. + Royalty charges/None	www.adonis.nl
Advanced Information Consultants, Inc.	All subject areas, including science, technology and business	Information not provided	$10–$12 Regular Rates plus costs. $20–$24 Rush Plus Costs. $30–$45 Panic Plus Costs. Additional costs may include copyright royalties, expedited shipping charges, facsimile charges, vendor fees and additional per page charges	www.advinfoc.com

Name of Service	Coverage	Delivery time	Charges	URL
Articles in Physics	Physical Science	Immediate	$15–$20 per article	ojps.aip.org/jhtml/artinphys/aipmain.html
ASM Library Document Delivery Service	Materials Science	Approximately two days regular service, rush service available	For charges inquire at ASM library – there is a two-tier schedule of charges for member or non-member and domestic (USA) including Canada and Mexico, or overseas	www.asm-intl.org/www-asm/library/matdoc.htm
BIDS Online Document Ordering System (BODOS)	Multidisciplinary	Information not provided	Mail £12.65 Fax £13.95	www.bids.ac.uk
Biomedical Information Service / BioMedical	Health sciences, especially medicine, nursing, dentistry, public health and health care delivery, mortuary science, pharmacy	Standard turnaround averages three to five working days. We also provide Next-day rush, Same-day rush, three-hour rush and one-hour rush service. Rush surcharges apply	Standard turnaround $6 plus delivery. Rush services from $11 per article plus delivery (next day) to $56 per article plus delivery (one hour)	www.biomed.lib.umn.edu/bishp.html

Name of Service	Coverage	Delivery time	Charges	URL
BIOSIS Document Express	Life Sciences	Regular delivery: articles mailed in three to five business days; rush delivery is also available	Copies from local / non-local sources: $11 / $15 + copyright. Shipping charges: USA & Canada mail: no charge. Airmail & express shipping: at cost. Fax (USA & Canada): $0.50 per page. Fax (other): $1 per page.	www.biosis.org/htmls/common/bde.html
The British Library Document Supply Centre (BLDSC) Photocopy/Loan Service and Urgent Action	Multidisciplinary	Requests processed within 48 hours of receipt. Urgent Action service between 2–24 hours, customer choice	Mail one photocopy/loan voucher (currently £4.76 including VAT, from 1st May 1997). Urgent Action mail three vouchers. Urgent Action fax 3.4 vouchers	www.bl.uk/services/bsds/dsc/
CAB International	Agriculture, forestry, human health, natural resources	Two to five days turnaround time for material held on site	Delivery by post: £10 per article (USA $20) + VAT in UK & EC. Delivery by fax: £17 per article (USA $40) + VAT in UK & EC.	www.cabi.org/infolib/libserv.htm

Name of Service	Coverage	Delivery time	Charges	URL
Capitol District Information	Legal and financial	Same day/within 24 hours	Contact Capitol District Information for prices	www.capitoldistrict.com/index.html
Carolina Library Services, Inc. (Carolib)	Multidisciplinary	Two to three days	Basic charges $5 per article, $0.25/page	www.Intrex.net/carolib
CAS DDS – Chemical Abstracts Service Document Detective Service	All sciences – with emphasis on chemistry and related sciences	One-hour fax, four-hour fax, 24-hour fax or courier. Usually mail and fax are sent within 24 hours $9.	US mail / UPS: no charge Domestic Courier: $8 International Courier: $3 + courier fee. Airmail: $2.50 Fax: $4 / $8. Loan: Rush: $10 / $20.	www.cas.org/Support/dds.html
CISTI's (Canada Institute for Scientific and Technical Information) Document Delivery service	Science, technology, engineering, medicine and agriculture	Normally two days for electronic orders.	Four hours for Urgent Service (fax) EST. Direct Supply copies per 50 pages per article: $9 if ordered electronically & delivered by fax or Ariel anywhere. $12 for non-electronic orders or courier delivery in Canada, USA & Mexico. $30 for non-electronic orders or courier delivery outside North America – plus copyright if applicable in all cases	www.nrc.ca/cisti

Name of Service	Coverage	Delivery time	Charges	URL
CSIR DocDel	Multidisciplinary	Information not provided	R46 handling fee plus actual cost of document. Other fees e.g. rush fees, fax fees may also be charged	www.csir.co.za/cls/docdelintro.html
Derwent International Patents Copy Service	Patents	Despatch within four hours is the fastest. Despatch within two to three days is the slowest	Depends on territory for delivery	www.derwent.com/patdelivery.html
Engineering Information Document Delivery service	Engineering and associated disciplines	24 to 72 hours	Documents indexed in Ei databases from 1991 $9.50 plus copyright fee. Other documents $14 plus copyright fee. Additional fees: postage at cost outside North America. Fax: $1 first page and $0.50 each additional page. Rush Service: $17. Documents over 40 pages $0.40 per page. Discounts for high-volume users.	www.ei.org/

Name of Service	Coverage	Delivery time	Charges	URL
Blackwell's Electronic Journal Navigator (EJN)	All – the system is not subject specific	Instantaneous delivery to the desktop	A subscription to the electronic journal must be held by the requestor although a pay-per-view option will be introduced during 1999	navigator. blackwell.co.uk
ELEKTRA (Elektronischer Aufsatzdienst = electronic article delivery service)	Mathematics, computer science, materials science and design and medicine. Other subjects are to follow	At most two hours from order to delivery.	Internal Bavarian circle: none. International (only from 1999 on): subito charges	elektra.informatik.tu-muenchen.de
FirstSearch Electronic Collections Online	Looking to cover all main subject areas	Immediate	Included in subscription price of journal	www.oclc.org/oclc/menu/eco.htm
FirstSearch	All subjects	Immediate delivery via Email. Other means range from immediate to three or five days mail service	Subscription to full text file	www.oclc.org/oclc/menu/fs.htm

Name of Service	Coverage	Delivery time	Charges	URL
FOI Services, Inc.	Covers medical device and pharmaceutical information acquired from the US Food and Drug Administration	If the document is in-house, it is generally shipped within two business days; same-day turnaround may be available depending on the time of day and length of document ordered	If the document is ordered on the website, the charge per document is indicated, and ranges from $20 to $500. If a document is not in our files (no charge for us to check availability) and must be handled separately, the charge is $39 service plus photocopying, shipping, and any direct charges imposed by the government	www.foiservices. com
GeoRef's Document Delivery Service	Geosciences, environmental, groundwater and engineering	Most orders filled within five to seven working days. Rush requests shipped within 24 hours	Regular order $14. Rush order $26. Page charge $0.25 per page. Specific charges for maps, cancelled orders, etc.	www.georef.org/ dds.html
German National Library of Medicine	Biomedicine and all fringe areas like molecular biology, bioengineering, molecular genetics, pharmacy, clinical psychology, hospital	Less than two hours to five working days	Vary from DM16 for regular processing to DM54 for Super-fax-service/delivery by fax	www.uni-koeln. de/zentral/zbib-med

Name of Service	Coverage	Delivery time	Charges	URL
Infocus Research Services	Document delivery from all major US library collections, government agencies, standards bodies and associations in all subjects	Normal service three to seven working days. Rush service 4–48 hours depending on delivery method	Basic charge $15 per article plus copyright fees. Discounts for deposit account holders and volume users. Rush charges extra	www.israweb.co.il/infocus/
INFOMAYDA	All information about Israel	One week	As per request	www.actcom.co.il/~atoz
Infonetwork, Inc.	All fields	10 days turnaround	$20 per article	www.doc-quest.com
Information Centre	Information not provided	Two hours delivery in central London	Postage £2. Courier in central London £7.50	
Information Express	Science and technology, engineering, medicine, chemistry, business and law	Rush orders: same day. Regular orders: California Sources shipped within 24 hours.	Base rates are determined by volume of orders and source of document. Price includes 10 pages of copying. Single document cost from IE Holdings: $8. Single document cost from California Sources: $10. Rush orders: $12 applied to base rate	www.express.com

Name of Service	Coverage	Delivery time	Charges	URL
Infotrac Web	Various – academic subjects	N/A – articles available immediately onscreen, or for Email download	Database charges: variable depending on database and user licence. No extra delivery charge	www.galegroup.com
Infotrieve	All fields	Mostly within one to three working days. Some items require extra time for retrieval, and the customer is always welcome to specify a deadline. Rush service is available and most documents are sent within a few hours, or by the next business day	Basic Cost $9.75 per article, plus copyright or purchase	www.infotrieve.com
ingentaJournals	Multidisciplinary	Information not provided	Depends on journal and publisher	www.ingenta.com
INIST	Science, technology, medicine, humanities and social sciences	Standard service: within five to eight days. Express: any order received before 12 noon (French local time) sent by express courier within two to four days. Fax: for any order received before 5pm (French local time), will be faxed within two hours	From UC48 for an article of less than 10 pages in standard service to UC216 for the same article in Fax service	www.inist.fr/anglais/welcang.htm

Name of Service	Coverage	Delivery time	Charges	URL
Instant Information Systems	Medical and pharmaceutical (all biomedical fields)	We offer a range of turn-around times from Super-Rush same day service to economy service.	From: $7.75 to $19.75 + $0.25 per page + copyright (if any). Fax charges: $1 per page (USA), $2 per page (International).	www.docdel.com/info.html
IRIS Document Delivery Services Ltd.	Information not provided	Items dispatched in under 24 hours in a working week	Information not provided	www.fdgroup.co.uk/IRIS.htm
ISI Document Solution	Scholarly and scientific articles	ISI Document Solution offers standard, internal 24-hour turnaround time with U.S. mail at no charge. Fax delivery (24 hour) is also included (for U.S., Canada & Mexico only). Delivery can be accelerated with 30-minute fax response or delivered via FedEx	The standard rate is $9.95 per article plus a copyright fee when applicable for U.S. customers. Foreign orders are $10.95 plus copyright. Rates for 24-hour fax outside US, Canada & Mexico is $10/article; 30-min fax is an additional $5 for USA, Canada and Mexico customers only. FedEx standard / priority delivery is $6 / $9 per shipment (USA, Canada and Mexico only; International rates vary)	www.isinet.com/prodserv/tga/tgadoc.html

Name of Service	Coverage	Delivery time	Charges	URL
JST (Japan Science and Technology Corporation)	Science and technology	Approximately two to three days for items in JICST's holdings and airmail delivery time	Minimum charge per article up to 10 pages $14. Each additional 5 pages $3. Location fee for JICST shelf mark/accession number of JICST, JICST-E, JISCT-EPlus file $2. Extended location surcharge per article $14. Fax delivery surcharge per page $1.40	www.jst.go.jp/EN/ JICST/ServiceGuide/ ext-serv.html
Kessler–Hancock Information Services, Inc.	Multi-disciplinary / science, technology and engineering	Standard delivery, 48 hour service and 24 hour service	$10 for standard. $20 for 48-hour rush. $30 for 24-hour rush. Faxing $1/page for domestic, $2 for international	www.khinfo.com
KR SourceOne/ UnCover	All subjects	For patents, two hours by fax. Mail and courier available. Other documents, two to three days from receipt of order to shipment from Knight Ridder offices (mail time not included)	Basic service: $12.95 plus copyright. Rush service: $26.95 plus copyright. Same day: $29.95 plus copyright	www.krsourceone. com

Name of Service	Coverage	Delivery time	Charges	URL
Legal Information Resources Ltd. (Sweet & Maxwell)	Law and Finance	Same/next day	Searches: £25 posted and an additional £1 per page if results are faxed. Plus publisher's rates for document delivery	www.smlawpub.co. uk/product/docdel.cfm
Linda Hall Library Document services	Science, technology and engineering	From 24 hours to within one working hour	Copy service: $11.50 for first 50 pages; $0.25 for each additional page. Rush services (prices given additional per document): from $6 to $100. FedEx, delivery: from $6 to $20. International fax: $5	www.lhl.lib.mo.us
LIVEDGARTM, a product of Global Securities Information, Inc.	SEC transactional data	Real-time	Database charges: $10 login fee, $1 per minute. Delivery charges variable	www.gsionline.com
Infotrieve's MEDLINE on the Web	Medical publications	Most articles shipped in one to two days	$8 (more for some services)	www.infotrieve.com
MicroPatent	Patent and trademark information, file histories, patent and trademark searches	Minutes	$4.95 per Standard patent (downloaded); $8.95 per patent Special Collection Trademarks; MarkSearch Pro System $50/day, $450/month or $3650/year; MarkSearch System $35/day, $295/month or $1995/year	www.micropat. com/

Name of Service	Coverage	Delivery time	Charges	URL
NIWI (Netherlands Institute for Scientific Information Services)	Data for secondary analysis (data archives), documents and bibliographic references, research information, science, biomedicine, Dutch language and literature, environment, history and social sciences	Four days, 24 hours, two hours	In Netherlands (one to seven pages / additional pages): Normal: Dfl7 / Dfl1. Express: Dfl17.50 / Dfl2.50. Combi express: Dfl24.50 / Dfl3.50. Outside Netherlands: Normal: per article, or per unit of 20 pages Dfl15. Express mail: per article, or per unit of 20 pages Dfl30	www.niwi.knaw.nl
Online Contents (OCL)	Many subject areas	One to three days	Hfl10 per article up to 10 pages and Hfl1 per extra page	www.pica.nl/obn
Patent Specification Delivery Service	Patents	Rush: same day fax (or if the publications is too large, per courier). Standard: post	Standard including delivery by post: Fl34. Other prices available on request	www.polyresearch.com
PFC Information Services, Inc.	Public Records	Usually five days	Variable	www.pfcinformation.com/
ProQuest	Multi-disciplinary including business, medical/health, engineering, sciences, etc.	Immediate	Subscription	www.bellhowell.infolearning.com

Name of Service	Coverage	Delivery time	Charges	URL
Purdue's Technical Information Service	Purdue's 14 school and departmental libraries cover aviation technology, biochemistry, chemistry, consumer and family sciences, earth and atmospheric sciences, engineering, humanities, social science and education, life sciences, management and economics, mathematical sciences, pharmacy, nursing & health, physics, psychological sciences, veterinary medicine	Standard turnaround time is two days, but most documents are shipped within 24 hours; rush service is available as required to meet the client's need	Photocopy or loan of Purdue-owned item is $14, plus copyright and shipping. Special orders for documents not available at Purdue are charged at cost plus $15. RUSH charge is $15. Domestic fax charge is $1 per page; overseas fax charge is $2 per page. Volume rates are available	www.lib.purdue.edu/tis

Name of Service	Coverage	Delivery time	Charges	URL
RAPID (Research And Professional Information Delivery) Services, University of New South Wales	All areas covered with emphasis on medicine, applied sciences, technology, engineering, law and social sciences	All areas covered with emphasis on medicine, applied sciences, technology, engineering, law and social sciences	Prices shown in Australian dollars. Items from NSW Library collection: $25. Other Australian held items: $45. Internationally acquired items: $60. Surcharges of $10–$20 for international fax, express post or couriers at cost	www.library.unsw.edu.au/rapid.html
RECAL Information Services	Prosthetics, orthotics and physical medicine and rehabilitation; includes seating wheelchairs and biomechanics	Mailed within 24 hours of receipt	£0.15 per page	www.recal.org.uk
Reedfax	Intellectual property	For patents in our database – 15 minutes. All others are usually available same day.	Email/web delivery of US patents $3. Email/web delivery of EP/WOs $6	www.reedfax.com

Name of Service	Coverage	Delivery time	Charges	URL
The Research Investment, Inc.	All subjects	Same-day rush service – same day. Rush service – within 24 hours. Standard turnaround from within our network – one to three days. Standard turnaround from our extended resources – up to four weeks for obscure international documents. Most extended resource items are supplied within one to two weeks	Base rate $12 plus copyright and/or purchases. Additional charges may be added for faxing, pages and special delivery requests	www.researchinvest.com
Library and Information Centre, Royal Society of Chemistry	Chemistry; all branches	Standard 48 hours, urgent action 24 hours	Members (individual or corporate) start at £4.99 (incl. VAT). Urgent action(s) extra. Non-members start at £9.99. Prices apply from 1 May 1999	chemistry.rsc.org/rsc/library.htm

Name of Service	Coverage	Delivery time	Charges	URL
SOCIOLOGY*Express	Sociology	Information not provided	$12.50 USA/Canada $15 International includes all postage and handling (first class mail) RUSH: overnight courier: base price, plus courier charges (billed at cost); fax: $10 + $2 per page (USA/Canada), $4 per page (International)	
TDI Library Services, Inc.	Covers all types of documents in every field of industry and human endeavour. (Examples: journal articles, abstracts, news articles, conference proceedings, dissertations, chapters from books, tables of contents, indices, patents and materials published solely on the internet.)	Same-day rush service (same day). Rush service (within 24 hours). Regular service (one to three days). 80 per cent of regular orders are completed within 24 hours, 77 per cent of rush orders are completed within one to six hours	Rush order: $24.50 (includes 10 photocopied pages) + copyright. Regular order: $11 (includes 10 photocopied pages) + copyright. Same-day rush: $35 (includes 10 photocopied pages) + copyright. Clean copy service: $10 per article. Colour copies: $2 per page	www.tdico.com

Name of Service	Coverage	Delivery time	Charges	URL
Theological Research Exchange Network (TREN)	Religion, theology, Biblical studies, ministry	For small orders (two or three titles) we can usually ship out within 12–24 hours. Rush orders are also accepted and shipped via overnight Express Mail through the US Postal Service	Paper copies are available for $0.15 per page. Microfiche copies are available for $5 per title. Shipping is $3.50 per order for USA customers. Non-USA orders are charged approximately $10 to $25 extra for most shipments	www.tren.com
Tuebingen Document Delivery	No limit to special subjects; everything available is delivered. Outstanding holdings in theology, religious studies, ancient near-East, South Asia	95 per cent of the orders are processed within three workdays	Non-commercial institutions and customers in Europe: via mail: DM8 (0.20), via fax: DM10 (0.50), via ftp: DM5 (0.20). Commercial institutions and customers outside of Europe via mail: DM15 (0.50), via fax: DM20 (1.00), via ftp: DM15 (0.50)	www.uni-tuebingen. de/ub

Name of Service	Coverage	Delivery time	Charges	URL
Uncover Document Delivery Service	Multidisciplinary	Try to fill in 24 hours. There are a number of faxes marked on the database as one-hour fax. These are always delivered within this time	Individuals: $25 per year (Reveal subscription) Academic / Corporate Site Licences: Cost based upon number of people wishing to use Reveal service. Basic service charge $10. Variable fax surcharge e.g. UK $3. Variable copyright fee averaging $4 or $5 per article	uncweb.carl.org/
Weldasearch is the main database name (there is no special name for the document delivery aspect). TWI library	Welding, brazing, soldering, thermal cutting, thermal spraying, hardfacing. Properties of joints etc. made by any of these processes. Testing of joints made by any of these processes	Around three or four working days	Copies are generally £5 per item to members and £10 per item to non-members. VAT and postage are added. Additional charges are made for fax delivery of £1.50 per page for members and £2.50 per page for non-members	www.twi.co.uk/

Research methodology tool-kit

Introduction

This tool-kit is concerned with the evaluation of document access systems. A document access system is any means whereby a user obtains the full text of a required document in the appropriate format.

The FIDDO evaluations of document access options were guided by the need to identify and synthesize assessments by/of:

1. Users
2. Managers
3. Systems

The relationships between these actors are illustrated in Fig. B1.

In a day-to-day working scenario (the plain lines), managers administer document access systems, and have a service relationship with library users. Library users make use of document access systems in their work, a relationship described in the diagram as 'practice'. These three relationships (indicated by the plain arrows) represent the field (the shaded area) for the analyst.

In the analytical scenario (the dashed lines), the analyst is concerned with how each of these relationships may be modified in the case of various systems, and hence needs information from the system, the users and the managers. These analytical relationships (indicated by the dashed arrows) are the ones described in this tool-kit. Information from users relates to their use of systems and to their service from the library;

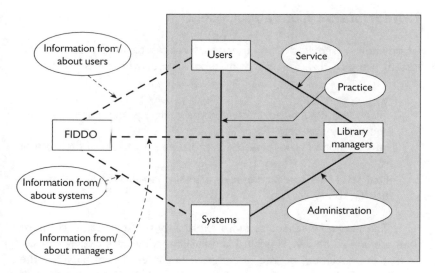

Figure B1. Overview of the context of the methodology tool-kit

information from library managers relates to administration of systems and to the library's users, and information about systems relates to how they are used and to how they are administered.

FIDDO-specific issues

For the substantive purposes of the FIDDO Project, the users were academic researchers and the managers were academic library staff in UK higher education. This was because FIDDO was sponsored by the Higher Education Funding Councils. The systems were a sample of those available at the time, including both those that were in common use and novel systems. The term 'systems' includes both particular products or services and the infrastructure that enables end-users to use them.

A number of factors, including unsuccessful pilots and time constraints, meant that the option of trialling various systems with both managers and users was impractical during the FIDDO Project. Hence, system trials were limited to users only; their administration was handled by FIDDO.

1. Information from/about users

Information is required from users that relates to library service and system use. For this, a field-trial method is used, whose basic structure is:

- initial semi-structured interview, assessing systems currently used and library service;
- introduction of a novel system, record kept by users of their use of it;
- final semi-structured interview, assessing novel system and potential for library service.

The interview schedules (with explanations in italic for each question) are copied below. The initial and final interviews are closely related, so that the maximum degree of comparison can be drawn between the two. In FIDDO, we found it useful to employ a qualitative data analysis software package (NUDIST v. 4.0) to support analysis of the interview transcripts.

In addition to the interviews, users are asked to record certain details each time they use the system during the trial period. The template for recording these details is copied after the interview schedules.

Although the interviews address the broad question of whether users prefer print or electronic format documents, it is possible to be much more precise in assessing user preferences. An experimental approach, based on the principle of 'paired comparisons' is used, whereby a sample of users is shown a series of pairs of documents (the same document in different formats), and asked to express a preference. The preferences are based on a series of readability variables, developed from the literature:

- ease of handling (size);
- effective layout, text print quality, graphic print quality (headings, spacing, colours, legibility, clarity of graphics);
- navigation aids (superstructure, contents list).

Standard statistical analysis techniques can be applied to the data.

Initial interview with users

I'd like you to imagine a time when you had a couple of hours, or perhaps a whole afternoon, free to focus on some research work you had in hand. You have time to search for and get hold of literature that you need for this research work.

*   Can you give an estimate of the number of papers you would scan for each one you would want actually to read thoroughly? Is scanning the abstract enough?
    [Aim of question is threefold: to get researchers thinking in 'research' mode; to emphasize the distinction between browsing and ordering documents; and to assess the information required before a document is ordered.]
*   Talk me through how typically you would get hold of a paper **for which you already had a reference** (if the journal was in the library? if not?)
    [Aim of question is to get a rich description of researcher's perception of their own current practice.]
*   How much does each article cost you or your department on average? Are these costs reasonable/when would they stop being reasonable? Who has control over the budget: library/department/end-user? (if the journal was in the library? if not?)
    [Aim of questions is not only to get the information, but to assess differences between researcher's perception and assessment of costs, true costs to them, their department and their institution.]
*   How much time do you have to dedicate to getting hold of a paper in the normal way – using your usual routes (i.e. time that you are actually concentrating on getting hold of the paper)?
    [Aim of question is not only to get the information, but to assess whether this time is noticed by the researcher to the extent that they can answer the question easily – have they thought about it before being asked?]
*   How long do you have to wait between ordering and receiving the paper, during which time you can be doing other things?
    [Aim of question is not only to get the information, but to assess importance of multitasking. Also to assess whether this time is noticed and counted – how important is speed of delivery? How is time an issue in document access?]

- In what format do/would you prefer to receive material? Why? (ease of reading/file compatibility/speed of download/other)
  [Aim of question is to assess perceived issues in print/electronic formats and conversion between them.]
- What are the best and worst aspects of the current system for document access?
  [Aim of question is to assess user's general reaction to the library service and particular systems.]
- Do you feel in control of your access to documents?
  [Aim of question is to assess user perceptions of the extent to which they believe their work is constrained by the service and systems used.]
- How easily does the current document access system fit into your overall way of doing things?
  [Aim of question is to assess perceived compatibility between service/systems used and the tasks which they are supporting.]
- Did you have to ask for help when first obtaining documents using the current system? Was that help forthcoming? Was it adequate, effective and easy to understand?
  [Aim of question is to assess both perceived difficulty of accessing documents and system/service features apparent to users to help them.]
- What problems do you think a new user might have when using the current system for the first time?
  [Aim of question is to assess the degree to which the systems are perceived as easy to learn in the context of the library service.]
- What do you use the library for? What would you like to use it for?
  [Aim of question is to assess the place of the library as an institution in the user's task-oriented world.]
- If you could have instant access to any document, would it make a difference to the quantity or quality of your research? In what way? Is it desirable?
  [Aim of question is to assess the perceived effects of the constraints of current systems on user's work.]
- Please describe your computer/printer/network configuration.
  [Aim of question is not only to get the information, but to explore researcher's technical knowledge.]
- Have you downloaded files from the Internet? How comfortable would you be/are you downloading files from the Internet and printing them out?

[Aim of question is not only to get the information, but to explore researcher's experience of and confidence in using networked information sources.]

Final interview with users

Note: This template may need to be adjusted depending on the features of the particular system being evaluated

Again, I'd like you to imagine the times when you used SYSTEM to (search for and) get hold of literature that you need for this research work.

- What were your general impressions of SYSTEM?
  [Aim of question is to get user's impressions of the system as they are structured by the user – that is, relatively unprompted by the researcher.]
- Did SYSTEM cover the kinds of subjects in which you wanted documents?
- Did SYSTEM cover these subjects in enough depth (i.e. did searches bring up enough hits)?
- Did SYSTEM cover these subjects appropriately (i.e. were the hits from quality journals, etc.)?
  [Aim of these questions is to assess the perceived coverage of the system, and its appropriateness to the user's needs. The coverage reported here may or may not be related to the 'actual' coverage.]
- If you could have access to any document via SYSTEM, what problems would still remain with it?
  [Aim of question is to assess user's views of aspects of the system other than its coverage.]
- Would/will you regularly use SYSTEM?
  If No – why not? Which alternatives are better? In what way are they better?
  If Yes – what would/will you do less of to make time to use SYSTEM?
  [Aim of question is to get user to compare the system with other methods of getting hold of documents, and so to tell the researcher which criteria are important to the user in such comparisons.]
- Were there particular issues with receiving documents in electronic format?
  [Aim of question is to get user's views on their experience of using electronic format, as compared (perhaps) with their general views on the subject as expressed in the initial interview.]

- Was it quicker using SYSTEM than it would have been to use the traditional way of doing things?
- Why? Which part of the process was quicker/better (or slower/worse?)
  [Aim of question is to assess whether time was an important issue in using the system.]
- What were the best and worst aspects of using SYSTEM for document access?
  [Aim of question is to assess user's general reaction to the system.]
- Did you feel in control of your access to documents using SYSTEM?
  [Aim of question is to assess user perceptions of the extent to which they believe their work was constrained by the system used.]
- How easily did SYSTEM fit into your overall way of doing things?
  [Aim of question is to assess perceived compatibility between system used and the tasks it was supporting.]
- Did you have to ask for help when first obtaining documents using SYSTEM? Was that help forthcoming? Was it adequate, effective and easy to understand?
  [Aim of question is to assess both perceived difficulty of accessing documents and system/service features apparent to users to help them.]
- What problems do you think a new user might have when using SYSTEM for the first time?
  [Aim of question is to assess the degree to which the system was perceived to be easy to learn.]
- Do you think having access to SYSTEM has/would have an effect on the quantity or quality of your research?
  [Aim of question is to assess perceived potential of the system in relation to constraints of current options, as identified in the initial interview.]
- Were there any technical issues using SYSTEM?
  [Aim of question is to assess user-perceived technical reliability of the system.]

Form to record details of use of trial system

Note: This template may need to be adjusted depending on the features of the particular system being evaluated

1. **Date of the document search/download:** ⬚

2. **Time of the document search/download:**

    Before 9.00 a.m. ☐
    Between 9.00 a.m. and noon ☐
    Between noon and 3.00 p.m. ☐
    Between 3.00 p.m. and 6.00 p.m. ☐
    After 6.00 p.m. ☐

3. **Did you search for specific articles for which you had obtained bibliographic details or references elsewhere?**   Yes ☐ No ☐

    If Yes:
    a How many items did you search for? ⬚
    b. How many of these did you find? ⬚
    c. How many of these did you download? ⬚
    d. How many of these did you print out? ⬚

4. **Did you conduct more open-ended searches for articles relating to a particular topic of interest?**

                                             Yes ☐ No ☐

    If Yes:
    a. How many relevant items did you find? ⬚
    b. How many of these did you download? ⬚
    c. And how many of these did you print out? ⬚
    d. Please indicate your assessment of the following:

    The number of items found

too many				too few

    The relevance of the items found

high				low

    The quality of the items found

high				low

5. How much time did you spend using the service?

Less than 15 minutes ☐
15 to 30 minutes ☐
30 to 45 minutes ☐
45 to 60 minutes ☐
Over 60 minutes ☐

6. Please indicate your agreement with the following statement:

Overall, I was satisfied that the results obtained were worth the time and effort when compared with other ways of getting hold of material.

Disagree   Neutral   Agree

☐☐☐☐☐☐☐

7. Did you have any problems while using the service?

Yes ☐   No ☐

If Yes, please comment:

....

....

....

....

8. Any other comments:

....

....

....

....

Thank you for taking part in this evaluation.

2. Information from/about library managers

Note: Because FIDDO's circumstances did not allow for library managers having direct experience of administering trial systems, information relating to the administration of such systems was directly available to the analyst.

Information is required from library managers on the service and administration aspects of document access systems. In order to contextualize the experience of the analyst (in administering the trials) within library service issues, library service managers are asked in semi-structured interviews to comment on aspects of a number of hypothetical document access models. Relevant models at the time of the FIDDO work were:

Model 1

Users search a new subject-based full-text database on the web, viewing those documents in which they are interested, with an option to print them out. There are options to view/print documents in text-only or in PDF format. All full-text is copyright fee-paid, and the database provider charges a flat-rate access fee, depending on how many simultaneous accesses are allowed. The average delay between a user's decision to have a (printed) document and actually having it is 10 minutes.

Model 2

Users search a known and familiar subject database on the web, ordering photocopies of those documents in which they are interested by clicking on the appropriate button. The documents are then sent by a supplier directly to the users via the postal service. The documents are available under the 'fair dealing' provisions of UK copyright law. There is a subscription charge to the database, plus a charge for each document ordered, depending on the supplier. The library can set the system to try certain suppliers for particular journal titles or publishers. The average delay between a user's decision to have a (printed) document and actually having it is three days.

Model 3

Users input their requests for documents to the university library via a web form, or via Email. The library decides on the best supplier for each article and makes the order. The document is delivered to the library, checked in and forwarded to the users via the internal mail. There is a charge for each document. The average delay between a user's decision to have a (printed) document and actually having it is five days.

Model 4

Users send their requests for documents via Email to a document supplier. The documents are supplied in PDF format as Email attachments within a couple of days if the item is in the supplier's collection, or between one and two weeks if not. There is a charge for each document, consisting of a flat-rate delivery charge plus a variable copyright charge depending on the publisher of the document. The documents are therefore copyright fee-paid.

A series of questions is asked for each model. The 'contexts of action' (see Chapter 2) of library managers are used to develop relevant questions. These questions guide library managers in the interviews toward discussing issues of system administration and library service. An example of a set of such questions is:

1. Who would you expect to pay? How?
2. Who regulates access?
3. What university/external infrastructure is necessary?
4. What is the role of the library?
5. Compared with journals-on-the-shelf, who wins and who loses? (for example: suppliers, libraries, researchers, students, no-one)

3. Information on systems

Clearly, much of the information already described relates to systems, but it relates to systems as they are used or administered by actors in the field (users or library managers). It is also necessary for the analyst to assess systems directly.

Relevant features of document access systems are:

- dedicated time – the time required to obtain a document in printed format, during which the user cannot undertake other tasks;
- delivery time – the time that a user has to wait while obtaining documents, during which s/he can undertake other tasks
- cost – the cost of accessing documents and (if necessary) converting them to printed format;
- coverage – the proportion of required documents that are available using the system.

In order to assess the dedicated and delivery time, and costs, a comparative experimental method is used. The time taken and cost to access documents using each of a number of systems are recorded by the analyst using forms based on those below, adjusted as appropriate. For example, the dedicated and delivery times and costs of document supply from local collections, British Library Document Supply Centre and a novel, commercial system could be compared.

A sample of at least 20 documents is selected, for example from a list of real user requests during the system trials (see 'Information from users'). The sample is limited to documents known to be available using all the systems included in the experiment. Each document is ordered or accessed using each system. The orders/accesses for any one document should be undertaken as close to simultaneously as possible for all systems.

Experimental testing of systems: Template for each request

(Please attach copy of bibliographic details of document to this form):

SYSTEM BEING USED:	
Starting conditions:	
Day and date:	
Time:	
Equipment setup used:	
Computer/printer/network:	
Library, distance to travel:	
Other details as appropriate:	
Dedicated time:	
Time for locating the required document, if necessary: (up to the point of making the request/clicking to download document/finding reference on OPAC)	
If the computer crashed or the server timed out at this point, then note that here:	
Time for requesting the required document: (keying in the details/clicking on a web page/visiting library and retrieving article from shelf)	
If the computer crashed or the server timed out at this point, then note that here:	

Time taken to download document (to get the full text on screen):	
Could the computer be used for other things during downloading?	
If the computer crashed or the server timed out at this point, then note that here:	
Delivery time:	
Delay between order and receipt of document during which time other work could be done:	
Printing / photocopying:	
Time that computer/user was tied up printing/ photocopying document:	
Time that printer was tied up printing document:	
Number of pages printed/photocopied:	
If the computer/printer crashed or the server timed out at this point, then note that here:	
PLEASE NOTE DETAILS OF ANY OTHER TIME SPENT	
Cost	
Total cost of printed/photocopied document	

The remaining feature of document access systems – coverage – is assessed using a different approach: citation analysis. The principle being used is that system coverage can only be assessed in relation to some measure of local demand, and that local citations of articles represent a valid indicator of that demand. Citation analysis is a widely criticized methodology, but can be used in this context as an indicator or proxy for local demand for journal titles. The use of citation analysis can only be valid where it is reasonable to assume that users publish their work in the scholarly format wherein citations indicate contributory influences to a piece of work.

A list of researchers' names is obtained for the user organization in question, and these are submitted to the Institute for Scientific Information (ISI) who, for a fee, will produce a database summarizing the citations in articles indexed on ISI databases that are by those researchers listed. These citations can be used to generate lists of journal titles that, on the evidence of the citations, have a significant influence on the work of the users (researchers) in question. It is then assumed that this past influence is related to demand for those journal titles.

The coverage of each document access system (in the form of a list of journal holdings) can then be compared with demand (as represented by the citation lists).

There are many problems with this methodology: it ignores the length of backruns demanded by users and covered by systems; journals do not represent the only form of either research publication or influence on researchers; and citations are used for reasons other than to indicate direct influence on a piece of work. However, it is difficult to conceive of another way of approximating demand without resorting to intrusive and equally indirect methods such as questionnaires.

Glossary and index of technical terms

The following glossary contains terms used in this book. This includes both terms coined specifically for the FIDDO research and terms in wider use. For a more extensive glossary, see: uksg.lboro.ac.uk/aaa.htm or www2.echo.lu/libraries/en/acronym.html

Term	Explanation	Relevant URL
Actual coverage	The proportion of user requirements, as measured by a standard technique such as citation analysis, that are met by a *document access system*.	
Actual time	The *dedicated* and *delivery* time necessary to use a *document access system*, as measured experimentally.	
Adobe Acrobat	De facto standard software for the electronic reproduction of page images.	www.adobe.com/
AGORA	An *eLib* phase three project, building a *hybrid library* management system.	hosted.ukoln.ac.uk/agora/
ALPSP	Association of Learned and Professional Society Publishers	www.alpsp.org.uk
Artel	*BLDSC*'s telnet-based requesting system	www.bl.uk/services/bsds/dsc/reqmeths.html
ArtE-mail	*BLDSC*'s Email-based requesting system	www.bl.uk/services/bsds/dsc/reqmeths.html
ASCII	Basic text-only file format	www.hut.fi/u/jkorpela/chars.html#ascii
ATHENS	A UK-based authentication management system, funded by *JISC*	www.athens.ac.uk/
BIODOC	A serials cancellation and CAS–IAS study at Cranfield University, UK, now carried forward into practice	www.cranfield.ac.uk/cils/library/libinfo/biodoc.htm
BLDSC	British Library Document Supply Centre	www.bl.uk/services/bsds/dsc/
BL inside	A service offered by BLDSC based on the 20 000 most frequently requested journal titles	www.bl.uk/online/inside/

Term	Explanation	Relevant URL
BUILDER	An *eLib* phase three hybrid libraries project	builder.bham.ac.uk/
CAS–IAS	Current awareness service – individual article supply	
CGI	Common Gateway Interface; a language for managing procedures in a World Wide Web environment	hoohoo.ncsa.uiuc.edu/cgi/
CLA	Copyright Licensing Authority; the UK's reproduction rights organization	www.cla.co.uk/
Context of action	A context to which reference has to be made in understanding the actions of an identified group	
DALI	Document and Library Integration project, a part of the Telematics for Libraries Programme of the European Union DG XIII	www.echo.lu/libraries/en/projects/dali.html
Dedicated time	The time that it is necessary to dedicate to using a *document access system*; time which cannot be used for another purpose	
Delivery time	The delay between requesting a document and receiving a paper copy; time which can be used for another purpose	
Document access system	A means of obtaining scholarly documents in paper format; it typically includes particular products, infrastructure, technology and budgetary arrangements	
Economic and Social Research Council	UK public grant-awarding body for higher education	www.esrc.ac.uk/

Term	Explanation	Relevant URL
EDD	Electronic Document Delivery	
EDDIS	Electronic Document Delivery the Integrated Solution, an *eLib* project	
Effective coverage	The coverage of a *document access system* as perceived and used by end-users	
Effective time	The *dedicated and delivery* time necessary to use a *document access system*, as perceived and used by end-users	
EiText	Electronic document delivery service offered by Elsevier Engineering Information during 1998	www.ei.org/
eLib	The Electronic Libraries Programme: A UK-based programme of development and research projects. The cradle of the concept of the *hybrid library*	www.ukoln.ac.uk/services/elib/
ERL	Electronic Reference Library; software offered by SilverPlatter Information to support use of the databases they host	www.silverplatter.com/product.htm
FastDoc	A document delivery research and development project, a part of the Telematics for Libraries Programme of the European Union DG XIII	www.echo.lu/libraries/en/projects/fastdoc.html
FIDDO	Focused Investigation of Document Delivery Options, an *eLib* supporting project investigating document access in the *hybrid library* environment	www.lboro.ac.uk/departments/dis/fiddo/fiddo.html

Term	Explanation	Relevant URL
Geobase	An Elsevier database focusing on geography and environmental sciences	www.elsevier.com:80/homepage/sah/spd/geoabs/menu.htm
Georef	A database produced by the American Geological Institute, focusing on geography and environmental sciences	www.agiweb.org/agi/georef.html
Geo–SL–BL	A *document access* system used during the *FIDDO* fieldwork, based on *SilverLinker* linking technology, *Geobase* and the *BLDSC*	
Headline	An *eLib* phase three project focusing on, among other things, issues of authentication in *hybrid libraries*	www.headline.ac.uk/
HTML	HyperText Markup Language, one of a family of markup languages, and the main code for the web in the 1990s	www.w3.org/
Hybrid library	A term coined within the *eLib* programme to highlight the goal of seamless end-user access to material regardless of format. Extended by *FIDDO* to include budgetary and other considerations.	mirrored.ukoln.ac.uk/lis-journals/dlib/dlib/october98/10pinfield.html
HyLife	An *eLib* phase three project looking at the user, management and evaluation aspects of hybrid libraries	hylife.unn.ac.uk
IFLA	International Federation of Library Associations and Institutions	www.ifla.org/
ILL	Inter-library loan	

Term	Explanation	Relevant URL
ILL–BLDSC	A *document access* system including university *ILL* units and *BLDSC*	
IP address	A number, based on the Internet Protocol, identifying a particular location on the internet	ftp://ftp.isi.edu/in-notes/rfc791.txt
IP domain	A number, based on the Internet Protocol, identifying a particular range of locations on the internet	whatis.com/domain.htm
IPIG	ISO ILL Protocol Implementers' Group, an international committee concerned with the implementation of the ISO 10160/1 ILL messaging protocol	www.arl.org/access/naildd/ipig/ipig.shtml
ISI	Institute for Scientific Information	www.isinet.com/
ISO	International Organization for Standardization	www.iso.ch/
ISSN	International Standard Serial Number	www.issn.org/
JISC	Joint Information Systems Committee, a committee of the UK Higher Education Funding Councils, whose subcommittee, Committee for Electronic Information, is responsible for funding the *eLib* Programme	www.jisc.ac.uk/
JSTOR	Major project and service allowing access to backruns of a number of journals	www.jstor.org/
Kinetica	Australian networked system supporting interlending	www.nla.gov.au/kinetica/
LAMDA	London and Manchester Document Access; a UK resource-sharing system that emerged from an early *eLib* project of the same name	www.man-bus.mmu.ac.uk/lamda

Term	Explanation	Relevant URL
LAN	Local Area Network	www.whatis.com/lan.htm
Library and Information Commission	UK grant awarding body, focusing on library and information research	www.lic.gov.uk/index.html
LIDDA	Local Interlending and Document Delivery Administration, an Australian research and development project, precursor of *Kinetica*	www.nla.gov.au/kinetica/
LINUX	A freely available *UNIX* variant	www.linux.org
Local holdings	Used in this book to denote the *document access system* including the journal holdings of the local university library, along with photocopying facilities	
MIA	See *Models Information Architecture*	
MALIBU	An *eLib* phase three project, looking at user issues in institutional settings of the *hybrid library*	www.kcl.ac.uk/humanities/cch/malibu/
MODELS	An early and influential *eLib* project which hosted a series of important workshops at which was elaborated the idea of the *hybrid library* and the *MODELS Information Architecture*	www.ukoln.ac.uk/dlis/models/
MODELS Information Architecture (MIA)	A schema to describe the entities and processes that go to make up the *hybrid library*	www.ukoln.ac.uk/dlis/models/models7/

Term	Explanation	Relevant URL
NAILDD	North American Inter-library Loan and Document Delivery; a project linked to the American Library Association	www.arl.org/access/access.shtml
NESLI	National Electronic Site Licensing Initiative; a UK initiative whereby publishers and higher education institutions can negotiate site licences for access to scholarly material	www.nesli.ac.uk/
NUDIST	Software supporting qualitative analysis, produced by QSR and marketed in the UK by Sage (Scolari)	www.qsr.com.au/
NT	Windows NT network operating system	www.whatis.com/windnt.htm
OS	Operating system	www.whatis.com/operatin.htm
PDF	Portable Document Format, a de facto standard file format for electronic page reproduction, used with the Adobe Acrobat software	www.whatis.com/pdf.htm
Perl	The scripting language for CGI	www.perl.com/
ProQuest Direct	A web-based database including access to some full text, marketed by UMI in 1998, then Bell and Howell Learning Information	www.umi.com/proquest/
Research Assessment Exercise (RAE)	Publication-based evaluation of the research output of UK higher education, linked to funding decisions	www.rae.ac.uk/

Term	Explanation	Relevant URL
Researcher	A term used by *FIDDO* to denote Ph.D. students, post-doctoral research assistants and academic faculty	
SearchBank	A web-based database including access to some full text, marketed by Information Access in 1998, then Gale Group	www.informationaccess.com/library/index. htm
SEREN	An *eLib EDD* project focused on the needs of libraries in Wales, and now integrated into the operations of Interlending Wales	seren.newi.ac.uk/user/seren/
SilverLinker	A system, marketed by SilverPlatter Information, for linking resource discovery with full-text access, and for managing that link; an early example of *hybrid library* technology	www.silverplatter.com/silverlinker/index.htm
TIFF	A standard graphics file format	www.whatis.com/tiff.htm
TLTP	Teaching and Learning Technology Programme, a UK higher education initiative	www.ncteam.ac.uk/tltp/
UNIverse	A research and development project looking at linking bibliographic data and services across Europe, a part of the Telematics for Libraries Programme of the European Union DG XIII	www.fdgroup.co.uk/research/universe/
UNIX	An open and powerful *operating system*	unixhelp.ed.ac.uk/
WebSPIRS	Proprietary software marketed by SilverPlatter Information to support the *ERL*	www.silverplatter.com/product.htm

Guidelines for library managers

The text included here is taken directly from FIDDO's final report to eLib. The guidelines have since been updated and are presented as Key Points in Chapter 9.

The following guidelines have been developed from the findings of the FIDDO Project as presented in its final report. One means by which these guidelines could be well-integrated into practice would be for them to be incorporated into university information strategies.

G1. In order that all options for full text be considered within a consistent framework, library managers should conceptualize full-text access in terms of document access systems (DAS). A DAS is any means whereby researchers can obtain a paper copy of a document, for example via library journal subscriptions plus working photocopiers, or via full-text web databases plus working computers and printers. Currently available DAS are all partial in terms of their effective coverage. If full-text access is considered in terms of DAS, then part of the library role should be conceived as combining them to provide a seamless, appropriate and flexible information service – a hybrid library.

G2. The hybrid library should not be conceived only as a technologically determined concept. Because they are all related, library managers need simultaneously to consider change along the following axes:
- central/decentralized document access structures;
- central/decentralized user-support structures (both technical and informational);

- central/devolved budgetary structures;
- mediated/unmediated requesting and delivery.

G3. In deciding between DAS, library managers should be guided (among other things) by researchers' criteria for using DAS. These criteria influence the effective coverage of individual DAS, and so are relevant in considering what service the library can deliver. The criteria can be summarized as:

- the level of meta information available via the DAS ('can I find out what is available?');
- the level of contextual information available via the DAS ('can I find out what else is available?');
- the time to learn and to use the DAS ('does it seem it worthwhile?').

G4. In deciding between DAS, library managers need to be aware of the demand patterns that they face. Interdisciplinarity is common but not overwhelmingly so. For this and other reasons, assessments of demand based on institutional structures such as departments are likely to lead to an inaccurate view of demand and an inefficient use of library resources. The appropriate unit of analysis for assessing demand is the individual researcher; this is the corollary of the unit of analysis moving from the journal to the individual article. However, management at these levels is not yet supported by established techniques. The complexity of the demand structure makes a central rather than a devolved information function appropriate.

G5. The central information function is rendered difficult by any substantial move to pay-per-document access arrangements, as compared with subscription models, since appropriate management mechanisms are not yet established. The reverse is also true. Library managers should support both:

- consortial subscription initiatives, with their associated authentication systems; and
- the development of management tools for pay-per-document regimes to enable fair and accountable budgetary control.

Regarding the latter, some such mechanisms currently in use, such as routing ILL requests through intermediaries, could be seen as exercises in suppressing rather than in managing demand. Such mechanisms should be reviewed; an over-reliance on precedent will be counter-productive.

G6. Library managers should review all procedures involved in ILL via BLDSC. The delay as experienced by end-users could be significantly reduced. Efforts should continue to automate the process and to enable delivery of documents directly to end-users. The library and/or the university internal mail are currently sources of major delay, nearly doubling the potential response time.

G7. In considering the coverage of various DAS, library managers should be aware that, according to the demand for journals, disciplines are not simply congruent with departments across several universities in a region. However, one potential DAS, the consolidated holdings of a region's libraries, may provide coverage for researchers at any one institution comparable to that afforded by *BLDSC*. In developing their strategies, library managers should consider regional resource sharing, although the consequences of formal arrangements on other means of document supply would have to be assessed.

G8. In considering their own local journal subscriptions, library managers should be aware that attempts to subscribe to a particular set of journals identified as core in any subject area are increasingly unviable. This is due to the tenuous nature of 'core' and 'peripheral' journal titles, for reasons including variations in demand in the same subject areas across institutions and significant degrees of interdisciplinarity. Therefore library managers should consider subscription-based services in the context of consortia rather than of an individual model of information resourcing.

G9. Library managers should prioritize desktop ordering and receipt of documents for researchers. This will become a minimum standard level of service. Researchers should not be expected to have to travel to documents (although the value of browsing in good research collections should not be under-rated). Instant access is required by some researchers some of the time.

G10. Support for users/systems should be integrated; if it is not integrated the spheres of responsibility need to be defensible and clearly explained to users. From research undertaken at institutions where convergence between libraries and computing support departments had not taken place, some advantages could be seen in such convergence to achieve integration in co-ordinating DAS user support. However, support structures should be appropriate to the user/system. Researchers' use of newer systems seemed to call for a distributed support structure; the notion of 'barefoot librarians' might be considered in this respect. Support should be centrally co-ordinated but, perhaps, increasingly distributed in delivery.

G11. Regarding copyright, librarians felt that 'fair-dealing' was essential to document supply in UK higher education. Technology should be seen as a way for it to be managed more efficiently and effectively, rather than as an excuse to abandon it. Librarians will need to work to ensure that this is the case. As copyright practice changes, so will the institutional role of libraries.

G12. Users and technologies continually change. Systems should be maintained to identify and allow for such change. The skills of library staff will need to change as their role changes. Librarians should take a proactive stance in these and other matters, for example, in relation to G5 and R2 (below).

Guidelines for people other than library managers

R1. Current budgetary structures and procedures hide a large amount of waste, especially when expensive researchers are called on to interrupt their work, travel to a collection and queue and photocopy documents. University budgetary arrangements should be reviewed to ensure that desktop ordering and receipt of documents for all researchers are made viable within the institution. Equal access for remote and on-campus users is essential.

R2. Management information from DAS suppliers should be appropriate to library managers' needs, configurable and in electronic format. Librarians should be involved in setting standards for such management information.

R3. Departmental equipment replacement cycles for researchers (including post-graduates) should be made explicit so that those negotiating with DAS suppliers can speak adequately for the users.

R4. Research practice is heavily influenced by the conditions imposed by grant-awarding bodies. Such research practice is the context in which information support functions. In considering research support strategy, the impact of research funding regimes should be taken into account. This implies that investigations into the (perhaps unintended) effects of the conditions of research practice imposed by grant-awarding bodies would be valuable. For example, what effect would any move away from formula-funding and towards short-term project funding have on scholarly communication patterns, or on university support structures? How does the UK Research Assessment Exercise currently impact on these support structures?

Index